# Women, Health and Poverty

# Women, Health and Poverty

**An Introduction**

Sarah Payne

HARVESTER
WHEATSHEAF

New York   London   Toronto   Sydney   Tokyo   Singapore

First published 1991 by
Harvester Wheatsheaf
66 Wood Lane End, Hemel Hempstead,
Hertfordshire, HP2 4RG
A division of
Simon & Schuster International Group

Typeset in 10 on 12pt Times
by Keyboard Services, Luton

Printed and bound in Great Britain
by Billing & Sons Ltd, Worcester

British Library Cataloguing in Publication Data

Payne, Sarah
    Women, health and poverty: An introduction.
    I. Title
    362.83

    ISBN 0-7450-0873-9 (cloth)
           0-7450-0874-7

    2 3 4 5   95 94 93 92

# CONTENTS

# PREFACE

As is always the case, many debts were incurred in the course of writing this book, and my thanks go to my colleagues and friends who have given me help and support. In particular I would like to thank Norma Daykin, Lesley Doyal, Lyn Harrison, Hilary Land, Jane Millar, Peter Phillimore, Peter Townsend and Sophie Watson for their interest and for reading various drafts and offering useful suggestions on this and earlier work.

Finally, but by no means least, my thanks go to the friends who have also lent their support. Most of all, I am grateful to Robert and Eleanor, who put up with my absences, listened, and generally put up with the stress of living with me while it was being written. In particular, my thanks to Robert, who was always interested, who took on much more than his share of childcare, and still found time to read and comment on various drafts.

As ever, the ultimate responsibility for the final version rests with the author alone.

# CHAPTER 1

# WOMEN AND POVERTY – AN INTRODUCTION

This book is about women and poverty, and the effects of the experience of poverty on women's lives. Women in the United Kingdom are more likely to suffer poverty than men (Glendinning and Millar, 1987; Millar, 1989a; Pahl, 1989). Throughout their lives women are more vulnerable to both poverty and deprivation, whilst there are more women than men living in conditions of poverty and deprivation at any one time. This vulnerability to poverty, however, is not restricted to women in the United Kingdom. In the United States, for example, a disproportionate number of the poor are women (Zopf, 1989) whilst in Sweden women form the majority of those dependent on state income support, and are more likely than men to have a standard of living which is below subsistence level (Vogel *et al.*, 1988). Evidence from other countries suggests that this over-representation of women among the statistics for the poor is mirrored throughout both the Western world and the so-called 'developing' countries (see, for example, National Council of Welfare, 1979; Cass, 1988; Bryson, 1988; George, 1988).

The exploration of women's poverty to date has tended to concentrate on the reasons for this vulnerability to poverty and deprivation, and on describing the nature of this experience. Whilst the study of poverty has continued for more than a century, traditional definitions and forms of measurement have largely been gender-blind and have focused on poverty as experienced by households rather than individuals. This has the tendency of obscuring the poverty and deprivation women experience within affluent households, and obscuring the extent to which women might experience greater

1

poverty than other members of poor households. It also tends to overlook the fact that poor households headed by women – in particular lone-parent households and those of lone older women – are significantly over-represented in the figures of household poverty.

Recent studies have begun to challenge these traditional definitions of poverty and deprivation, and traditional ways of measuring the depth of such conditions in society (National Council of Welfare, 1979; Scott, 1984; Pahl, 1980; Land, 1983; Glendinning and Millar, 1987; Brannen and Wilson, 1987; Wilson, 1987a; Daly, 1989). However, such challenges to traditional thinking have yet to be wholeheartedly incorporated in newer surveys, and have failed to redefine official statistics of poverty and income distribution.

This book explores not only the causes of women's poverty and deprivation but also the effects of such experiences on women's lives and, in particular, the effect of poverty on women's health. The link between poverty and poor health is well established – both through statistics which demonstrate the inverse relationship between occupational class and mortality and morbidity (Townsend and Davidson, 1982; Whitehead, 1987; Black Report, 1980); and through studies which more directly link poor health – both physical and mental – to circumstances of deprivation, such as poor housing conditions, damp, overcrowding, inadequate nutrition, and so on (Strachan, 1986; Graham, 1984; Hyndman, 1990).

However, one of the interesting paradoxes in health studies is that of the poor health of women in comparison with their greater longevity. Women in Britain have an average life expectancy at birth of 77 years, compared with a life expectancy for men of 71 years. Yet throughout their lives women consult doctors more often, and are more likely than men to report themselves as suffering illness. Self-report surveys such as the General Household Survey reveal women's greater perceived morbidity and their greater use of primary health care. Some of these visits may be accounted for by women's reproductive role – visits for ante-natal care, contraception, post-natal check-ups and so on – and some are accounted for by women's responsibility for child care – women consulting on behalf of another member of the household, most often a child. Yet even after allowing for those attendances which are not associated with women's own poor health, women visit doctors more often than men and report more symptoms of ill health and restricted activity. To some extent this poorer health may be associated with women's greater longevity itself – the result of health problems in those later years. However, illness in later life cannot entirely account for the difference between men and women either, as adult women at all ages report more health problems than men, and are treated more often for illness, both physical and mental (Verbrugge, 1986; Popay and Jones, 1988; Whitehead, 1987; Doyal, 1979; GHS, 1990).

The question arises whether this greater morbidity can be explained by women's greater vulnerability to poverty? Popay and Jones (1987) identify two models of explanation for women's poorer health over their longer lifetime: the artefactual model, which seeks to explain such differences through reference to women's greater tendency to see themselves as ill; and the social causation model, which argues that women suffer genuinely poorer health as a result of the stress of the roles they are called upon to play. Popay and Jones challenge both of these models as being too simplistic, arguing that it is not only the number of roles women hold in society but also the nature and quality of these which is important. In particular, both the quality of normative gender roles and the access to resources to fulfil these roles contribute to women's poorer health.

This book is a review of the evidence relating to the part played by poverty and deprivation – material and social – in determining women's health experience. The labour women perform, the expectations that are held of them, and women's position in both the domestic and public economy, do produce stress. This is related in part to the quality of that role, and partly to the conditions in which women's domestic and caring labour is carried out: in addition, economic and social deprivation have a direct impact on health potential which cannot be ignored. This includes not only the experience of poverty itself, and health risks associated with living on a low income, but also the threat of poverty. Such a model focuses on the causes of women's poverty and of women's vulnerability to poverty. It has long been observed that the poor are not a static group, and that households move in and out of poverty over time, as their circumstances change. For women, this movement in and out of poverty is related to the fundamental cause of women's poverty – their economic dependence on men, and the sexual division of labour which results in women's secondary position in the labour market and their first position in the home.

Thus there are two themes to this book: what causes women's

poverty – both the actual experience of poverty and deprivation, and the threat of poverty during the course of a lifetime – and what the relationship is between poverty and women's health.

## Women and poverty: definitions and causes

The study of poverty and deprivation requires, firstly, a definition of these terms and, secondly, a consideration of how the extent of poverty and deprivation suffered by a population might be measured. Clearly these two issues are related – definitions of what constitutes poverty will by their nature determine the amount of poverty found in a society, and also where it is found. In the area of both definition and measurement, the failure of traditional studies to focus on gender specific experience has important consequences.

Early studies of poverty in Britain identified two forms of poverty – primary poverty, being below subsistence income, and secondary poverty, where income was above subsistence level but was spent unwisely (Rowntree, 1922; 1941; Alcock, 1987). However, these measures of income and subsistence needs were applied to households as a collective unit, whilst individual consumption within households was ignored. The assumption underlying this 'heroic simplification' (Galbraith, cited in Land, 1983) is that resources within households are shared equitably, with the result that situations where resources are not shared are obscured. As Land writes: 'Thus all members of a poor household are poor, and no-one is poor in an affluent household.' (Land, 1983, p. 49).

Research has increasingly demonstrated the fallacy of such an assumption, as women are seen going without during times of need, in order to provide for partners and children, and as women are denied access to resources by partners with greater economic power within the household (Graham, 1984; Whitehead, 1987; Charles and Kerr,1988; Brannen and Wilson, 1987; Pahl, 1980; 1983; Daly, 1989). The economist's 'black box' approach to the household (Pahl, 1989), treating the household as if it was an individual for the sake of analysis, is not a mere simplification necessary to the study of poverty but one which results in misrepresentation of the extent and degree of poverty within the population, and inaccuracies in the identification of who the poor are.

This focus on the household as a unit of both income and

consumption has continued throughout later poverty research, including the major piece of work by Townsend in the 1960s (Townsend, 1979), later studies by him (Townsend *et al.*, 1987) and even in new attempts to measure poverty and deprivation, for example, in the kind of measurement based on a 'consensus' definition of deprivation (Mack and Lansley, 1985).

Thus one sense in which the definition of poverty and deprivation fails to take account of the specific experience of women is through the focus on households as units of consumption, with no analysis of ways in which different members of a household have different access to the resources of that household, relating to the differential economic power of each sex, and of parents and children. This cannot be resolved simply through the incorporation of a measure of differential spending on behalf of different members of a household, as expenditure itself must be reclassified into necessity and luxury or leisure items, and as some responsibilities for expenditure bring stress and deprivation of other kinds, rather than true economic power (Pahl, 1989; Land, 1983; Graham, 1987a). For example, having control of the household's income during periods of shortage – as many women do – brings responsibility for making ends meet and providing for the needs of the household under difficult or impossible conditions, but it does not bring independence. This is an extremely complex scheme to unravel, the more so as the allocation of both purchasing power and resources within the household is not necessarily static or easily observed – women and men may take for granted the assumptions of how resources are to be divided, the going without by one or both partners, and so on. This question of how resources are allocated is complex and subtle: it is also one which has serious consequences for the health chances of different members of the household. Again, these are not straightforward to observe – it is not only the denial or allocation of material resources, but also the responsibility, stress, and threat of denial which complicates the picture of possible influences on the health of individual household members.

The work of Townsend has been significant in developing a definition and means of measuring two states – poverty and deprivation. Relative poverty has been defined as existing where the individual or household does not have the economic resources with which 'to obtain the types of diet, participate in the activities and have the living conditions and amenities which are customary, or at least widely encouraged or approved, in the societies to which they belong' (Townsend, 1979, p. 31). It is thus a definition based on economic resources, but it relates these to the material and social resources which can be purchased and which are commonly accepted within society.

The definition implies the further meaning of relative deprivation – being without those material or social conditions which are taken for granted by the wider society – and indicates the relationship between poverty, which is measured in financial terms, and deprivation, which is more directly related to the actual lack of certain conditions or amenities. This distinction is important, as it allows deprivation to be measured when it is unrelated to income – for example, when black households are denied access to good housing through the operation of racism rather than through lack of income.

Such a distinction is crucial in the understanding of women's experience of poverty and deprivation – for women may suffer deprivation even where they do not suffer poverty, firstly, through being denied access to the resources of the household and, secondly, through being denied access to amenities and conditions taken for granted by male society. For example, women rarely have access to a car, and less than a third of the female population holds a driving licence (Sinfield, 1986). Within the household, the car might consume a large proportion of household income, and yet this resource is concentrated in the hands of the male partner (Graham, 1987a). In both poor and affluent households, such a division of resources is uneven and represents a form of deprivation on the part of women.

In addition, women are also denied access to many of the amenities and social activities commonly enjoyed by men. Women are unable to participate freely in leisure activities such as sport, social outings and political activity as a result of the way women's movements are restricted. Limited access to private transport, the cost and lack of safety of public transport, less leisure time, the informal curfew resulting from violence against women and poor design of public space (Deem, 1988; Jones *et al.*, 1986; Matrix, 1984) all add up to restrict women's participation in leisure and social activities, whether or not women have equal access to the funds needed for such participation.

Thus relative definitions of deprivation and poverty must take account of the different experience of men and women. This is further illustrated by the inclusion of different kinds of 'income' in the assessment of poverty. Townsend's measurement of income in relation to poverty incorporated a number of forms of income beyond cash resources. Income from relatives and friends, in the form of loans, gifts and other financial or material support, was incorporated in the 1960s survey, as were benefits-in-kind, such as garden produce. Whilst the household remained the central unit of measurement, the inclusion of benefits-in-kind demonstrates the extent to which women's domestic labour has yet to be understood or valued as real work: the savings produced by growing vegetables on an allotment were included, yet the savings produced through women's domestic labour in food preparation, cleaning and other household tasks were not.

What Delphy calls the production of 'use-values' (Delphy, 1984) through women's domestic labour is still ignored in the calculation of household poverty – and yet the performance of this work has a significant impact not only on the level of poverty suffered by a household, but also on the woman's own experience of poverty and deprivation, for domestic labour simultaneously benefits the household whilst depriving women of the time and energy for leisure pursuits and brings women into closer contact with some aspects of deprivation, such as poor housing. In addition, responsibility for domestic labour and childcare restricts women's availability for paid employment which might offer increased financial independence or relief to both her own and household poverty.

Turning to the measurement of deprivation, Townsend developed an index with which to measure household experience of deprivation. Questions about material and social resources perceived as commonly approved by society – a Sunday lunch or inviting children's friends to tea – were seen as revealing those households suffering forms of deprivation. Again, the focus on household deprivation reveals nothing about specific ways in which women suffer deprivation within the household – not sharing equally in the food which is consumed, for example. And, as Land has pointed out, some forms of deprivation – being without hot water for example – have more serious implications for the woman trying to cook and clean, and be responsible for childcare, than for the man who uses hot water only for his own hygiene (Land, 1983).

Townsend, in a more recent work (Townsend *et al.*, 1987), suggested a four-fold categorization of women's risk of deprivation: women who are unpaid carers, women in poorly paid employment, women who are lone mothers and older women living alone. However, these categories are incomplete and overly simplistic, for such types are not and cannot be mutually exclusive. Women may be, and mostly are, unpaid carers without paid employment when they are lone parents, whilst even women who do have paid employment outside the home may suffer deprivation through the unequal allocation of household resources. The earnings of women's paid employment are often crucial in keeping a household out of poverty (Land, 1983; Glendinning and Millar, 1987), and this is a fact of women's contribution to household life which should not be underestimated. However, women's earnings are typically not treated in the same way as those of the male partner, and poverty or deprivation for women can exist, in relative as well as absolute terms, alongside this earning capacity. Women's pay is typically spent on household necessities, and only more rarely and in smaller amounts on women's own needs (Pahl, 1989; Brannen, 1987). The money women earn also may result in similar amounts being deducted from the contributions to housekeeping made by male partners. Whilst for women a paid job may bring some relief from poverty or deprivation experienced within the household, this may simply be as a result of greater control over the allocation of household expenditure, and greater reliability of income (see, for example, Graham, 1987a). It does not of necessity result in freedom from poverty itself, and in relative terms within the household women may remain deprived as their income simply frees more of their partner's income for his own consumption.

A similar list of factors predisposing individuals to poverty was produced by Field (1981): when someone is prevented from working, is responsible for children or is over retirement age. These factors share a common relationship to the labour market – individuals who are excluded from the labour market as a result of childcare, sickness, disability and retirement are vulnerable to poverty.

Although Field failed to make a distinction between the resulting risk factors for each sex, for women this relationship to the labour market is of central importance in understanding both the immediate causes of women's poverty – low pay, responsibility for children, or other dependants, old age – and the underlying causes – women's perceived and actual economic dependence on men through the operation of a sexual division of labour, in which women's position is defined as primarily domestic, and only secondly in terms of the labour market.

It is this definition of women primarily through their domestic role and the home and family, which structures women's economic dependency on men. This sexual division of labour encompasses women's low pay (and educational opportunities), women's inferior pension rights, women's position within social policy, and in particular the payment, or lack of payment, of state benefits to women, whilst also justifying higher male earnings, higher male pensions, and the lack of childcare facilities within British society. So long as women continue to be seen as only secondary workers in the labour market, with a prior attachment to the home, they will continue to be seen as economically dependent on men. And it is this perceived and real economic dependence on men which creates women's actual poverty and their greater vulnerability to poverty during the course of their lives.

The immediate causes of women's poverty are therefore the result of this 'heroic assumption' of women's ability to rely on the economic support of men. In terms of poor households, women as lone parents and lone older women suffer poverty because there is no man with higher earning power or pension rights on whom to depend, whilst state benefits are paid at levels which assume that there should be. In addition, opportunities for women to move out of this dependence on state benefit or poor pensions are restricted by the same assumption of women's primary role – the low earnings of women and the scarcity and cost of alternative forms of childcare.

In terms of women's poverty within households, the higher earning power of men is assumed to be shared equally between men and women, parents and children. In many cases it will be, but this cannot be taken as automatic, and whilst women have less earning power and less opportunity to earn, and their domestic work is unrecognized in economic terms, women remain vulnerable to poverty within the household.

## Cause and effect: women, poverty and health

This introduction to the causes of poverty for women highlights the need for a definition and form of measurement which is capable of reflecting women's economic position. Such a definition then incorporates both the immediate causes of women's poverty and deprivation, and the deeper underlying causes, and thus highlights women's greater risk of poverty and deprivation. Chapter 2 takes up this question of defining and measuring poverty, and examines the ways in which women's experience has been obscured within both official statistics and traditional poverty research. Chapter 3 looks at ways of measuring women's poverty, and examines the evidence relating to women's greater rates of poverty and deprivation.

✶ The second theme of this book is that of the consequences of poverty for women. What effect does poverty have on those who suffer it? The experience of poverty and deprivation is likely to have a wide-ranging effect on the lives of women, men and children who are poor, and one effect in particular is that of health.

The relationship between poverty, deprivation and health is complex, and account must be taken of the experience of poverty over time, as well as the way the stresses of being vulnerable to poverty – living on the margins, or in economic dependency and uncertainty – take their toll on health. Women are not only more likely to be poor, they also spend a larger proportion of their lives in poverty and deprivation (Millar and Glendinning, 1989; Bradshaw and Morgan, 1987; Walker, 1987). It is this complexity which neither the 'snapshot' approach to poverty – looking at numbers in poverty – nor an approach based on listing categories of those who are poor can account for without reference to the impact of gender over a lifetime.

↛ Women's poorer health experience during the course of their lives relates to both physical and mental health. Whilst women consult doctors more often for physical ailments, these are typically chronic illnesses rather than acute, and as such are more likely to result in periods of ill health rather than short episodes of illness which are life-threatening.

In addition, women also consult doctors more often for problems associated with mental illness. Each year approximately 40 per cent more women than men are admitted to psychiatric hospital for treatment as an in-patient, whilst women are twice as likely to be treated by their general practitioner (GP) for what are termed the 'minor' psychiatric illnesses and to be prescribed psychotropic drugs (Cochrane, 1983; Dunnell and Cartwright, 1972; Barrett and Roberts, 1978; Skegg, Doll and Perry, 1977; Graham, 1985; McPherson and Anderson, 1983).

Again, most psychiatric diagnoses are indicative of chronic illness over time as opposed to acute life-threatening forms of ill health, although in some instances where psychiatric diagnosis might be invoked – for example, suicide, alcohol and substance abuse – women remain under-represented. The diagnoses associated with the over-representation of women in figures for treatment for mental illness are those of depression and anxiety-related disorders: for example in statistics for new admissions to psychiatric hospitals women outnumber men by three to one for depressive illnesses, whilst diagnoses of schizophrenia are evenly distributed between the sexes. This too leads to interesting questions relating to the nature of women's lives, and whether women's higher representation amongst figures for depression and anxiety relates to the fact that more women live in conditions of poverty and are vulnerable to the threat of poverty over the course of their lives. In addition, women's economic dependency on men may extract a large price in terms of stress and ill health, showing up here as psychiatric diagnosis.

Thus the patterns of illness exhibited by women throughout their lives might explain their greater longevity, despite greater morbidity, as they are illnesses which do not increase the rate of mortality. The question which remains is why women should suffer higher rates of these forms of illness – both physical and mental. The answer must be sought in women's lives, in terms of both the actual experience of men and women, and the psychological impact of this experience.

However, as with poverty, traditional analysis of links between health and socio-demographic data have focused on male mortality rates, and have obscured the relationship between socio-economic circumstances and health experience for women. Discussion and research on the association between health and social factors have been dominated by a focus on mortality linked with occupational class. For example, the major review of official statistics carried out by the working party chaired by Sir Douglas Black (Black Report, 1980; Townsend and Davidson, 1982) concentrated on the mortality rates of men and, less often, women, in different occupational classes. For women, however, occupational class is assessed in a complex fashion: for married women, the occupation of their husband is used, whilst for single women, their own occupation is used. In addition, the occupational structure in which women's jobs are located was originally designed on the basis of a ranking of men's occupations and as a result the peculiarities of a large proportion of women's jobs – part-time, in fewer occupations and industries and dominated by employment in the service sector – are not reflected in the overall structure.

This domination of male health statistics and second-hand occupational status for a large proportion of adult women has been increasingly criticized in recent years (Macintyre, 1986; Hart, 1989; Arber, 1989; 1990b; Roberts, 1990). The Decennial Supplement – which relates mortality statistics to socio-demographic data to produce rates of death amongst different social and occupational classes – produced data from the 1981 census for both men and women, including figures for women's own occupational classification. However, so long as the existing occupational hierarchy reflects a disposition based on male employment, and details for married women's employment are only collected on a small proportion of women's death certificates, data on the links between social and occupational class and mortality for women will remain limited.

Arber (1990a) describes this failure to analyse inequalities in women's health as a further example of the 'black box': the focus on men and male occupational structures obscures the ways in which women's health and mortality differs. It is a focus which is replicated in the practice and discourse of the medical profession (Doyal, 1979; Barrett and Roberts, 1978), and also in occupational health research and health and safety at work legislation (Daykin, 1990). This restricted approach to health inequalities is demonstrated also by research in the field of mental health, which was dominated for many years by studies of the links between rates of schizophrenia amongst men and their social class, despite equal numbers of women and men who receive this diagnosis throughout the Western world (see, for example, Faris and Dunham, 1939; Turner and Wagenfeld, 1967; Goldberg and Morrison, 1963).

The outcome of this focus on male rates of mortality and morbidity, and male systems of social classification, is an obscuring of the structural causes of inequalities in health for over half the population, and it is also a methodological absurdity. If we want to demonstrate and understand inequalities in health in relation to material structures, the links between women's health and the lives they lead are not only needed to complete the picture, they are central as a tool of explanation. The research on schizophrenia and social class debated throughout the 1960s and 1970s the role of drift: do schizophrenic individuals slip down the social scale as a result of their illness? The focus on male schizophrenics meant that the picture would never be complete, given the other 50 per cent of this diagnostic group, while an insistence on measuring women's social class by her father or husband's occupation wherever possible means that the extent to which schizophrenia leads to poorer occupations for women is concealed. As Mary O'Brien writes, 'it is an axiom of feminist understanding that the dogmas of male supremacy invade all human institutions and pervade all modes of discourse' (O'Brien, 1983, p. 16).

Health research has also been limited by its narrow focus on measurements of health which are more accurately described as measurements of illness and death. Again, the issue of gender is important here, for if women live longer but report more ill health and visit medical practitioners more often, the ways in which each sex experiences health needs to be considered separately for the links with poverty and deprivation. These questions of the way in which health is measured, and the way this measurement is then linked to measurements of socio-economic status by indicators such as occupation, housing and car ownership are taken up in Chapter 4.

Chapters 5 and 6 examine in greater detail the evidence relating to health, measures of illness and death, and poverty and deprivation. The chapters are divided along the lines of physical and mental health, with each chapter looking in depth at one aspect of the health experience. This is an uneasy resolution of a particular problem – how to divide the material into sections of manageable length, in relation to themes which are in fact linked. Organizing the material along the lines of physical and mental health reflects the division in the medical profession between what are presented as two kinds of health. The arguments for a holistic definition of health which is informed by concepts of wellness, rather than the absence of illness, and which recognizes the interrelationship between physical and mental well-being, makes this division unfortunate. One reason for this separation is that the research evidence on the links between poverty and health is similarly divided, although increasingly the many and varied effects of low income and poor housing, for example, are reported together. A further rationale is that there is a substantial critique of the concept of mental illness, and a major feminist contribution to this, which must be incorporated in the debate on the impact of poverty and deprivation on mental health.

Chapter 7 then takes up the themes of oppression and health. Throughout the book the focus is on gender – the ways in which women experience poverty and deprivation, and the ways this experience affects their health. However, the goal is to highlight gender as one dimension of health experience, not to prioritize women's experience of poverty as being greater or more significant than that experienced by men, nor yet is it to prioritize gender over and above the ways in which other discourses – attached to disability, race, sexuality and age, for example – also construct the experience of poverty and deprivation. Chapter 7 focuses on the ways in which other forms of discourse operate to pattern the experience of some groups.

The final chapter also ends with a review of the role of social policy in constructing women's economic dependency. Social security or State Income Support is the major source of income for a large proportion of the poor in Britain, and for many is also the cause of their poverty. Inadequate levels of benefit, combined with regulations which construct the 'poverty trap', mean those who have no other source of income or only inadequate earnings are poor. For women, the rules and methods of benefit payment help construct their economic dependency, and explain why being a mother, older woman or unemployed inevitably and inexorably lead to an existence in or on the margins of poverty. Whilst in recent years changes to the benefit system as a result of membership of the European Community and Equal Opportunity Directives have altered the regulations in favour of some women claimants, in practice little appears to have changed (Lonsdale, 1990), and the large majority of women claimants remain dependent on the poorest benefits of all – means-tested and non-contributory benefits such as Income Support and Severe Disablement Allowance. The real value of benefits has declined (Loney and Bocock, 1987), and one of those most valued by women – Child Benefit – has been frozen for most of the past decade. In 1991 the benefit for the eldest child was raised, whilst that for the second and subsequent children remained frozen. Even so, this increase is pitifully short of the value by which this benefit has been eroded in the past few years.

Women's poverty is not a new phenomenon, nor is it one which looks likely to disappear in the immediate or even near future.

# CHAPTER 2

# A QUESTION OF MEASUREMENT

There are two questions which this chapter seeks to answer: does the form of measurement used in poverty studies and official statistics underestimate the number of women who are in or on the margins of poverty; and does the form of measurement used blind us also to the short-term and long-term health effects for women of such poverty and deprivation?

This chapter examines in more detail the ways in which poverty and deprivation have been defined, and these definitions operationalized to produce measures of the prevalence of poverty in different societies. Why do we care about defining and measuring poverty? Firstly, because the use of different definitions carries substantial implications for the way in which poverty is then measured, and thus has a major effect on how many are seen to be poor in any society, at any point in time, and which groups are most vulnerable to poverty. And, secondly, because the definition used also implies underlying causes of poverty and deprivation, whether a remedy is seen as necessary, and if so, what this might be.

Recent concerns, amongst some commentators at least, over increasing numbers in poverty and the severity or depth of this poverty, relate not only to the problem of more poverty, but also to concern over how it is being measured. During the 1980s the method of assessing poverty shifted from a count of the number of households and people on low incomes to a measure based on income distribution. This resulted in a fundamental shift in how poverty was defined. At the same time social security benefits have been increasingly divorced from the concept that they should reflect basic income needs in society, even though this concept at best only approximated to a measure of 'subsistence' (Townsend and Gordon, 1989).

Suggestions that the income of the poor had risen more than the income of the wealthy in the 1980s, as a result of the 'trickle down' effect of Conservative economic policy were revealed as inaccurate by the end of that decade. The reworking of income figures to remove a statistical error demonstrated that the incomes of the lowest decile had in fact grown by 2 per cent, not 8 per cent as originally claimed, a far slower growth than that of the more affluent in society. (DSS, 1990; Johnson and Webb, 1990a; 1990b; Townsend and Gordon, 1989).

Amidst this background of concern that the numbers in poverty are actually growing, and the dispute over the measurement of poverty in government statistics, the need for a redefinition of poverty becomes ever more pressing. Recent feminist approaches to the meaning and measurement of poverty have demonstrated the need for a definition which is capable of expressing the experiences of women in poverty and the way women are specifically vulnerable to poverty and deprivation as a result of the construction of gender and the operation of discourses of femininity (Millar and Glendinning, 1987; 1989; Lewis and Piachaud, 1987). Such a gendered definition would do more than allow the investigation of women in poverty, it would demand it. It is more than a question of finding a way of defining poverty that is gender free. It is also a question of finding a definition which highlights the ways in which the experience of each sex differs, the reasons for this, and how therefore we are to set about measuring the experience of both men and women. Such an approach also carries implications for how women's poverty might best be remedied.

Unfortunately, research on poverty relies heavily, through necessity, on official statistics to examine the prevalence of poverty and deprivation in society. These statistics have increasingly been shown to be inadequate. Such figures do not tell us enough about the numbers of people living in or on the margins of poverty, the depth of their poverty, the related impact of material and social deprivation and how people move in and out of poverty. The lack of regularly produced figures relating to actual income received and levels of social security benefit means household poverty is impossible to calculate. Those figures which are made available show the distribution of income by different groups – income groups and different house-holds (DSS, 1990), whilst the Family Expenditure Survey gives figures relating to consumption of various items and services (DOE, 1990 Family Expenditure Survey).

However, as measures of poverty, these statistics are problematic, to say the least. Figures on income distribution tell us more about inequalities than poverty – although they do not tell us enough. So whilst such statistics may be useful as a measure of which groups are worse off, and changes in the structure of the poorest 10 per cent of society in comparison with the richest 10 per cent, their value even here is limited. Figures relate to households rather than individuals, they tell us nothing about the distribution of resources within house-holds, or how this income translates into purchasing power, or differences within this lowest income group. Thus the gaps between the lowest 1 per cent and the other households in that decile are hidden, as is the way in which this inequality translates into con-ditions of life. The use of deciles further underestimates the extent to which the value of income varies – the poorest spend more both proportionately and in absolute terms on the necessities of life as they are less able to take advantage of economies of scale, bulk purchasing and cheaper out-of-town shopping, for example. The way a purchase tax such as Value Added Tax has a disproportionate effect on the income of the very poor, and the fact that for such people a measure of inflation such as the Retail Price Index under-estimates increases in their cost of living are similarly ignored in such a focus on income distribution (Fry and Pashardes, 1985; IFS, 1986). Once such a measure is taken to represent poverty, it becomes inevitable that 'the poor are always with us', for it will always be possible to divide society into the poorest 10 per cent, and the richest 10 per cent and so on. We are left to argue about how such income and wealth may be measured, whilst the focus on inequality of income distribution implicitly alters the question of policies to remedy poverty, and prevents an examination of where current social policy might be failing those in poverty or on the margins.

The precise definition of poverty and deprivation are vital ques-tions, therefore, both in relation to abstract notions of equality and distributional justice, and also, quite simply, in relation to the way definitions set the agenda for measuring the numbers of poor, identifying who they are and reasons for their poverty, and the way policy intervenes in this process. The variety of approaches to defining and measuring poverty cannot be viewed simply as the unproblematic application of principles to statistics but as an intrinsically political statement about the society in which we live.

The rest of this chapter considers in more detail different definitions and forms of measurement of poverty and deprivation, and highlights some problems inherent in both traditional and newer style approaches to the question. The aim of the chapter is to consider how theories of poverty have developed over time so as to leave unacknowledged the specific experience of women. This is not to argue that it is only women who suffer poverty – clearly there are many men also living in circumstances of severe poverty and deprivation. In particular, a large proportion of the poor are men and women living as couples, mostly with children. Nor is the goal to reduce the causes of poverty and deprivation to a function of gender – clearly other dimensions of inequality are important. What is intended is a discussion of the way women share a specifically gendered vulnerability to poverty and deprivation which means women are more frequently poor and suffer the threat of poverty throughout their lives.

## Defining poverty

Charles Booth and Seebohm Rowntree are often credited with beginning modern social research into poverty. Booth's interest developed partly as a result of sensational reporting of destitution in the nineteenth century – the writings of Henry Mayhew (1851) and Andrew Mearns (1883), for example (cited in Fraser, 1984). Booth undertook a comprehensive study of the living and working conditions of people in London, publishing a seventeen-volume report on his findings, in the late nineteenth century. He reported widespread poverty in the city of London – finding up to one third of the population in or on the margins of poverty in his initial research (Fraser, 1984; Mack and Lansley, 1985), using a definition of the poor, as those without means 'according to the normal standards of life in this country' to allow a healthy physical existence (Booth, 1888, cited in Mack and Lansley, 1985, p. 27). Booth operationalized his definition by relating this minimum to a level of income, set at between 18 shillings and 21 shillings per week.

A more detailed approach to the identification of a poverty line was developed by Seebohm Rowntree, who studied the lives of a sample of the population in York. This led to the construction of a method of assessing poverty in relation to an income-based measure of need. Absolute poverty is defined as being without even the bare minimum required for survival, and Rowntree operationalized this concept by outlining the requirements for merely physical efficiency, and then translating these needs into an income with which they could be purchased. This subsistence definition is then infinitely capable of updating in line with changes in prices – once the original list of nutritional requirements and minimum clothing needs has been established, the cost of each item can be calculated and turned into a level of income required to keep the household or individual out of poverty.

Rowntree refined this concept to distinguish between two kinds of subsistence poverty. Primary poverty was defined as poverty resulting from an income too low to buy the necessities for the maintenance of physical efficiency, whilst secondary poverty was defined as that which results when an income which is of itself sufficient is unwisely spent. The calculation of a subsistence poverty line relied on everything being bought at the cheapest price available – and unwise shopping which resulted in secondary poverty might simply mean the failure to go as far as the cheapest market for the goods.

Initially, Rowntree attempted to define a level of subsistence poverty which truly represented the absolute minimum needed by the individual or household to sustain life: and expenditure on transport, leisure activities such as a day out in the country, concerts and reading, toys for children, political association or trade union membership, tobacco, alcohol and clothes other than everyday wear were not included in the total costs allowed. Such a strict minimum, rather than a relative definition which recognized these needs as socially conditioned, was adopted to strengthen the findings, and demonstrate the proportion of the population who were objectively in extreme poverty, through no fault of their own. However, as Mack and Lansley (1985) point out, the subsistence or absolute definition of poverty brings problems. In particular, the 15 per cent Rowntree found to be living at or below the poverty line, using a subsistence definition, were in fact surviving, which makes the reality of such a subsistence definition questionable. The problem is that mere physical efficiency cannot be defined so neatly, and rates of activity and ability fall off slowly, rather than being observable in a distinct cut-off point. Whilst poverty may bring ill health and higher mortality, the relationship between health – and death – and poverty is complex. Despite the existence of evidence that poverty brings higher rates of both morbidity and mortality, those who are not poor also die from disease, whilst the poor do not suffer an immediate deterioration in health that is directly measurable. Many of the health problems associated with poverty and deprivation will be long term and chronic rather than acute, whilst much depends on how health is defined. This demonstrates some of the difficulties inherent in Rowntree's subsistence definition, and suggests that Rowntree's definition and measurement was, after all, intrinsically relative, if fairly stringent (Mack and Lansley, 1985).

Subsistence definitions have a long history, and are implicit in the operation of alms and relief in previous centuries, most notably in the 1834 Amendment to the Poor Law (Thane, 1982). Subsistence definitions are also widely used in developing countries to assess the extent of poverty. However, as the country develops the definition of subsistence also grows (George, 1988). Similarly, Rowntree later developed his definition of subsistence to include such things as union dues, a newspaper or public transport costs (Rowntree, 1941; Mack and Lansley, 1985). Coffee and tea were also included in his list of necessities, whilst he acknowledged the insignificant impact of these on the body's physical efficiency and survival.

This suggests that these subsistence definitions are in fact relative definitions disguised in the attempt to emphasize their objectivity and, as Rowntree saw it, to reduce challenges to his findings based on the argument that the poor are simply bad managers, feckless or spendthrift.

What then is the distinction between an absolute or subsistence definition of poverty and relative poverty? The idea of a relative dimension to the meaning of poverty can be dated back to the writings of Adam Smith and Karl Marx – although, as George (1988) points out, these are strange allies which suggests that the process for each of operationalizing such a definition and the implications it may have for economic policy would differ substantially. The modern concept of relative poverty is generally associated with the work of Townsend. In particular, his study of poverty in the 1960s, defined relative poverty as follows:

Individuals, families and groups in the population can be said to be in poverty when they lack the resources to obtain the type of diet, participate in the activities and have the living conditions and amenities which are customary, or at least widely encouraged, in the societies to which they belong.

(Townsend, 1979, p. 31)

This was not merely an enlargement of a subsistence definition of poverty, along the lines of Rowntree's own reformulation or the changing definition in developing countries, as the list of basic necessities gradually widens with economic growth. The fundamental distinction lies in the way relative poverty is defined specifically in relation to what is enjoyed or accepted by the majority of the population: thus it is only through direct observation and reference to the living standards of others that those in poverty are identified. This is essentially distinct from a gradual addition of extra 'needs' to a subsistence definition, because it has as a starting point not the individual or household but the wider society to which they belong. Thus poverty is defined explicitly through reference to the society in which it is found, rather than through some notionally objective and universal system of needs which is, however, implicitly located in social needs.

The issue of defining poverty as a comparative concept has received growing attention, as international boundaries increasingly seem less relevant than corporate ones, and the need to develop an internationalist perspective becomes more urgent. The division between absolute or subsistence definitions of poverty used in developing countries and the relative meaning the term acquires in the so-called developed world leads to strange and difficult comparisons (George, 1988), and, as Sen argues (1983), it is important to recognize the value of retaining an absolute sense in which poverty is also defined, to maintain the visibility of absolute starvation and destitution, in both developing countries and in the developed world.

However, adopting a relative approach to poverty in the Western world does not relieve us of the problems in measuring the extent of this. How are we to measure poverty if it is relative – the fundamental question being of course, relative to whom? And who should decide on the definition? The work of Joanna Mack and Stewart Lansley (1985) for the London Weekend Television programme,

Britain', opened up the discussion further. Whilst adopt-
elative approach to poverty and deprivation, they argued
I for a 'consensus' definition, where the opinions of a sample
g    of the population are used to construct an index of deprivation.

Definitions of poverty, material and social deprivation carry implications for how each are to be measured, and some of the difficulties which must be overcome in order to operationalize such
definitions.


## Measuring poverty

The focus of both Booth and Rowntree in these early studies set
trends in the measurement of poverty which remain important. In
particular, two aspects of their work have persisted despite challenge and innovation – firstly, the focus on income as a means of
measuring poverty, based on the concept of a 'poverty line': an
income level below which all can be said to be in poverty, and
secondly, the focus on the household as a unit of consumption,
within which resources are assumed to be equally shared between
all members.

Rowntree's careful documentation of minimum needs for the
maintenance of physical efficiency referred to nutritional and housing needs, minimum provision for clothing, and required people to
budget carefully, using the cheapest markets and so on (Rowntree,
1941; 1922). Costs were then translated into an estimates of income
needs for different household structures, thereby introducing two
important components to the study of poverty.

On the question of the household as a basis for measurement of
poverty, whilst needs were seen as individual – and different for an
adult man or woman, a teenage girl or young boy for example –
these needs were then collapsed into household types and compared with the income actually coming into the household. Rowntree's description of secondary poverty – a household whose income
is sufficient, but spent inefficiently leading to poverty – allows a
recognition of poverty as a result of differential access to household
resources. For example, where one person has control of the financial resources and overspends on goods such as alcohol for personal
consumption. Secondary poverty might therefore reflect women's

position in households where the husband or father's prior claim on the household's income resulted in resources not being shared equally. However, the definition of secondary poverty did not set out explicitly to highlight women's unequal access to household resources, and the household remained in other respects the 'black box' (Pahl, 1989) of analysis where all resources going into the home are deemed to be shared. This remains a powerful assumption today, as demonstrated for example in the structure of social security benefits (Pascall, 1986; Alcock, 1987). It is also central in some of the research on poverty carried out more recently, as in a study of unemployment in three European cities:

> One can collect information on income at the level of the individual person, the family or the household. The first is clearly unsuitable for a study of poverty because members of a family generally share their income; a doctor's wife or an architect's children may have no personal income of their own but this does not mean they are in poverty. (Mitton *et al.*, 1983)

Such a comment is not only inaccurate, it demonstrates the importance of this assumption that households share their resources, for it is precisely because women are seen as the economic dependants of men that their poverty within the household needs exploration. It seems almost churlish to point out the bias in the additional assumption that the doctor is, by definition, male.

The second key factor is the focus on income and the translation of needs – the list of items for minimum efficiency to be maintained – into a financial statement about the level of income required to meet those needs. Whilst the first stage in the survey requires documentation of what people actually consume, or need to consume, in order to subsist, these are always then related back to an income needed to meet these needs.

This income required to meet minimum needs is defined as the poverty line. In this way, society can more easily be reduced to statistics demonstrating the numbers or proportion of the population in poverty at any one time. Such a measurement might then be refined, for example, to take account of what are termed 'the margins of poverty' – those whose income is slightly above this minimum income level, but still so low as to indicate economic hardship and a vulnerability to poverty, particularly if circumstances change even marginally. It thus becomes possible to estimate the proportion of the population in or on the margins of poverty.

One way in which this is often expressed is in relation to the level of government social security benefits. Thus the proportion of the population dependent on social security benefits might be used to describe the extent of poverty in society, whilst those whose income is up to 40 per cent higher than the level at which income support is paid might be said to be 'on the margins' of poverty.

However, there are a number of considerations which are important in the way such figures are interpreted. The use of social security benefit levels is often justified in that they are said to be representative of a socially defined poverty level. In this way, it is argued, the line used is relative, in that these are the levels which society agrees are the bare minimum for members of that society. Such an argument has little ground in reality. In fact, the levels at which new social assistance benefits were set as a result of the Beveridge report had little to do with an assessment of actual needs, and have been described more as 'an historical accident' (Mack and Lansley, 1985, p. 8). The fact that benefits as a whole were not drawn up to reflect a detailed calculation of need for different household types means that even if the benefit was a fair assessment of need for some groups in the population, there is no reason to suppose that it would be a good measure for another group. And whilst successive increases in the level of benefits were until the 1980s linked with increases in average earnings, and thus to some extent were related to wider standards of living, from the mid-1980s onwards even that link has been destroyed (Townsend and Gordon, 1989; Loney, 1983). To see social security benefit levels as some expression of a consensus in society on acceptable minimum income levels would be a serious miscalculation, although in some respects using numbers of those dependent on benefit has been justified as the only figures indicative of poverty in a society where more detailed official statistics are not forthcoming.

There is the further problem that those benefits not based on insurance were seen by Beveridge, when they were created in the 1940s, as short term, both in the scope of who they were to cover – as increasing numbers in the population would be covered by insurance-based benefits – and short term in that those dependent on these benefits would not remain so for long periods of time. In the event neither assumption was justified, and increasing sectors of the population are dependent on these means-tested benefits on a long-term basis (Loney, Boswell and Clarke, 1983; Hill, 1990).

Recent studies have confirmed this suggestion that a poverty line drawn at the level of means-tested benefits reflects only those in extreme poverty, whilst actual benefit income is too low for even barest needs (Townsend, 1989; Stitt, 1990). A more generous definition of poverty is supported both by those on benefit and a wider population (Townsend, 1989). Using state benefit levels to measure poverty is problematic in that the numbers of those in poverty are seen to reduce if levels of benefit drop. When benefits become less generous, a situation familiar in Britain in the 1980s, then the poverty line also comes down, and low earners who are not dependent on benefit will correspondingly no longer be counted as poor. Clearly this is a nonsense, which is exemplified by any attempt to measure changes in the numbers of poor over time, using such a definition.

A further dilemma introduced by the use of a poverty line, to describe those in or on the margins of poverty, is that wherever the line is drawn, the cut-off point is artificial. There will always be those whose income is slightly over the income level and who will be defined as not poor, whilst their circumstances may be substantially the same as those whose income is slightly under the poverty line, and who are deemed to be poor. Using a two-stage approach to poverty including a marginal poverty line reduces this problem to some extent. Similarly, the depth of poverty suffered by those whose income is well below the poverty line is obscured, and differences between those just above or on the poverty line and those at the very bottom of the income scale are not accounted for.

The issue of income itself, however, is not without problems. There are a number of difficulties in accounting for the most simple of incomes – such as weekly wages, salaries and benefits. For example, income from these sources may not be received on a regular basis, for many people their take-home pay may vary every week or month as a result of overtime payments, piece-rates or bonuses, or where their hours of work depend on factors beyond their control. Benefits may similarly vary, and are often unreliable. Should the researcher adopt an accounting approach, attempting to match both income and outgoings for the same period of time, regardless of when it is actually received? Or should she focus on the flows of money in and out which may be responsible for short-term poverty, and increase difficulties of management which can result in greater costs – the need to borrow short term funds from high interest rate money lenders for example?

These problems are compounded by attempts to widen the definition of income to more realistically represent the flow of financial resources. In particular, measures of income need to recognize that all households, and perhaps especially those which are poor, may have or depend on other resources – borrowing, financial gifts and gifts in kind (Glendinning and Craig, 1990) – and the contrasting recognition that other forms of income accrue more generally to the higher income groups. Studies which focus entirely on earned income, social security benefits and interest income are likely to underestimate the gulf between the rich and poor. Widening the meaning of the term income to include other resources such as gifts, loans, occupational welfare, fiscal welfare, and the production of goods at home gives rise to the question of how such resources are to be valued and incorporated in a statement of income. Townsend's study in the 1960s attempted to do this, listing five different types of resource and specifically excluding 'services carried out by members of the household for the benefit of the household itself' (Townsend, 1979, p. 223).

The issue of the reality of a cut-off point for income, however this is finally added up, led to a search for a measure of deprivation which would reflect the impact of poverty and could be compared with levels of income, suggesting the extent to which a cut-off point obscures discrepancies.

Deprivation is defined by Townsend as a distinct concept:

> people may be said to be deprived if they do not have, at all or sufficiently, the conditions of life – that is the diets, amenities, standards and services – which allow them to play the roles, participate in the relationships and follow the customary behaviour which is expected of them by virtue of their membership of that society                                     (Townsend *et al.*, 1987, p. 4)

Deprivation, then, is also relative: the very term implies a group of people who are without the resources with which to lead a way of life taken for granted by a majority of the society in which they live and, by definition, a group who do have such resources.

The way in which deprivation can be measured has itself formed the focus of debate. Townsend (1979) constructed an index of deprivation, using a list of variables which were seen as representative of those items which would be generally accepted as customary or approved by society. The list included such items as inadequate footwear, shortages of fuel, no television or refrigerator, not having had a holiday, and, 'for the housewife only, no new winter coat in the past three years' (Townsend, 1979, pp. 414–15).

The focus of this list was the standard of living commonly accepted by society, although the list itself was drawn up by Townsend in consultation with other academics and social commentators. This list was then compared to the income measures used in the survey, to assess whether deprivation could be related to poverty. Townsend concluded that there was a point of income below which the household's deprivation score climbed dramatically – in other words, a suitable cut-off point could be found, where income below a certain level had rapid effects on participation in society, living standards and levels of deprivation.

Such a cut-off point would need to be reviewed regularly as it would clearly change in relation to income distribution as well as items to be included in such an index. For example, whilst increases in the proportion of people on state benefit might be an important factor, of greater significance is the extension of the time people are dependent on benefit, given that levels of benefit are not paid to cover long-term dependence.

The research carried out by Townsend and others in the 1980s implies that there continues to be a clear association between income and deprivation, and that below a certain level of income the overwhelming majority of households suffer multiple deprivation (Townsend, 1989; Townsend and Gordon, 1989). In addition, this level of income sufficient to prevent deprivation was found to be at least 50 per cent higher than rates of benefit being paid, and, in the case of lone parents, nearly 70 per cent above government rates of social security (Townsend, 1989).

Such a measure of deprivation – based on access to goods and services – has a number of strengths. For example, it may be compared more accurately with a list of goods and services which social security benefits are supposed to provide, and thus be of value in relating levels of state benefit to the meaning of poverty, rather than an abstract income level. It has the advantage of being able to go beyond figures to describe the impact of an inadequate income on people, and it also is capable of reflecting single deprivation – access to housing for example – as well as multiple deprivation resulting from low income. Thus intervening factors such as sexuality and discrimination in housing against gay men and lesbians can be incorporated. Further, by differentiating between material deprivation – a lack of material goods such as good housing or adequate food – and social deprivation – restricted social participation – the nature of links between these two areas can be explored. Finally, a measure of deprivation may also reflect the impact of continuous poverty and erratic income in a way that a 'snapshot' approach using measures of financial resources alone cannot.

However, Townsend's deprivation index from the original study came in for criticism. In particular, critics were concerned that the list represented the researcher's own beliefs regarding a minimum standard of living and made no allowance for the extent to which households exercised choice (Piachaud, 1981b). A rejoinder from Townsend argued that there was a significant association between low income and the index of deprivation which suggested an income barrier to satisfying needs, whilst the significance of culture and choice is precisely that there are strong pressures on the individual or household to conform to such living standards because they are commonly approved (Townsend, 1981).

The work of the Breadline Britain survey attempted to go beyond this, by using a 'consensus' approach to construct a list of variables which represented a minimum standard of living (Mack and Lansley, 1985). Their approach was similar to that of Townsend, in that they constructed a list of items which would equate to a deprivation index, but they asked a sample of the population to rank items according to whether they were necessary: thirty-five items were selected by a majority of this structured sample as being indicative of a minimum standard of living. The list included material goods, such as an indoor toilet and bath, a refrigerator and washing machine, and social items such as leisure activities, holidays and outings for children, although the survey focused on possession of these items, rather than their quality. There was a high degree of consensus over those items seen as necessities for a minimum standard of living, when the sample was divided according to class, or gender – thus women and men shared similar perceptions of the minimum needed in society (Mack and Lansley, 1985). However, the sample was too small to make the same assessment of perceptions according to ethnic group.

The fact that there was a high degree of similarity in answers from different groups was seen as supporting the concept of relative deprivation, and the possibility of outlining a standard of living widely seen as a minimum for all in society.

The survey followed up this list of necessities by asking the sample whether they had the item in question, and if not, whether they went without because they did not want it, or because they could not afford it. The result of this was a measure of deprivation according to a popular definition of what this means. The single item most often gone without through lack of money was reported as a holiday.

These findings were then related to the population as a whole, producing some stark figures as to the depth of relative poverty in Britain: suggesting some 5 million adults and 2.5 million children were living in poverty (Mack and Lansley, 1985, p. 90). Mack and Lansley found 23 per cent of the population in or on the margins of poverty, compared with 30 per cent found in Townsend's larger study (1979), and 28 per cent found by Rowntree at the turn of the century.

However, the crucial issue which this survey highlighted is that of choice – should a measure of deprivation include only those items which people claim to go without through lack of money, or should the question of effective choice mean that we cannot distinguish between those who are deprived for various reasons. For example, the 1986 English House Condition Survey found that those people living in the poorest accommodation – suffering overcrowding, damp and lacking basic amenities – were less likely to say they wanted to move to better housing than those who were less deprived. This lack of desire to move may simply be a realistic appraisal of the likelihood of such an event occurring – the issue of the power individuals have to change their circumstances, and reduce their deprivation, is an important one. Mack and Lansley (1985) adjusted their estimates of poverty for this element, which they termed 'low expectations'.

The issue of choice remains a sticking point in later studies, and is important in particular in relation to the operation of gender. In the London survey Townsend *et al.* construct an index of deprivation which is broken down into material and social indices, each of which is weighted for impact, but does not reflect adequately the ways in which the experiences of women and men differ (Townsend and Gordon, 1989).

Finally, the recent comparative studies of poverty and deprivation – for example the EEC funded National Reports on Anti-poverty Policy in member states (Brown, 1984), has lent urgency to the search for a definition which is comparable from one country to another. One answer to the problems of how to assess poverty in different countries – both developed and comparisons between developed and developing countries – has been to use an internal assessment. Thus a measure relating to income inequality inside each country has been used in the European programme of research, whilst other studies have focused on the concept of a standard income using scales of household equivalence (Mitton *et al.*, 1983; Millar, 1989; Brown, 1984), but the problem of comparability remains.

These difficulties highlight the fact that if defining poverty is hard, operationalizing a definition is harder still, and the links between the two mean that we shift between idealized and abstract questions of what we are seeking to uncover, and realistic and pragmatic questions of how that is to be done in the real world.

This chapter began with an outline of the two questions which constitute the focus of this discussion. Does the form of measurement used for both poverty and deprivation underestimate the number of women who are poor, or deprived, and obscure the gendered experience of these conditions; and does the form of measurement obscure the short- and long-term health effects for women of such experience? These questions are highlighted in the problems inherent in the ways in which poverty and deprivation have, to date, been measured.

## The problems of measurement

### Income and poverty

The focus on income as the central means by which poverty is measured is not without problems. As discussed above, the use of an income level and a cut-off point below which people or households are poor gives rise to a false dichotomy, the poor and the not-poor, when in many cases those just above and just below the line will be substantially similar in terms of access to resources and standards of living.

Income alone also fails to convey in sufficient detail the meaning of poverty – what it is like to live in circumstances of deprivation. There are advantages though. One is that a measure which is expressed in financial terms – a weekly income for example – can then be related to other measures similarly expressed. If we are interested in examining women's poverty this potential for comparison is particularly valuable.

For example, a definition of the poverty line at £50 per week would allow us to examine the likelihood of women being in poverty if they rely on earnings alone. Women's earnings are on average two thirds of men's, yet this fact in itself, whilst indicating women's inequality in society, does not tell us about vulnerability to poverty. If women earn on average less than the poverty line, women will be in poverty if they are the sole earners. This is of course more complex – poverty lines are expressed in relation to different household types. Nonetheless, a measure of the money needed to keep a household out of poverty is indicative for women's vulnerability. Single women in paid employment may earn on average more than the poverty line for that type of household, however, the income level needed by a lone mother to keep the household out of employment rises to reflect the larger household and increased needs. Yet women's earnings do not increase in line with the number of people dependent on them, whilst the opportunities for women to enter paid employment simultaneously contract.

This highlights the reasons for women's poverty in relation to an income level – women are poor because they are low paid, receive low pensions, or inadequate state benefits for example.

This focus on income has a negative impact on our understanding of women's poverty – it brings out the relationship between women's economic position and their vulnerability to poverty, but we need then to move one step further back to consider the origins of women's economic position – economic dependency.

A second consideration in the focus on income as a measure of poverty is that of how income is to be calculated. As described earlier, increasingly research has moved beyond simple household income to look at other ways in which financial resources accrue. Occupational welfare, for example, is a form of income in kind which employers pay to their employees and which has an impact on household income. Different kinds of occupational welfare relate to occupational status and the nature of the paid employment.

Employees in higher status employment, for example, are more likely to receive high-paying pensions, school fees for children, private medical insurance; whilst the company car or subsidized meals might be a 'perk' for employees of many different grades, and lower occupational groups have far fewer, and less valuable, benefits, such as clothing, for example (Sinfield, 1986; Townsend, 1979).

Occupational welfare is not only class related, though. Women in all sectors of employment receive fewer benefits – partly because benefits are defined in male orientated categories, and partly because few women work in the higher paid jobs. Part-time workers – the vast majority of whom are women – are far less often covered for sick pay and maternity leave, for example. (Sinfield, 1986; Dex, 1984; Brannen, 1987; Callender, 1987; Groves, 1987).

Similarly, fiscal benefits accrue through the tax system more often to men than women – more men own houses and receive tax relief on their mortgages, while there is no such relief on the forms of tenure where women as heads of household are more frequently found in the private and public rented sectors (Watson and Austerberry, 1986; Watson, 1986). Other fiscal benefits which should be added into a calculation of income include tax relief on private pension schemes, and again, more men than women are able to take advantage of these (Land and Ward, 1986; Lonsdale, 1987; Groves, 1987).

These are forms of income which should be included in the attempt to measure women's poverty. As has been described, Townsend (1979) also included in the 1960s survey a measure of gifts, loans and the production of resources such as home-grown produce, which saves the household money. The inclusion of these realities is valuable exercise for a measurement of women's poverty, but one important issue remains unresolved.

Women's domestic labour is that work carried out in the home without remuneration. It involves both housework – cooking, cleaning, washing clothes and so on – and childcare or care for other dependants. Estimates of the value to the husband and children of the housewife's labour have been produced by insurance companies keen to sell, to the spouse, life insurance for these women. Such estimates are calculated on the basis of the cost to the household of employing someone to perform the various tasks women carry out on behalf of their partner and children, and have been put by one company at over £10,000 per annum (Legal and General, 1990, *What is a Housewife?*). This figure may appear low given the skilled nature of such work and the long hours that both childcare and housework consume. Oakley (1974), for example, estimates up to 72 hours per week spent in housework. This suggests that the value of the housewife's production for home consumption (Delphy, 1984) which should be included in figures for income adds £200 a week on to estimates of a poverty line. Whilst this may appear unrealistic given current income levels, it does at least have the impact of acknowledging the value to the household of women's unpaid labour and of highlighting one of the major reasons for women's own poverty and deprivation, both material and social: their responsibility for this unpaid work in the home restricts labour market participation, perpetuates the myth of the 'breadwinner's' wage and women's economic dependency on a male, and restricts women's opportunities for leisure both inside and outside the home, and participation in political life.

The final question here is the extent to which a focus on income, as opposed to deprivation, prevents an examination of the relationship between health and poverty. Overcrowded, damp, poorly heated housing is more readily associated with poor health than low income. Restricted access to good quality accommodation, and a greater reliance on private rented housing, where the worst problems are found, or owner occupied housing in run down areas, or where there is no money left to ensure repairs are carried out or the heating is switched on, increase the likelihood of deprivation for women. In addition, inefficient heating systems, often found in the public sector, may lead to deprivation even where income is above the poverty line. These are effects which are likely to be experienced differently by the adults in the household.

## The household unit

The majority of studies on poverty and deprivation have followed the tradition laid down in the research of Rowntree, that of focusing on the household as the unit of consumption by which both income and poverty are assessed.

Such studies have developed sophisticated techniques with which to measure the income which goes into the household – to account for the earnings, gifts, loans, and goods and services-in-kind which are received by different members of the household. These measures are carefully constructed to ensure the study is reflecting the complexity of financial resources which go into the household. It is ironic that the second half of this equation – what happens within the household in terms of how income is used – is then reduced to the most simplistic of assumptions: that resources are shared equally. One illustration of how inaccuracies can result is the inclusion of occupational welfare as a form of income for the household as a whole, when it is initially received by the person in employment and will most often remain under that person's control. A simple example is that of the company car, most often a male 'perk', it also is mostly used by men, for work and for leisure, whilst the majority of women in this country have not got a full driving licence (Sinfield, 1986). The importance of this ownership of 'perks' is demonstrated by what happens on the breakdown of a relationship – most importantly in relation to private and occupational pensions, where women may lose their right to future income (Land and Ward, 1986; Land, 1986).

As described earlier, Pahl likens this approach to income study to the 'black box' – where all that goes on inside the unit of consumption is treated as unproblematic, and ignored for the purposes of study (Pahl, 1989). This has the result, quite obviously, of summarizing the occupants of households as poor or non-poor, not in relation to the access each one has to resources, but in relation to a theoretical notion of what they should have access to (Maclean, 1987).

That this 'black-box' approach might conceal inequalities is suggested by a growing volume of research on women's experience of poverty within the household, the way resources are actually shared and the way women report changes in their standard of living on the breakdown of a relationship (Graham, 1987a; Brannen and Wilson, 1987; Charles and Kerr, 1988; Pahl, 1989).

## The experience of poverty

One feature of poverty obscured by the 'black-box' assumption is that of how households alter their behaviour in times of shortage, and in particular, the different experience of men and women within a poor household. Land (1983) described different ways in which households divide income, which have different implications for women's access to the household's finances. One feature of this was the complexity of such studies – attempts to classify different systems of financial management used by households found that there are a vast range of methods beyond the simple types first outlined. However, one aspect of household finances highlighted by such classification systems is that women are more likely to have control of restricted income, and men are more likely to keep control when the income is high. Thus in households where the major income comes from state benefits, women more often have responsibility for managing the money, whilst in households where the main source of income is earnings, men will more often control the finances (Wilson, 1987a; 1987b; Land, 1983; Daly, 1989). The terms, 'responsibility', 'control' and 'managing' are important indicators of this relationship between money and power – for the task of surviving financially on a low income, such as state benefits, is hard work, whilst having control over higher earnings is a source of power, and the two cannot be equated. Thus it is that men retain control over income and women manage benefit: and for women poverty is a different experience, in that it draws on their skills as a manager, a 'good housekeeper', and exacts a price in terms of stress, anxiety and sheer hard work. As Daly (1989) points out, managing to survive on a minimal income is exhausting both mentally and physically. The need to buy only from the cheapest shops, hunt for bargains – every day for cheaper food as well as for items of clothing and domestic goods – means often going some distance, whilst public transport or private cars are too expensive, and walking must be substituted. Such 'managing' also creates an emotional burden – the worry of finding goods, entertaining children with no toys, keeping their minds off their hunger, taking them with you to the shops, and feeling guilty about everything. (Daly, 1989; Glendinning and Craig, 1990). This is the reality of 'managing' a low income for many women, and whilst men too will have worries, and be worn out by the burden of poverty, we are beginning to talk of a qualitatively different experience, which must therefore be reflected in the research process.

*Equal shares*

In addition to the ways women's experience of the same low income may differ, women may also not receive an equal share of the household's resources. There are two aspects to this, which are less separate than might appear.

One way in which women might go without is that they are denied access to the household's resources, and this highlights how women even in an affluent household may be poor in terms of their own living standard. This may occur in a number of ways, for example, there remain a number of women who do not know how much their partner earns, including those who knew once but who do not know of increases, bonuses, and so on (Land, 1983). Many men will see these extras as theirs by right – received for additional work, or increments for merit. Research suggests that the money women receive from their partner's for 'housekeeping' does not always rise in relation to inflationary increases paid by the employer (Land, 1983).

However, women will also go without in order to provide more for their children or partner – the concept that some resources, particularly food, should go first to men and children whilst women can cut back on their own intake remains a strong factor in poor households (Charles and Kerr, 1988; Graham, 1987a; Brannen and Wilson, 1987). It is mirrored throughout society however, in terms of who gets the choicest parts of the meal – the best quality meat, for example – and who gets the largest piece, the biggest steak (Charles and Kerr, 1988; Wilson, 1987a).

The other side of this is demonstrated by the way women after the breakdown of a relationship talk of feeling richer despite a lower income (Maclean, 1987; Graham, 1987a; Daly, 1989). This relates partly to their undisputed access to the household resources – although many will still deny themselves in order to provide for children (Daly, 1989), and partly because women can then choose differently (Charles and Kerr, 1988). There are marked differences in the kind of food men demand – cooked evening meals rather than salad, for example – which have further implications on the distribution of resources and the impact of poverty on women's 'management' of the household budget. Women living alone with their children report being able to buy cheaper sources of nutrition, and eat better as a result despite the overall decrease in their available income (Graham, 1987a; Wilson, 1987a).

It is also the case that women will see household income differently, according to the source. Thus men's earnings are seen, by both partners, to be primarily his, although some will be paid to the woman for household purchases, and some will be spent by the man on joint costs such as housing and bills for fuel for example. However, women are more likely to see their own income from paid employment outside the home as belonging to the household and are more likely to spend it on goods for domestic consumption rather than individual (Pahl, 1989), and are more likely to offset their wages, rather than the joint income, against childcare costs (Brannen, 1987). Women's and men's perceptions of income and the allocation of resources are deep rooted and bear part of the explanation both for cases of absolute denial by men of money and of women going without.

Thus women are less likely to buy goods for themselves out of either their own earnings or their housekeeping, whilst men have some money kept aside for their own personal use. This results not only in the way women deny themselves or are denied new clothing – one woman in Pahl's study found difficulty in buying herself a new pair of tights from her own earnings (Pahl, 1989) – but also it is clearly related to women's access to leisure activities both inside and outside the home. Women's leisure is primarily either cheap or free, reading from the library, for example, or is derived from goods shared by the household anyway – watching the television – and which can be combined with other work; or it is productive, such as knitting. Men's leisure pursuits, on the other hand, are more widespread, and more likely to involve activity away from the home (Deem, 1988; Pahl, 1989).

This suggests that the impact of an income which is not shared needs to be examined in relation to both material and social deprivation. This leads on to the next issue: that of how the actual experience of deprivation for each sex may also differ.


## Deprivation and gender

Lists of items which together might be said to constitute an index of deprivation, or a standard of living below which constitutes poverty, are an attempt to reflect the conditions of life which are enjoyed by the majority or are seen as the minimum living standard in a society. As we have seen, various ways of drawing up this list of goods, services, activities and so on, have relied on academic and social observation, and the opinions of a cross-section of the population. In general, however, measures of deprivation have focused on items enjoyed by the household as a whole, or by children, but rarely by one or other adult member alone. Questions relate to whether the household has a refrigerator or washing machine, but do not consider the different impact on each sex of the lack of such a resource (Mitton *et al.*, 1983; Mack and Lansley, 1985).

For example, not having a refrigerator means the person responsible for buying and providing food – most often the woman – must plan meals accordingly, and will spend more time shopping; not having hot water or a bathroom means different things to the man who uses hot water for washing and shaving in comparison with the woman who is responsible for childcare, the washing of clothes and cleaning the house.

Deprivation indices which do not take account of either specific needs of men and women, or of the ways the same lack will affect each sex differently as a result of their domestic obligations, are failing to document the prevalence and true meaning of deprivation. Recent attempts to separate and account for material and social deprivation as distinct phenomena are similarly problematic. The crucial test of any index must inevitably be whether it highlights or disguises standards of living for each sex, and where these might differ, and this can only be done by relating an index to the actual lived experience of women and men.

Townsend's index of material and social deprivation, used in the recent survey of poverty in London (Townsend *et al.*, 1987) therefore goes some way towards meeting these criticisms. For example, recognizing the problem with heating for women or other adults at home all day – by scoring this twice where there are adult carers – is a major step forward. Deprivation in the workplace has been measured in the past, but it is only recently that women's 'workplace' – the home – has been recognized as a site of deprivation, and that women who work full time in domestic labour are at home all day and thus suffer more from housing deprivation. Townsend resolved this by repeating the housing deprivation score for those who were not in paid employment and who performed more than twenty hours a week of caring for dependants. However, whilst there remains a question over how the extra weight of such caring in deprived circumstances might be assessed, difficulties also arise in this new appreciation of women's domestic labour. For example, there is the issue of how to treat women who do have a paid job but who also carry out the domestic labour of the household, as the majority of women in paid employment do (Sharpe, 1984; Brannen and Moss, 1987). The meaning of housing deprivation for women is that for both those in paid employment and those at home all day, their housework is harder – it is more difficult to clean an overcrowded house, to remove damp and mould, to dry clothes, to turn poorly repaired and decorated accommodation into a pleasant environment.

Similarly the score for locational deprivation – the deprivation of a poor environment and difficulties caused by lack of local facilities – is also scored twice in Townsend's study for those working at home caring for dependants. Again, this is an improvement, but is insufficient as it does not attempt to measure who will suffer more if shops are further than ten minutes away in households where the woman has paid employment outside the home.

The list of household amenities is not weighted differently for men and women. Both sexes, if they live in a household without a washing machine, receive the same score and this fails to reflect who carries the added toil of washing clothes by hand or going to the launderette, often with children in tow, both in homes where the woman has a paid job and where she does not.

Thus recent studies have attempted to take account of ways in which women might suffer deprivation as a result of their caring and domestic obligations at home but as yet they have not yet gone far enough. The importance of these obligations in a discussion of the health effects of poverty and deprivation cannot be overstated, for the extent of the physical and emotional toll on women in these conditions can easily be overlooked.

This highlights the complexities of household behaviour and resource allocation, further demonstrating the inadequacy of a 'black-box' approach to an understanding of society. The simple household approach assumes women's economic dependency needs are met; research which goes inside this black box and examines who gets what within the household shows us how much this assumption is at odds with the reality for many women. This assumption that women's economic dependency needs are met within the household is not confined to economic and poverty research: it is central to the operation of the labour market – the breadwinners' wage, for example, and women's lower earnings; it is central to the payment of state benefits and as such it is central to an understanding of the causes of women's poverty. It is precisely because women are assumed to be economically dependent on men that women are poor.

## The 'snapshot' approach to poverty

It is not only the question of what is measured and how, but when. Using income as a measure of poverty requires a rethink in terms of what is included, and focusing on the household as a unit of consumption requires a more substantial shift to highlight access to resources and different kinds of consumption. But in order to measure women's experience of poverty and deprivation we need to move towards a more long-term approach to the analysis of income and living standards. People move in and out of poverty during the course of a lifetime, in relation to employment status and earnings and the number of dependants they have. Periods out of the labour market – in sickness, old age, during maternity and child-rearing, and during unemployment – have a marked effect on income and poverty, whilst the mismatch between earnings or benefits and the needs of those dependent on this income is a further cause of poverty.

These events come and go so that the numbers of people in poverty at any one time underestimates the proportion of the population who will spend some period of their lives in poverty or circumstances of deprivation.

Some groups, however, are more vulnerable to poverty and deprivation. People in the lower occupational groups are more likely to suffer periods out of the labour market as a result of poor health and disability, unemployment and redundancy, and of pregnancy in employment where the job is not protected. At the same time, the lower earnings of these groups will mean fewer resources to fall back on and fewer opportunities for alternative financing – loans for example.

The movement in and out of poverty, and on and off state benefit paid at short term rates, will result in greater difficulties with each new episode of poverty, whilst returning to the labour market does not reduce poverty, due to the backlog of needs which must be met, for example for new clothes or domestic appliances. The Social Fund system brought in in the 1986 Social Security Act, in which claimants may receive loans for needs which cannot be met from weekly benefit, means that a return to paid employment is even less likely to mean an end to poverty than ever before, whilst simultaneously reducing opportunities for saving and providing against the next period of dependence on state benefit.

Thus exposure to poverty can begin at an early age – to children born to those dependent on state benefit – and continue throughout life up to an old age spent on the state pension, which is supplemented by means-tested benefits because it is so low. This life cycle in effect represents a vulnerability to poverty which results from the operation of the labour market and state benefits, and which means working-class people are more vulnerable to poverty throughout their lives.

However, as a group women are particularly prone to this vulnerability to poverty. Women spend a larger proportion of their total lives in poverty (Millar and Glendinning, 1989), and this carries very strong implications for the way poverty must be measured if we are to encapsulate women's experience of poverty and the experience of living with the threat of poverty.

Focusing on vulnerability means moving away from a snapshot approach to poverty – how many of the population are poor at any one time – towards considering lifetime income and resources, and the total period spent in poverty or on the margins. This needs to be done if we are to consider the nature of the relationship between health and poverty, for it is not only the periods spent in poverty that exact a cost in terms of health, but also the threat of poverty and deprivation over time, and the effect this has.

It is also true that the health impact of poverty and deprivation is rarely immediate and observable – it is the lifetime toll of poor nutrition and damp housing that correlates to higher rates of mortality, not six months as part of a life span. It is important to know not only who the poor are at any one time, but what proportion of them were born to poor mothers, what proportion of their lives have been spent in poverty and which part of their lives was spent in poverty. Five years spent in poverty during childhood might have a more substantial effect on adult health than five years in poverty at a later age. Recent research on the links between ischaemic heart disease amongst adults and socio-economic circumstances during childhood suggests that childhood poverty does indeed carry long-term implications for some conditions (Kaplan and Salonen, 1990). For women, poverty during puberty and inadequate nutrition at this time may also lead to greater risks of still birth and health problems for any children they may have in later life.

Income is, therefore, transient and there are crucial differences in the way this changes over time for each sex. This movement in and out of poverty is central to an analysis of women's experience of poverty, and the health impact of this. It depends, however, not purely or even primarily on a direct relationship with the labour market, but on a secondary relation to this labour market, that is, women's movement in and out of economic dependency in relationships and the extent to which their economic dependency needs are met.

If we examine this in relation to the life cycle, despite drawbacks in an approach which attempts to typify or generalize the lived experience, the different vulnerabilities of each sex becomes clearer. In childhood and early adolescence, before the arrival of children, the experience is somewhat similar, although female children are likely to receive less in the way of resources in the parental home, and are expected to contribute more to the domestic labour of the household. Young women will also mostly earn less than young men. However, differences become even more marked with the arrival of children.

Once children are born the position of men and women alters substantially, for, as carers, women become economically dependent on either a male partner, the State or another adult, such as their own father. Their relationship to the labour market becomes indirect rather than direct, and their access to resources is mediated through another, either in private, as women become economically dependent on their partner, or through the public agency of the social security system. Even where women take only a short period out of the labour market, their employment status has substantially altered as a result of the need to find a paid job which can be managed alongside responsibility for children. Thus women mostly return to paid work part time, in jobs which are less well paid and carry fewer benefits such as sick pay, often taking jobs near to schools or childminders, while the time out of the labour market has a 'de-skilling' effect reducing their earning power (Main, 1988; Hunt, 1988a).

Women become vulnerable to poverty when they become economically dependent on men and thus lose direct access to earnings gained in the labour market. The underlying causes of women's poverty are that women are determined as the economic dependants of men in the structure of the labour market in the payment of wages and the payment of state benefits. Alongside this assumption of economic dependency lies the reality of women's lives – both for women who are outside partnerships with men, and for women who are inside relationships where resources are not shared, either because the 'breadwinner's wage' is too little for those who rely on it and women choose to go without in order to provide more for others, or because women are denied access to household resources. Thus women's vulnerability to poverty is the result of this myth that men are the providers and women often face the choice of poverty inside a relationship or outside.

## A feminist definition?

It would not be enough to leave a critique of traditional methods of measuring poverty without putting in place an alternative model. Such an alternative tool of measurement would require a focus on individual experience of deprivation within the household – looking at both material and social components of a standard of living approach. In terms of material deprivation, any measure used would need to include items highlighting experiences which may differ for each sex, where the list might either include different items or weight items differently to reflect who was most affected by the lack. Measures are increasingly being developed to reflect the extent to which individuals suffer social deprivation or isolation. This is a valuable addition to an understanding of the various dimensions of relative poverty and deprivation, one which also needs an approach which highlights gender. Measurements of social deprivation need to include access to social activities and public space, access to time for leisure, the money to pursue leisure and the energy for such activities; although as a corollary to this the kinds of social support women and men get could also be included.

This need to distinguish between the experiences of women and men requires a shift of focus to the individual within the household, using a measure of the resources which are available to them for their needs. Millar and Glendinning (1989) suggest a more valid measure would compare women's incomes with the expenditure for which they are responsible and they cite a study in which the proportion of women in poverty increased by 50 per cent when this method was used. As suggested earlier, women's earnings could be used to measure the threat of poverty – the extent to which women would be in poverty if reliant on their own earned income. Women's rates of pay could also be used to calculate the time taken to earn the resources needed to sustain themselves and their dependants – again, a measure which would highlight the gulf between men and women (Millar and Glendinning, 1989).

A new measure of poverty would also have to find a way of incorporating the value to others of the work women do in the home. Scott (1984) recalculates women's earnings on the basis of the total hours women work, rather than hours in paid employment. On this basis, the vast majority of women world-wide are poor (Scott, 1984).

### Conclusion

Limitations of traditional studies in highlighting women's exposure to and experience of poverty mean that the impact on women's health of such factors is also underestimated. The effect of this 'black box' in poverty research is to obscure the depth and underlying causes of women's poverty, the accentuated risk for women of suffering poverty throughout their lives, and the impact of this poverty on health, both physical and mental.

# CHAPTER 3

# WHY ARE WOMEN POOR?

Women have been the poorer sex throughout this century, and have formed a substantial majority of the poor since poverty was first recognized or measured. Women were the majority of recipients of poor relief in Victorian times, and the majority of those in the workhouse and other institutions, such as the lunatic asylum (Thane, 1978; Showalter, 1987; Lewis and Piachaud, 1987).

Women have also made up the majority of the poor in later surveys – as lone older women in poverty, lone mothers, and as one member of a two-adult household. Whilst the poverty of old people and children has long been recognized (Glendinning and Millar, 1987; see, for example, Townsend, 1957; Townsend, 1979; Marsden, 1969), this has not been related to gender and women's position more generally. Thus observations that older people and lone parents are more often poor than other groups in society, and the recognition that lone older women and lone mothers are poorer than lone older men or lone fathers, have failed to produce a recognition of the role played by gender in this process.

Recent feminist analysis has drawn attention to this weakness, linking women's experience of poverty, and their greater risk of poverty throughout their lives, to their experience as women in patriarchal and capitalist societies. One aspect of this critique has been the argument advanced by some that a 'feminization of poverty' has taken place. Thus Scott (1984) argues that women's poverty has increased and that women are now at more risk of poverty during their lives. Similarly Zopf (1989) has argued that women's poverty in the USA has grown because of increasing numbers of women

who are lone mothers, and that women are now the greater proportion of the poor as a result of a rise in the number of women bringing
up children alone (Zopf, 1989).

This representation of women as a growing army of poor under-
estimates the extent to which women have always suffered poverty
and deprivation, and the invisibility of women's experience, both in
society and amongst those who hold the measuring stick. Thus
women have formed a constant proportion of those in receipt of
state assistance: in 1908, women represented 61 per cent of those in
receipt of Poor Law Relief, whilst in 1983 women were 60 per cent
of those on supplementary benefit, the means tested social security
benefits which predated Income Support (Lewis and Piachaud,
1987). Clearly comparisons over time are not easy to make, given
not only the difficulty of obtaining figures from the early part of this
century, but also the difficulty of obtaining figures of a comparable
nature today. It is becoming increasingly hard to monitor trends
over recent history at a time when methods of counting the poor are
changing and are disputed. However, anecdotal evidence from
women trying to manage low incomes with large families demonstrates not only the depth of poverty amongst women at the beginning of this century, but also the consistency of the reasons for
their deprivation. A central criticism of the traditional measures of
poverty is of the focus on the household as a unit of consumption
(Pahl, 1989; 1980; Wilson, 1987b; Brannen and Wilson, 1987). Evidence from women in the early part of this century suggests that the
pattern of women going without – either to allow more for others
or where women are denied equal shares – existed, and was well
known, at the beginning of this century (Pember-Reeves, 1913;
Llewellyn Davies, 1915; Hewitt, 1958). A study in 1895 documented the poorer diets of women in comparison with men, and
female children in comparison with male children, especially in low
income households (Oliver, 1895, cited in Pahl, 1989). However,
poverty research has continued to assume a division of resources
within the household which is equitable and agreed – a consensus
model of the family, rather than a conflict model (Millar and Glendinning, 1989). Thus women's experience of denial is seen, both in
the study of poverty and in the household itself, as voluntary and
self-sacrificial, rather than imposed, and as a legitimate and natural
resolution to income difficulties (Land and Rose, 1985; Millar and
Glendinning, 1989).

Similarly, women's earnings have remained low in comparison with those of men, despite the introduction of equal opportunities legislation in the latter half of this century. Thus in 1886 adult women in full-time employment were paid on average 52 per cent of male earnings (Lewis and Piachaud, 1987); in 1988 women's earnings were on average 67 per cent of the figure for men (Social Trends, 1990). This represents a gain of a mere 15 per cent over the course of the century, whilst women continue to receive on average only two-thirds of male rates of pay.

The feminization of poverty thesis, which argues that women's poverty has increased in this century and that women have formed a growing proportion of the poor, is therefore misplaced.*What has happened however is that women's poverty has become more visible. Changing demography means that women are now more likely to be poor as a result of lone motherhood, marital and relationship break down, and old age, and less often poor within large family households (Millar, 1989a; Graham, 1987c; Groves, 1987; Land, 1969). Women who are poor, as a result, are more easily counted and more readily observed, although the extent of the poverty women continue to experience within households remains obscured by both poverty research and government statistics. Further trends in recent years, however, suggest that women's risk of poverty, and the severity of that poverty, are growing, as a result of changes in the labour market and in social policy. Changes in the payment of social security and the increasing privatization of benefits such as maternity pay, sick pay and occupational pensions, have had a significant impact on women's risk of poverty. Similarly the restructuring of the labour market, and changes in the availability and cost of childcare, also carry specific implications for women (Millar, 1989a, Room *et al.*, 1989; Andrews and Jacobs, 1990). The increasing marginalization of women's employment, poorer pay and conditions of employment, and cuts in real rates of social security, suggest that whilst paid work as a source of income for women is becoming more limited, social security benefits are increasingly unlikely to prevent serious poverty and deprivation.

The so-called demographic time bomb, where fewer young people are entering the labour market, means that in Britain and other Western countries older female workers are increasingly needed. Employers have responded to the need for skilled women in clerical and office work with the introduction of workplace nurseries, longer maternity leave and longer periods in which a woman's job is held open. However, these moves to retain women employees have been concentrated in the private sector, and amongst women in higher occupational groups, and women have not benefited equally from these moves. Class and other factors – race, disability, age and sexuality – also divide women and structure the gulf between those who occupy these different sectors of the labour market.

How then can we assess the risks of poverty for women, as opposed to those for men, and how can the impact of gender be disentangled from factors of race, class, disability and age, in their significance for poverty? One way of examining women's risk of poverty lies in a focus on the factors which create poverty. We need to move from the direct causes of poverty – low pay or inadequate state benefits, for example – to the underlying ones. And it becomes possible to fit gender as a factor in poverty into a model where race, class, age and disability also figure. The key questions to be addressed in this chapter, then, are: what are the causes of women's poverty, both direct and underlying, and what are the relationships between these factors and risk factors for other groups in society?

One approach to this is through a more detailed appraisal of the sources of income, wealth and poverty to see what differences there are between the sexes in how they come to be rich or poor. Mary Daly, in her book on women and poverty in Ireland (1989) notes that a crucial difference between the sexes lies in their distribution amongst the very rich and the very poor – thus whilst both men and women suffer poverty, more men than women enjoy affluence and wealth at the other end of the scale: if some men are poor, some are also very rich (Daly, 1989). This gives an insight into the way gender might operate in the creation of risk factors for poverty. Thus the different sources of wealth and income are not evenly distributed and, crucially, women are more often dependent for their income on relationships, whilst for men, the primary source of income is earnings.

Women's poverty is related not simply to the actual distribution of resources in society, but the mechanisms through which this distribution operates. People are rich or poor according to their receipt of – and their ability to obtain – resources in one of four different ways: wealth, and income from wealth; earned income and the labour market; state benefits; and resources from others – most commonly intra-household transfers and divisions, but also inter-household transfers, such as between parents and adult children.

Using these as origins of wealth or poverty, the distinction between the opportunities each sex has to maintain a standard of living above the poverty line becomes more clear, as does the role played in each of these four spheres by other factors.

This distinction between different origins of resources does not mean a focus entirely on cash income. Some resources will be received as welfare benefits, gifts or services by others: for example, occupational welfare services or presents from relatives, including money, goods and time – a relative looking after children to enable a parent to go out for either paid employment or leisure. Other inputs which constitute resources include services within the home carried out by a member of the household – unpaid domestic labour and the tending of sick or infirm relatives, for example.

Not only should such resources be included as a form of income and thus part of the overall total which determines poverty (Townsend, 1979); many resources also have implications for access to further income or wealth – for example, credit is more easily obtained by those with capital, whilst having someone to care for children increases access to the paid labour market.

It is the circumstances in which the distribution of these different kinds of resources is negotiated or determined which creates women's greater vulnerability to poverty (Millar, 1989b). Access to resources within households is influenced by the way all resources are brought into the house, for example by earnings or benefits (Brannen and Wilson, 1987). Assessing intra-household distribution should also take account of resources which are 'brought in' by women's production of use values through domestic labour (Delphy, 1984; Millar, 1989b): this is not usually recognized in the transfer of other resources within the household, either time or financial. Different stages of household formation are also important factors in the distribution of income, often in combination with levels of income (Atkinson, 1985). Thus not all women are equally disadvantaged within the household, and the presence, age and number of children, in conjunction with the resources available to the household are also significant factors.

It is crucial to recognize the extent of the limits to this generalization of household behaviour. If the economists' 'black box' is inadequate for pinpointing the ways in which women's share of resources is mediated by gender, it is also inadequate as a representation of the many ways in which households differ. The question of how resources are distributed within the household may be ethnocentric, in that some black women are far less likely to live in two-parent households, particularly Afro-Caribbean women, whilst women from Asian backgrounds are more likely to live in larger household types, with several other adults present. The reasons for this differentiation are complex, relating to the political history of slavery and colonialism (Thorogood, 1987). Sexuality – and the division of resources between couples and children in gay and lesbian relationships similarly suggests that any attempt to break down the model of household behaviour must start with a recognition of these differences, mediated by class, race, sexuality, and so on. The 'black box' approach to the household is under-pinned by a notion of the white, heterosexual family, and is in-adequate for an understanding of the specific experience of any individual in society.

In negotiating access to resources, there are crucial differences in the way each sex views their earned income. Men more often retain part of their earnings for personal consumption, even when money is tight (Townsend, 1979; Graham, 1987c), whilst women tend to use their own earnings for household rather than personal expenditure (Brannen and Moss, 1987; Millar, 1989b; Pahl, 1989).

Thus it is not simply a question of women who do not have paid employment who are denied access or who deny themselves access to household resources. This question of the way households treat resources is extremely complex – earnings and social security bene-fits are paid to individuals, although benefits are more clearly related to household composition or assessment unit in the calculation of the total to be paid. Expenditure can be both individual or joint, in terms of the mechanics of shopping, paying the money or writing a cheque, but it is complex to untangle the distribution of benefits and burdens associated with this. Buying goods and resources for daily living, paying for services consumed, and making major outlays are all forms of expenditure which may have different kinds of respon-sibility attached to them, and the money may come from different sources. Thus differences may not only be in terms of who has access to the resources purchased, but also who takes the responsibility for making a purchase and who has the power to make decisions over what is bought. In addition, household costs vary over time, which may affect either purchasing behaviour and responsibility, or may act to increase or decrease the deprivation suffered by some members of the household if such changes in needs are not recognized (Brannen and Wilson, 1987; Wilson, 1987b; Pahl, 1989; 1983).

The approach to women's poverty used here examines the factors which determine access to resources in each of four ways in which these are accumulated. It starts from the origins of wealth and poverty and the factors through which access is mediated. If we assess the relative importance for each sex of each of these sources, it becomes possible to locate gender as a factor alongside other factors such as race and class. The intention is not to prioritize these – to argue that women are poorer than working-class men, or than men who are black or from ethnic minority groups. Clearly there are likely to be substantial differences between a white middle-class woman and a black working-class man in their experience of poverty, and the extent to which each is vulnerable to poverty. However, to argue that one is more disadvantaged than the other prevents what is the more useful task: an evaluation of the part factors such as race, class and gender play in determining the access of individuals to resources from different sources.

This approach differs from those of studies which have recognized women's poverty as one aspect of the distribution of poverty in general. In such approaches women's experience of poverty has tended to be related to the inadequacy of state provision for these groups – state pensions, social security programmes for single parents, and, for younger women bringing up children, the lack of childcare facilities which would enable these women to work. However, without an explicit reference to the means through which resources are distributed, these accounts of women's poverty remains descriptive rather than analytical.

The last chapter described models of vulnerability to poverty which are based on access to the labour market and responsibility for the care of dependants (Townsend, 1987; Field, 1981; 1987), and the way such lists of risk factors tend to overlap: thus women who are responsible for children either as lone parents or in the two-parent household are less often in paid employment, or are in part-time employment as a result of women's primary childcare role in all Western societies. There are however, further gender-based distinctions – for example, men are more likely than women to find paid employment after a physical disability (Maclean and Jefferys, 1974). It is also not simply a question of absence from paid employment but also of what people receive in the labour market. For women, the issue of earnings versus childcare costs is often crucial in their decision whether or not to seek paid employment, as typically the opportunity cost of women's labour outside the home, in terms of alternative childcare, is seen as a cost to the woman, paid out of her wages (Brannen, 1987; Martin and Roberts, 1984; Sharpe, 1984).

If a list is drawn up of different stages in the life cycle or different causes of poverty the underlying links are overlooked. Thus to describe women's poverty simply in terms of each group of women who are most at risk of poverty – lone mothers, women who care for children or other dependants, women as low earners or older women living alone – means the relationship between the factors causing poverty for each group is obscured.

## Poverty in the United Kingdom

In order to address the question of why women are poor we need to firstly assess levels of poverty in the United Kingdom and the representation of women. However, immediately the problems described in the previous chapter return to the centre of the debate. The definition of poverty and methods used to measure it remain problematic, particularly in view of the availability or otherwise of figures from government sources to describe poverty in the United Kingdom in the 1980s and 1990s.

The preceding chapter concluded that poverty must be defined as a relative term, from the basis of a standard of living which is generally accepted as the minimum in society. There are various ways in which this can be determined, using either a sample of the population or a group of experts. In each case, a consensus is being sought to reflect 'wider society', and as with all consensus approaches suffers from the lack of voice of significant minorities or those without power to determine the agenda. Thus, in describing poverty, the caution expressed in the last chapter in relation to the limitations of both official statistics and much of what constitutes poverty research must be reiterated. In some respects it is the same caution which applies to discussions of health, and inequalities in health, in that we are presented with an imperfect set of statistics which are routinely criticized but are used, on the basis that it is all we have!

However, the ways in which women's access to resources is mediated by gender carries further implications for the measurement of poverty. This was described in more detail in the last chapter, and whilst the fact remains that available data focuses on household income, some steps forward can be made by breaking income and wealth figures down further into four distinct areas, as seen later.

The other problem to bear in mind in this discussion of who the poor are, in official statistics, is that these figures present a 'snap-shot' of numbers in poverty at any one time. Again, as described earlier, people move in and out of poverty, and the health effects of poverty must be related to periods of time spent in poverty and under the threat of poverty. For example, a study of premature death in two areas of North Tyneside revealed strong associations with long-term unemployment and poverty and early death (Philli-more, 1989). In particular, the research found that those who had died under retirement age in more affluent areas were more likely to be 'new recruits' who had led the majority of their lives in poorer circumstances.

## Who are the poor?

The simplest measure of poverty in the United Kingdom is that which uses as a poverty line the level at which means-tested state benefits have been set. Using this measure, those on or below this income level are described as poor, whilst those whose income is up to 40 per cent above the poverty line are described as being on the margins of poverty. This higher rate partly expresses the small savings and earnings which are disregarded in the calculation of benefit, and is partly used as a response to evidence suggesting that this higher level is equal to a 'deprivation threshold', below which people's participation and consumption drops notably (Townsend, 1989; Oppenheim, 1988).

One source of such figures in the past was the series, Low Income Families, last produced by the then Department of Health and Social Security in 1988. This revealed that in 1985 a total of 15.4 million people in Great Britain were living in or on the margins of poverty, a figure which represented 28.5 per cent of the population (DHSS, 1988). Of this figure, there were 2.4 million people living below the level of state benefits, nearly 7 million who were depen-dent on means tested state benefits and 6 million people whose income was over this level, but less than 140 per cent above the poverty line. Thus, using the state assistance level as a poverty line reveals 4.5 per cent of the population in extreme poverty, and well over a quarter of the population in or on the margins of poverty in 1985.

The figures, however, do not reveal the proportions of men or women in these poor households – how many were two-adult households, lone adult households or lone parents. A very large proportion of all families with children were in poverty, and this gives an indication of the poverty of women in these families, alongside other members of the household, although again we do not know details about the distribution of resources within these poor households. Studies would suggest women are likely to experience greater poverty within these households: as women in low-income households are more likely to be responsible for managing the budget, taking a large part of the strain of this, and as although both parents are likely to go without in order to provide for children, women are likely to have least of all (Evason, 1980; Graham, 1984; Glendinning and Craig, 1990; Daly, 1989).

The statistics also clearly do not include the poverty experienced by some members of an affluent household. In addition, the figures do not tell us about the depth of poverty – households with an income below the poverty line are classed together. Thus the household with an income only 1 or 2 per cent below the line share the same category as households where the income is only half the means tested baseline. Similarly, households which are only 1 per cent above the basic poverty line are classified in a different way to households on the poverty line, and are implicitly seen as less poor.

Furthermore, we know nothing of the length of time the household has been in poverty, yet this will have a serious impact on the standard of living a household can enjoy. Whether the household has savings left, unpaid bills, or major household appliances which need replacing affect the meaning of the poverty suffered by different households (Sen, 1983), a concern made more urgent by the system of discretionary Social Fund loans. Thus income alone increasingly tells us less about the severity of poverty, unless it is combined with an assessment of such other considerations. And as the household appliances and goods of long-term claimants become more worn and are replaced with loans which reduce the net value of benefits, such measures will increasingly reflect only the minimum of those in poverty.

Using these figures alone therefore implies a satisfaction that levels of state benefit represent a minimum income which will keep a household out of poverty. Such assumptions are seriously flawed: one study suggests that levels of means-tested state support may be up to 61 per cent too low to finance the needs of the household (Townsend, 1989). Similarly Stitt (1990) suggests that current income support levels can finance only 50 or 60 per cent of the needs of the household as described by government or 'neutral' guidelines for minimum needs.

This deficiency in social security benefits suggests that using state benefits as a poverty line for households seriously understates the size of the poor population and the depth of the poverty they experience. And in no sense does it account for or describe the poverty experienced by some members of both poor and affluent households which is greater than the poverty of others within that household.

Despite these limitations in figures for people and households on or below the poverty line as defined by state benefits, the statistics were valuable indicators of minimum levels of poverty in the population and of trends in poverty over time. However, the series Low Income Families Statistics was last published in 1988, and it has been replaced by a new report, Households Below Average Income. The new statistics are based on data from the Family Expenditure Survey, and are thus based on a sample of the population. The report uses average incomes for households of different sizes, using what are called 'equivalence scales' to compare different household types, so that the income of a single retired adult living alone can be compared with a household of two adults and two children. The figures give details for households in different income groups – the lowest 10 per cent of the population up to the lowest 50 per cent.

The new series was justified on the grounds that the Low Income Families' (LIFS) figures did not sufficiently describe the distribution of income across the population. In particular, it was claimed that LIFS had the effect of increasing the numbers of those in poverty every time the benefits were increased, and thus they reflected general rising living standards rather than poverty itself.

The figures themselves do give greater detail on the make-up of those on the lowest incomes. The figures are based on people within different household types: thus, in 1985, 56 per cent of the lowest decile were people living in households with two adults and children, 15 per cent were people in pensioner households, 13 per cent were in single households without children, 9 per cent were in two-adult households without children, and 7 per cent were in lone-parent households. If these proportions are compared with the population as a whole, then some groups appear more likely to be poor than others: in particular, lone parents and families with children. There were also more households where the head of the household was unemployed, sick or disabled.

The report produced by Johnson and Webb (1990a) which focused on low-income families revealed slightly different distributions and gives a more direct indication of the extent to which certain groups are over-represented in figures for poverty, rather than below average income. In 1987, of those people living in or on the margins of poverty, 31 per cent were pensioners, 34 per cent were living in households comprising two adults and children, and 11 per cent were living in lone-parent households (Johnson and Webb, 1990a). By comparing these proportions with figures for the population as a whole, both pensioners and lone-parent households were substantially over-represented in the figures for those in poverty.

The tables in the Households Below Average Income series also demonstrate the importance to those on lower incomes of state social security benefits. In 1985 75 per cent of the income of this decile came from social security, compared with 19.3 per cent of the population's income as a whole (DHSS, 1988).

However, again the figures in this report fail to be a complete measure of poverty. One problem lies in the aggregation of individuals, and different benefit assessment units, into households. Using the household as a basis once again assumes shared resources, and this is quite explicit in the report. The opening pages of the first report state:

> the unit of the analysis is to be the individual so that all individuals receive equal weight . . . all members of any one household will occur at exactly the same point in the income distribution since they are all taken to have an income level determined by the income . . . of the household as a whole.    (DHSS, 1988, p. 2)

This aggregation also has the effect of reducing the overall total of units in poverty, if the household rather than benefit assessment unit is counted (Oppenheim, 1988). The new series also means that it is no longer possible to judge the effects of poverty policy by the

government's own standard – as figures no longer show the proportion of the population falling below the means-tested poverty
line. Furthermore, the new figures begin with 1981, and the increase
in numbers dependent on state benefit between 1979 and 1981 is
thus incorporated into the baseline (Oppenheim, 1988).

Although establishing trends is clearly a difficult and suspect task,
given the problems of the changing basis of figures and new methods
of calculation and presentation, the figures in the Low Income
Families series suggest an increase in the proportion of the population in or on the margins of poverty, from 22 per cent in 1979 to
29 per cent in 1985. The population on or below the poverty line
increased in those years from 12 per cent to 17 per cent, whilst the
proportion who were very poor, that is below the poverty line,
increased from 3.9 per cent to 4.4 per cent (Low Income Families
Statistics, 1986; 1988). Although the LIFS' data was not produced
after 1988, a study commissioned by the House of Commons Social
Services Committee on the same basis revealed a further increase in
the proportion of the population in poverty in 1987, with 34.3 per
cent of the population living in or on the margins of poverty (Johnson and Webb, 1990a). Over the past decade there has been a
significant increase in the numbers of poor, from less than a quarter
of the population in 1979 (22 per cent) to over a third in 1987
(Townsend, 1990b).

Figures based on the share of income gained by the poorest 10
per cent, initially suggested that between 1981 and 1985 the poorest
had become relatively better off, increasing their share of total
income by 8.3 per cent as opposed to a 6.4 per cent increase amongst
the population as a whole. This appeared to indicate that the poor
had done rather well in the first half of the decade. Some doubts
were expressed (see, for example, Townsend and Gordon, 1989),
and in 1990 a reworking of the figures in a report produced for the
Social Services Select Committee pointed to statistical errors which
had over-counted this gain. New statistics revealed that the income
of the lowest decile had only grown by half as much as the overall
increase between 1981 and 1985 (Johnson and Webb, 1990a). In
fact, the income of the poorest 10 per cent has increased by a mere
0.1 per cent, after housing costs have been taken into account,
between 1979 and 1987 compared with an increase in income of 23
per cent for the population as a whole (Oppenheim, 1990). Clearly,
the poor are becoming relatively worse off.

Another way of measuring the poor is to look at those who are in receipt of state benefit. This certainly is a statement of only the minimum figure of the poor, and it may be that non-claimants are found more in one group or another. However, given this caveat, figures for income support claimants show that the largest single group of those dependent on state benefit are older people, who make up 39 per cent of all claimants. Lone parents account for 16 per cent, people with a disability 6 per cent, the unemployed 31 per cent, families on income support 4 per cent and others, such as those on training grants, 4 per cent (DSS,1989). Again this does not tell us directly about women's experience of poverty, which can only be inferred. Women make up the larger proportion of the older population, and in particular the very old, who are the most likely to suffer poverty (Sinfield, 1986). Women are the vast majority of lone parents, accounting for over 90 per cent of these (Millar, 1989a; Social Trends, 1989). Women are also the majority of those suffering a physical disability (Lonsdale, 1990), partly in association with older age.

These figures for poverty, based on government statistics and representing the minimum number of those who might be counted as poor using other methods of measurement, fail to identify who the poor are in any more detailed sense. The extent to which women are over-represented is obscured, as is the representation of black individuals and households, or of people with a disability. The following sections pose the question from another direction, the distribution of resources, to assess the impact of gender on access to resources.

## Resources

### Women and wealth

Despite the existence of a substantial feminist critique of the measurement of poverty, there is little on the subject of women and wealth. This is primarily the result of the difficulty of obtaining data on wealth ownership, which similarly limits our knowledge on the ownership of wealth according to other parameters, such as race. However, problems also exist in determining the relationship between ownership on paper and actual ownership in terms of decision-making power. For example, some wealth has been redistributed within families as a result of tax liabilities (George, 1988), and this may be one of the major ways in which women's share of wealth has increased this century (Harbury and Hitchins, 1979). This is a difficulty which is likely to become more pronounced in the wake of the changes to income tax which allow women to hold assets separate to their husbands and offset the tax liability for these against their own tax allowance. However, although this new access to their husband's wealth may be significant for some women, as a whole this is a change which is likely to affect only a small part of the total wealth in the country.

The term wealth includes financial assets such as savings and bank deposits, stocks and shares, land, and other material investments. It can also include the value of housing and pension rights, although this wider definition of wealth has the effect of changing, to some extent, the pattern of distribution of wealth.

How, then, is wealth distributed in the United Kingdom? The simple fact is that there is a remarkable degree of concentration of wealth in few hands: the top 1 per cent of the population in 1987 owned 18 per cent of the country's marketable wealth, whilst the top 10 per cent owned over half of all marketable wealth (Social Trends, 1989). Owner-occupied housing is now the largest single proportion of marketable wealth, with over a third of the total wealth in the country being represented in dwellings, net of the mortgage debt, compared with 21 per cent in 1971. Financial assets represented 18 per cent and stocks and shares 10 per cent of total marketable wealth in 1987 (Social Trends, 1990). However, the inclusion of housing underplays the concentration of the power which attaches to wealth in the shape of land and larger shareholdings (George, 1988).

This is an important fact, for not only does wealth add to income, and the potential for income, it also creates considerable opportunities for power when held as land or in substantial blocks of shares. However, the little that is known about women's wealth holdings indicates that inequality here is just as important as in other areas.

One of the greatest changes in relation to women's patterns of wealth is in the move towards owner-occupied housing being held in joint names by two adults (Harbury and Hitchins, 1979). Thus one of the major ways in which women's share of wealth has increased in this century, and in particular in the past few decades, is in the area of housing, an asset which represents one of the least powerful forms of wealth. Women in owner-occupied housing may share ownership of the unmortgaged portion, and are most likely to gain sole ownership in the event of their partner's death (Holden, 1990). Given the greater longevity of women this is one indication of an increase in women's access to a particular form of asset.

Despite this, on the breakdown of a relationship women are most likely to lose their home, either when they leave, as in a violent relationship, for example, or simply where they cannot afford the mortgage repayments (Sullivan, 1986; Watson, 1988; Watson, 1986). The means to this most accessible form of wealth are constrained by women's lower earnings, their restricted entry to the labour market when caring for children, their greater dependence on either male earnings or state benefits, and discrimination against lesbians and black women. In addition, the poverty of older women and their lack of pension rights means many older women who do acquire a house on the death of a partner will be unable to maintain the value of the asset through necessary repairs, and may have to sell the house. Finally, the operation of social security rules in relation to the payment of benefits to older people in residential care can mean the house has to be sold, and any capital above the maximum allowed for the payment of benefits being offset against the costs of care. With more older women dependent on state benefit as a result of inadequate or non-existent pensions, this again has a greater impact on older women than men.

The argument advanced for the privatization of public companies has often been that it will result in a wider share ownership. Although in fact small shareholders are few in number, there has been a growth in share ownership since the early 1980s. However, again men are more likely to own this form of wealth: in 1988 25 per cent of men owned shares compared with 18 per cent of women (GHS, 1990). In every age group and every social class women are less likely to own shares, with the widest divisions being amongst 35–44 year-olds, and in the unskilled classes (GHS, 1990). Although the figures do not detail the extent to which women own shares on behalf of others, to avoid tax, what we know of the distribution of income suggests that more women are likely to own shares on behalf of a man than vice versa.

Thus women's wealth depends more frequently on relationships than on earnings, whilst their ability to retain some forms of wealth is similarly predicated on their remaining in the relationship, and on their earning potential and domestic responsibility.

The other forms of wealth are primarily, in the United Kingdom at least, acquired through inheritance, whilst only a small fraction of wealth is accumulated through entrepreneurial activity (Harbury and Hitchins, 1979). Thus the main source of inherited wealth is fathers, and to a lesser extent, husbands. Women tend to outlive their husbands, which may result in inherited wealth, although wealth can also be left in trust for children, or left directly in some proportion to offspring. Women's share of wealth in Britain has increased since 1920 but as a result of transfers and joint mortgage, rather than a result of increased inheritance of other forms of wealth (Harbury and Hitchins, 1979). Patterns of inheritance in relation to housing, the most rapidly growing form of wealth holding, indicate that this form of wealth mostly remains in small family groups, and is most often passed to the surviving spouse initially. Women's greater longevity ensures that they are the more frequent recipients of this form of inherited wealth, whilst both daughters and sons are likely to inherit on equal terms when the wealth from the house is passed to the next generation (Munro, 1988). However, this in itself is likely to represent an inequality, as female children are most likely to have spent time caring for an aged parent in their final years, a 'labour of love' or duty which increases women's financial dependence on their partner or the State in those caring years and in their own old age, as a result of decreased participation in the labour market. The financial implications of such labour fail to be reflected in a division of housing inheritance which is made equally between all children (Menchik, 1990; Holden, 1990).

Although the concentration of total wealth appears to have reduced in this century, this has primarily been a transfer from the very rich to the rich, and the transfer of resources from men to women has been either in the shape of gifts to avoid tax liabilities, or housing which is a precarious asset to hold on to in circumstances of limited earnings or limited pensions. The nature of intra-household transference of wealth remains a 'black box', just as in intra-household income transfers, and the limited data on wealth in Britain and in other countries refers mostly to household ownership of wealth rather than individual men or women. Clearly we need to know much more, not only about actual ownership of both the wealth that brings economic power and other forms of wealth but also, as with household income, the significance of intra-household transfers of wealth in terms of actual power over it.

## Women and the labour market

Women continue to earn less than men, despite the introduction of equal pay and sex discrimination legislation over fifteen years ago. It is a picture which has changed little over time, and which seems set to continue: in Britain in 1990 women working full time earned on average only 77 per cent of male earnings (New Earnings Survey, 1990).

Women who work part time are likely to be even further behind when their pay is compared to that of men. In 1989 average gross hourly rates of pay for women in part-time manual employment were only 62 per cent of average gross hourly rates for men in full-time manual employment, whilst women in part-time non-manual employment were earning only 50 per cent of the male non-manual hourly rate (New Earnings Survey, 1990). This inequality in rates of pay understates the true differential, given men's greater opportunity to increase take-home pay with bonus and overtime additions, and given that men more often have the higher tax allowances, even where tax allowances are transferable between partners.

In addition to cash income from paid employment, employees stand to gain other benefits in the form of occupational welfare and 'perks', terms which cover a wide and growing range of resources which are available to some employees. This welfare can be grouped in three categories; cash benefits, non-cash benefits-in-kind and welfare services such as counselling.

Cash benefits differ from simple earnings in that they are not related to hours worked but to the employment contract and are paid in special circumstances. Two major cash benefits have been transferred from the State to the employer in the past decade, and both are only payable where certain conditions are met. The employer is now responsible for the payment and administration of Statutory Sick Pay (SSP), and Statutory Maternity Pay (SMP), to employees who meet the eligibility criteria. SMP is paid at a higher rate to women who have been in their current paid full-time employment for more than two years (over 16 hours a week). This qualifies a woman for six weeks leave at 90 per cent of her pay, together with 11 weeks at a lower rate. Further benefits to women meeting these criteria are that they also have the right to have up to half-a-year in maternity leave, the majority of it unpaid, and their job will be held for them. Not only are these benefits meagre compared to those received by women in other European countries (Hewlett, 1987; Women of Europe, no. 31, 1990), not many women qualify (Daniel, 1980). Although women in younger age groups and up to the time of the birth of their first child are likely to be in full-time employment rather than part-time employment, there are also a substantial proportion who will have been unemployed, on short-term contracts, or on a youth training scheme, and also a number who will not have had two years continuous employment with the same employer. Women who return to work between children do so mostly as part-time employees, who have no rights to the higher rate SMP if they work less than 8 hours a week, and will only be eligible if they work between 8 and 16 hours a week if they have had continuous employment with the same employer for more than five years.

There is also a class dimension, however, and those women who do qualify for maternity pay and maternity leave are more likely to be in non-manual and professional occupations (Brannen and Moss, 1987; Daniel, 1980).

Statutory Sick Pay (SSP) is similarly confined to those employees who meet eligibility criteria, and again this restricts it to certain categories of employees and occupational groups. SSP is paid to employees whose contract of employment is for more than three months and who earn enough to pay National Insurance contributions. The criteria again have the effect of limiting the proportion of women who are eligible for SSP, because of the large number of women working in part-time and low-paid employment below the National Insurance threshold. In addition, both SMP and SSP assume employment in the formal labour market, and exclude all those working in the informal economy, such as homeworkers, those working in family businesses and those in casual employment which are sectors of the labour market which account for a substantial number of female workers. Women with a disability who have a child are particularly likely to be excluded from higher rates of maternity benefit as a result of their lower likelihood of being in full-time paid employment, and are particularly likely therefore to have the poverty associated with disability intensified when they have children.

Employment is also the source of future affluence or poverty, and the shift of pension arrangements from the public to private sector carries implications for women's poverty in old age. The introduction of an occupational pension scheme by the state in the 1970s, and the move which related pensions paid to earnings over the best twenty years of the working life substantially improved women's prospects for a reasonable pension after retirement. The provision of a state pension is particularly crucial to those employees not covered by the private pension market. Female employees, being mostly low paid, part time and irregularly employed due to absences from the labour market for periods of their lives, are least often covered by private pension plans. In 1988 only 54 per cent of all women in full-time employment were members of their employers' pension schemes, compared with 64 per cent of male employees, whilst 23 per cent of women employed full time were in jobs which were not covered by such a scheme, compared with 21 per cent of men in employment without a scheme (GHS, 1990). In addition, a large number of occupational pension schemes exclude part-time employees, the vast majority of whom are women (Kidd, 1989).

The role of the state occupational pension scheme, SERPs, was substantially reduced in the 1980s, with a shift of emphasis to the private market to provide pension plans both through employers and on an individual basis, in the shape of personal pension plans. In addition, SERPs itself was modified to make final pensions dependent on earnings over the working lifetime rather than the best twenty years, which has the effect of reducing the final pension payable for all those whose earnings have fluctuated and who have spent periods out of the labour market. At the same time, the amounts paid under SERPs to widows and widowers are reduced by one half. Thus the contraction in the state scheme severely increases the risks of poverty in old age for women, whilst the cost of a personal pension plan which will produce a reasonable pension for women working fewer years and more part-time hours is prohibitive for the majority of those in need. In addition, personal pension plans are not required to provide benefits for widows and dependants, and a woman may not even know that her partner has transferred to a plan which does not provide such benefits. The sum effect of these changes is a seriously increased risk of poverty for women beyond retirement age (Land and Ward, 1986).

Non-cash occupational welfare in kind includes a wide range of resources which the employee might acquire. Some are well known: subsidized canteens, health services on the work premises, employer-subsidized private health care, the company car, and help with private school fees, for example. These non-cash benefits can represent substantial forms of income which need to be accounted for in a measurement of the distribution of income and wealth (Townsend, 1979; Titmuss, 1963; Sinfield, 1986; Oakley, 1986). Again, those who gain most in cash-equivalent terms are the higher paid, and women gain least from such forms of income, as a result of the distribution of women in the lower-paid jobs in the labour market. Some of these benefits – and in particular a subsidized canteen – also act to diminish deprivation experienced outside the workplace, which further adds to the gap between men and women.

A third form of occupational welfare has more recently been identified as one of the benefits of employment, and is made up of services such as counselling, advice, convalescence, retirement and sick visiting. These personal welfare services are similar to those often carried out in the past by personnel departments. However, there has been a growth of interest by employers in this form of occupational benefit both in Europe and in the USA (Challis and Hutchins, 1990). There are a variety of ways in which these services can be viewed. For example, providing advice on healthy eating and programmes to reduce alcohol intake are both individualistic – in that they focus on the person rather than their surroundings – and have benefits for the employer as well as (or possibly more than) the worker herself. The overwhelming majority of the firms providing such services are larger employers, with a large workforce and are more often found in male-dominated industries such as engineering. Whilst it is to be questioned whether such occupational welfare is a total 'good' in terms of reduction of poverty, some of the benefits – for example, debt counselling and support in sickness or convalescence – might have important implications, particularly for health. Alternatively, some of the costs of this kind of welfare are borne more by some employees. Dulcie Groves has described the dilemmas of women caring for adult dependants at home, in trying to keep this a secret to prevent it affecting their prospects for promotion and to prevent their performance at work being judged suspect as a result of their caring responsibilities (Groves, 1987). These are feelings which are similar to those of mothers in paid work (Doyal, 1979). This need to conspicuously demonstrate to both employer and colleagues that caring responsibilities do not interfere with abilities at work means that some aspects of this occupational social welfare could present a burden for women in employment. Although this final form of welfare constitutes only a minor part of occupational benefit expenditure, it will be interesting to see how welfare in this area develops, and how the benefits and burdens are distributed.

So, women both earn less than men in manual and non-manual jobs, and receive less in the way of other benefits and non-cash income. What accounts for women's position in the labour market?

The vast majority of women have paid employment at some time in their adult lives, and most are in the labour market for considerable periods. The years since the Second World War have seen an increase in the proportion of the labour force who are women: from 37 per cent in 1971 to 43 per cent in 1988 (Social Trends, 1990). In 1987 51 per cent of all adult women in the United Kingdom were economically active, compared with 75 per cent of all men (Social Trends, 1990). Thus over half of all adult women were in the labour force, compared with 32 per cent in 1921 (Lewis and Piachaud, 1987). This increase is largely accounted for by a rise in the number of married women who are economically active, from 8.7 per cent in 1921 to 45.5 per cent in 1981 (Lewis and Piachaud, 1987). The labour force participation of women with young children has increased primarily as a result of women returning to work more quickly after the birth of a child than in previous years, and of more women returning to paid employment between the births of their children. However, this has largely been an increase in the participation rate of middle-class women, whilst working-class women have had a much longer history of combining childcare and domestic labour with paid employment outside the home (Hunt, 1988a; Land, 1981).

Despite this increase in overall rates of participation, however, women's paid employment has taken a particular shape which sets it apart. Women returning to paid employment after having children are largely employed in part-time work, and it is this form of employment which has been the fastest growing sector in the labour market over the past forty years or so. As a result, 43 per cent of all women in employment in 1988 were in part-time work (GHS, 1990).

Part-time employment has advantages for married women, in that it can be combined with childcare, even though this is at the cost of what is termed the 'double burden' of domestic labour and paid employment, adding up to a substantial working week (Sharpe, 1984; Oakley, 1976). Thus, two-thirds of all economically active women with dependent children worked in part-time employment (GHS, 1990). Although fewer lone mothers are likely to be in paid employment, those who do have a paid job are more likely to work full time (Rimmer, 1988). A major reason for both lower participation and the higher proportion in full-time employment is the prohibitive cost of childcare combined with lower hourly rates for part-time employment: in order for it to be economic sense, a lone mother often has to work full time.

In terms of the kinds of paid work women do, there is a concentration of women in certain industries and occupations, in particular employment in the service sector, for example in catering, cleaning, hairdressing, selling and clerical services, and in health, welfare and education (New Earnings Survey, 1990). The work women do outside the home mirrors to a large extent the unpaid work women carry out inside the home: domestic labour such as cooking and cleaning, and tending and servicing work such as nursing, education and social work.

Women's part-time employment is also concentrated in these service sectors and low-status occupations. Women working part-time make up 54 per cent of the workforce in catering, cleaning, hairdressing and other personal services, 32 per cent of the workforce in selling, and 24 per cent in education, welfare and health.

There are also a large number of women who are homeworkers, in both manufacturing and service-based industries such as computer-related employment. Homeworking is associated with appalling rates of pay – one survey found women being paid the equivalent of 50 pence per hour for boring, repetitive work (Bagilhole, 1986), others have also documented the low pay, alongside other forms of deprivation: isolation, inability to control the flow of work which is determined by the employer, lack of security and lack of benefits, such as holiday pay and travel costs delivering the finished work, and the costs of production such as heating and lighting. Again, it is most often women with young children in this kind of employment, as a result of childcare responsibilities and the difficulty of finding affordable childcare. In addition, other groups of women

are significantly more likely to take this kind of work – Asian
women who prefer to work at home because of racism and language
barriers, women with a disability who have greater difficulty getting
to paid employment, for example (Westwood and Bhachu, 1988;
Huws, 1984; Hakim, 1987; Allen and Wolkowitz, 1987).

Women in paid employment are most often found in the lower
tiers of occupational hierarchies: they are most likely to be shop
assistants or typists rather than managers, nurses and auxiliaries
rather than doctors, lower grade teachers rather than heads of
departments or schools, social workers rather than team managers,
and so on.

Thus at one level women suffer lower wages because they are
more often at the lower end of the occupational scale, they are part-
time rather than full-time employees, and in the poorer paid sectors
of the labour market – service industries rather than manufacturing.
Women work more often in small companies and organizations, in
the less unionized occupations, and as part-time employees with
shorter service records they are more often unprotected by employment legislation.

However, the question remains as to why women are found in
lower paid occupations. Women's involvement in the labour market
cannot be understood without reference to the position of women
more generally. Women's work histories reveal a pattern of paid
employment interspersed with time out of the labour market – when
children are young, and when caring for other dependants. Women
continue to hold paid employment after marriage or setting up in a
relationship, and work during the early months of pregnancy. Only
half of all adult women may be entitled to maternity leave (Daniel,
1980), and not all who are entitled will return to their paid employment after their child is born. Those women not eligible for maternity
leave will be without a job to go back to, whilst the lack of childcare,
particularly for younger children and babies, combined with an
ideology in which women are more likely to see themselves and be
seen as mothers who should stay at home, especially whilst they
have young children, means that very few women return to their
previous job after their first child. In a study by Daniel (1980) only
7 per cent of women had returned to full-time employment eight
months after their child was born. Thus the birth of a first child
signals not only an absence from paid employment, but also a loss of
the woman's job, with consequences for her subsequent return to

paid work. Women's work histories reflect this temporary absence from the paid labour market which results in a 'de-skilling' of women (Main, 1988; Stewart and Greenhalgh, 1984). Thus women leave the labour market in early adulthood with the arrival of their first child, and when they do return, the majority take up part-time low paid and low-status jobs (Elias, 1988; Martin and Roberts, 1984; Joshi, 1987). However, the negative effects of this break in paid employment extend beyond the loss of earnings in an absence from the labour market and lower income during the period of part-time paid employment. Having a part-time job carries an effect on women's prospects for later full-time employment. The loss of status incurred in returning to part-time work has a negative impact throughout the rest of the woman's work history, and the kinds of full-time jobs women move on to, when their children are older, have more in common with their part-time employment than their earlier full-time employment (Elias, 1988).

The result, therefore, of women's caring responsibility, is dramatically to reduce their earning potential not only in terms of their restricted opportunities for paid employment and fewer hours, but also because it draws women into lower paid employment, with fewer benefits, fewer perks and fewer opportunities for improvement. But why are women's jobs – both part time and full time – concentrated in occupations which receive the lower rates?

Women's work is often described in terms of the 'secondary' labour market, where jobs are less stable, poorly paid, with fewer benefits and less security, in comparison with a primary labour market where jobs are well paid, with a range of valuable benefits, security and stability (Baron and Norris, 1976; Beechey and Whitelegg, 1986). This picture of the dual labour market has more value as a description of differences rather than as an explanatory model of how groups of the population – women, and black and ethnic minority people for example – come to be employed in the secondary sector. In terms of trends, this kind of division appears to be growing as a result of restructuring labour markets and employment (Room *et al.*, 1989).

The structure of women's employment as a whole does seem to fit this picture. Women are not only more often employed in part-time, low-paid and insecure jobs than men, but the discourse of women's participation in the labour market is one of secondary attachment to employment. Women are seen as taking paid jobs as an addition to their primary roles – either before the arrival of children and the fulfilment of their vocation as mother, or after the arrival of children, as a temporary phenomenon, to add to family income. Thus, despite the economic reality that a large proportion of families need women's earnings to lift the household above the poverty line, women see themselves as working for luxuries, or on a temporary basis, rather than permanently. Pollert (1981) described how female factory operatives in the 1970s described themselves as temporary, even after being in the job for over twenty years. Similarly, in Brannen's study (1987) on women returning to paid employment after maternity leave, a quarter of the women described themselves as working for 'luxuries', even where the majority of their earnings were spent on essentials. One of the essentials that typically comes out of the woman's earnings is the cost of childcare, again reflecting the ideology of women's primary attachment to the home, in comparison with their partner's employment. And indeed, the 'breadwinner's wage' remains a strong concept indicative of this differential view of male and female employment, which also legitimates differential access to household resources.

One aspect of this denial of the importance of women's earnings to the economic survival of the household – which is widening in line with increased rates of mortgage interest affecting middle-class households – is the paradox of women's economic dependence on men. Women are *not* simply economically dependent, and their own earning power is often necessary to lift a household out of poverty (Land, 1981; 1983; Mitton *et al.*, 1983). Given the way women spend their own earnings on household needs (Brannen, 1987; Pahl, 1989), the woman's employment also often increases the spending power of their partner. Paradoxically, however, these same earnings are too low for women to manage alone if they have children. This situation of women's poverty wages which are too low, being insufficient to even approach subsistence if they are trying to support other dependants, is likely to become even more apparent over the next decade as women's employment becomes more marginal and increasingly insecure (Millar 1989b; Room *et al.* 1989).

The relationship between race and gender in the labour market leaves black women in poorer jobs, which are low paid, and which have poorer conditions. Black women are more likely to work in unskilled and semi-skilled occupations, in unsociable hours, and in jobs which are less protected and are less likely to offer benefits such as sick pay and maternity pay. One way in which poverty in employment has a direct bearing on health for black women is the greater economic pressure to work during pregnancy and to return to paid employment after having a child (Bryan *et al.*, 1985). In addition, black women more often are employed in marginal work where time off for ante-natal care is more difficult to obtain, and poorer outcomes of pregnancy are highly associated with economic determinants such as these.

## Women and state benefits

The third way in which resources are acquired is through state benefits. As we have seen earlier, women are more likely to be dependent on state benefit than men – as partners in a two-adult household, as lone mothers and as older women with inadequate pension rights. Not only are women more likely to be dependent on benefits, they are dependent on the poorest benefits: the non-contributory means-tested benefits, in particular Income Support (Pascall, 1986). The operation of state benefits, then, is crucial to an understanding of women's poverty.

Feminists have long observed that the operation of the social security system rests on a fundamental assumption of women's economic dependence on a man, and the payment of benefits both reflects this explicit assumption of women's primary domestic role, and reproduces ideologies of gender (Pascall, 1986; Alcock, 1987). The operation of state benefit is not only a mechanism through which women remain poor, but also a mechanism through which the discourse of women as economic dependants is reinforced.

The system of contributory benefits is built upon assumptions of a particular pattern of participation in the labour market and on the concept of short-term absence from paid employment as a result of unemployment and temporary sickness. In order to qualify for benefits the employee must have recent experience over a period of several years of full-time employment in a job where the pay is high enough to qualify for National Insurance contributions. As such, it is built on an assumption of a work pattern which most clearly matches that of the adult able-bodied male: a full-time and permanent attachment to the labour market (Land, 1986; Land and Ward,

1986; Kidd, 1989). As a result, women are less often eligible for unemployment benefit, Statutory Sick Pay, and sickness benefit paid from social security. Maternity benefit stands out as a form of benefit which although designed to pay women during their absence from employment whilst pregnant and caring for a child, remains fitted to the male model of paid work: the short term for which it is paid (18 weeks) gives it more in common with sick pay, although even sick pay covers a longer period, of up to 28 weeks before the claimant switches to invalidity benefit.

This modelling of the contributory benefit system on full-time employment does not unwittingly reflect male working patterns: Beveridge was quite explicit in his description of married women's economic dependency on a male partner, who would either be in paid employment or who would claim the benefit on behalf of the household during any absence from the labour market. The Beveridge report stated:

> the great majority of married women must be regarded as occu-pied on work which is vital though unpaid, without which their husbands could not do paid work and without which the nation could not continue. In accord with the facts the Plan for Social Security treats . . . man and wife as a team . . .
> (Beveridge, 1942, p. 50)

Beveridge's vision of women as the economic dependants of men, whose primary function is to work at home as mother and house-wife, is quite clear, if factually incorrect. A large number of married women were already working in a variety of ways to contribute to the support of the household, and had been for some time (Land, 1981). The concept of husband and wife as a 'team', sharing re-sources equally, had also been revealed as a myth in many house-holds (Pember-Reeves, 1913, Spring-Rice, 1939). Despite this, the assumption of married women's economic dependency on their husband was built into the system and matched the rhetoric, if not the reality, of the time.

However, Beveridge's initial ideal was for the means-tested social assistance system to wither away, as more and more of the population were drawn under the net of contributory benefit either through their own contributions or, in the case of married women, through their attachment to a man (Beveridge, 1942; Loney *et al.*,

1983). This trend failed to materialize, and the emphasis on means-tested benefits has hardened since 1979 (Loney *et al.*, 1983; Hill, 1990). The policies of the Conservative government in the 1980s and early 1990s have brought increasing numbers dependent on the means-tested benefits, primarily income support, as a result of increases in those with insufficient contributions and changing rules in determining eligibility for contributory benefits since 1979.

For women, this shift towards even greater reliance on means-tested benefits has important consequences, as the assumptions built into the system carry an impact for the poverty of women. One group in particular highlights the impact of Beveridge's assumption of women's economic dependency on men, that of lone mothers.

The Beveridge report identified children as a priority – so long as they were born within marriage, and incentives were provided to place a 'premium on marriage in place of penalizing it' (Beveridge, 1942, p. 52). Incentives took the form of children's allowances and, for working women, a maternity benefit paid at a higher rate than sick pay to prevent the 'mothering function interfering with her work and her work function interfering with her childrearing' (p. 52). Although this higher rate of maternity benefit was dropped in 1953 (Wilson, 1977), the report again is reinforcing the primary role of women as mothers, and the idea, still with us today, that women cannot be both good parents and good employees (Doyal, 1979). However, women who had children out of the proper state of wedlock were left out of Beveridge's provisions: 'The interest of the state is not in getting children born, but in getting them born in conditions which secure to them the proper domestic environment and care.' (p. 135)

This thinking, which continues to be reflected in current New Right analysis, means that the vast majority of women bringing up children alone rely on state benefit. Where women are lone mothers as a result of a breakdown in a relationship, they may continue to be economically dependent on a man through maintenance payments. However, the difficulty of ensuring these are paid at an adequate level, even where a court ruling has been made, increases women's reliance on the State, whilst the net effect of maintenance payments offset against state means-tested benefits often results in little or no gain for the women in financial terms. A new amendment to social security legislation in 1990 proposes to deduct maintenance payments from the earnings of absentee fathers.

Such a tactic is of limited value, and fails to address the problems of men who cannot afford to pay maintenance – where the inequalities between women from different income groups before marriage will only be replicated in inequalities after breakdown of a relationship; nor does it answer the needs of those women who have not been involved in a relationship and who have chosen to bring a child up alone. The idea of making men pay merely reinforces the assumption that women should be financially dependent on men both in and out of relationships, and that the solution for the State is simply one of matching responsibility, rather than positive action to support all who care for children and increase the opportunities for either parent to care or to enter paid employment, if they wish. In this respect the UK system is modelled on the marginal support system of the United States' Aid for Families with Dependent Children, rather than the system operated by some European countries to support both parents at home and parents in paid employment (Women of Europe, 1990; Hewlett, 1987).

This assumption of women's economic dependency on a man and the desire to match a woman with a man who should be responsible for the maintenance of both her and her children is made clear in the operation of the 'cohabitation rule'. A change to social security rules in the early 1970s meant that women's entitlement to benefit became dependent on non-marital relationships. Thus women who were not married or separated could be refused benefit where they were deemed to be living with a man in a domestic or sexual relationship. Although the emphasis was on equity with married couples, the introduction of 'snoopers' with instructions to assess the relationships of lone-women claimants emphasized sexual liaisons: in effect, the assumption of the married woman's dependence on her husband was extended to all women involved in a relationship. Although the cohabitation rule applies to both men and women, and to a number of benefits including widow's pensions, in reality the rule has been most often applied to women on income support (Pascall, 1986); and the assessment of cohabitation has most often been based on the existence of a sexual relationship even where the couple are not living together (Lister, 1973; Pascall, 1986).

In Britain, arrangements for women bringing up children alone have been added on to existing benefits for families (Kidd, 1989), and as a result lone mothers are particularly vulnerable to poverty: as Pascall says, 'the breadwinner/dependant model makes poor social security where there is no breadwinner' (Pascall, 1986, p. 199).

Most lone mothers remain stuck in a poverty trap where childcare is unobtainable and unaffordable, part-time work would constitute a net loss in income and even full-time employment would need to be very well paid to make a real difference to net income. Social security legislation in 1988 made it more difficult for women to climb out of the poverty trap by changing the conditions of the earnings disregard for those on income support. Prior to this date, the costs of childcare could be offset along with other expenses against earnings. Despite the increase to earnings allowed, the effect of removing the cost of childcare as a genuine expense of paid employment not only resulted in preventing most lone mothers from taking paid employment and gaining, it also underlined the ideological position of state policy, and the Conservative government in particular. Perhaps not surprisingly, the rate of participation in the labour market for lone mothers has decreased since 1979, when Margaret Thatcher came to power: in 1977–79, 22 per cent of lone mothers worked in full-time employment and 24 per cent had part-time jobs, compared with 17 per cent in full-time employment and 22 per cent in part-time employment in 1986–88 (GHS, 1990). The greatest fall in labour market participation has been amongst those lone mothers most dependent on social security benefits – single or 'never-married' women – of whom only 14 per cent have full-time jobs now, compared with 25 per cent in 1977–79 (GHS, 1990). The employment position of lone mothers is likely to deteriorate further still, as a result of reduced employment opportunities for women and the restructuring of the labour market (Room *et al.*, 1989; Millar, 1989a, Kidd, 1989). The poverty trap has become even more severe for this group of women (Rimmer, 1988).

Even where women are eligible for contributory benefits, the value of these benefits is likely to be low as a result of a poorer contribution record and lower pay, where benefit is related to earnings as in Statutory Maternity Pay (Millar and Glendinning, 1989). Unemployment benefit is also affected by this assumption of women's domestic role: in order to qualify as available for employment, women have to persuade benefit offices that they have made adequate arrangements for childcare, while men do not (Pascall, 1986).

The vulnerability of all who are dependent on means-tested

benefits has increased as a result of other changes to the social security system in the 1980s, bringing more people into poverty. Some of these changes have had a disproportionate effect on women.

The long list of cuts in the benefits available to women during pregnancy and after the birth of a child has resulted in a substantial increase in the risk of poverty at a time when high standards of nutrition, decent housing, warmth and clothing are all crucial for a healthy outcome of pregnancy and for good health in early childhood. In 1979 Piachaud calculated the cost of bringing up a child to be 50 per cent greater than the amounts paid in social security at the time. Since then supplementary benefit has been replaced by income support and discretionary loans have replaced special needs payments, whilst child benefit has been frozen over successive years. The universal maternity grant has been replaced by discretionary means-tested payments. The weekly cost of the medically recommended diet for pregnant women represents nearly half of the amount paid in income support to a single person over 25, whilst a woman under this age would experience even greater difficulty in meeting the nutritional requirements (Oppenheim, 1990). The additional cost of maternity clothes, baby clothes and equipment is even more difficult to finance on the low levels of income support or maternity benefit (Oppenheim, 1990; Durward, 1984; Roll, 1986). There is little indication that even the narrowest view of the objective of maternity benefits – 'ensuring the health of the mother and baby' (Roll, 1986, p. 4) is being met.

Changes to the UK social security system during the last decade have also arisen as a result of Directives from the European Community on equality. This has resulted in substantial changes in the rule – if not the operation – of some aspects of the system. Until 1983, only men could apply for benefit on behalf of the household. Since that date either partner may apply, although the majority of claimants in two-adult households remain men. This is partly the result of men's reluctance to lose the 'breadwinner' role and partly the result of the operation of a system whereby preferred claimants are those with the greater attachment to the labour market, which leads to a preference in favour of the male partner (Pascall, 1986).

Until 1986 married women were not eligible for Invalid Care Allowance (ICA), payable to men of any marital status and to single women. This assumption of the naturalness of caring for married women and their economic dependency on a husband was challenged in the European Court by a British woman in 1986, with the result that married women can now claim ICA. However, the rules regarding the payment of the allowance have been tightened considerably, and whilst it is valuable in that it maintains women's state pension rights, the amount itself is too low to represent real compensation for loss of paid employment (Land and Ward, 1986), and the virtual dissolution of the SERPs scheme means even this meagre benefit to women claiming ICA is minimal.

Another overt form of discrimination was the restriction of the non-contributory invalidity pension to only those married women who failed a housework test. These conditions have also been abolished and the Severe Disablement Allowance (SDA) is now paid to either sex. Again the rules under which it is paid have been tightly drawn. However, whilst these changes are important steps forward in the apparent equal treatment of men and women, the continued aggregation of adults into assessment units, cuts in specifically female benefits, such as benefits during maternity and child benefit, the privatization of large parts of the sick pay, maternity pay and pension systems all result in less equality for women and a downgrading of women's already meagre benefit rights.

Women claiming a disability benefit further suffer from the underlying assumptions written into the division of contributory and non-contributory benefits. Because of contribution qualifications and women's work histories, there is a gender-based division in the claiming of benefits. Women make up the majority of those claiming the non-contributory SDA, whilst men make up the majority of those claiming the contributory Invalidity Benefit, which is paid at a higher rate (Lonsdale, 1990).

A final important source of state benefits for women is the system of child benefit. Eleanor Rathbone campaigned during the middle of this century for a system of family allowances to relieve both children and women of poverty. Despite threats to the benefit and the way it is paid, it remains an important source of income for many women. It has been frozen over a number of successive years in the 1980s and early 1990s, although a new benefit, of an additional £1 for the first child was introduced in the autumn of 1990.

Policies over the past ten years in both employment and social security have contributed to a worsening of the position for women

(Millar and Glendinning, 1989; Andrews and Jacobs, 1990). However, the fundamental assumptions on which the system was built remain embedded in the system as it is today. The assumption of women's economic dependency on men, and as a consequence the design of benefits which reinforces this dependency and, given the reality of women's lives, women's poverty and deprivation, was a reflection of widely held beliefs at the time (Wilson, 1977). The changes to the system in the 1980s, despite responses to European Directives on equal treatment, have simply reinforced this subordination of women's needs to those of 'families' (Land and Ward, 1986).

In addition, the sheer inadequacy of benefits means that over and above this assumption and reinforcement of women's economic dependency, the poverty of state benefits means that all who depend on them are likely to be poor (Berthoud, 1989; Bradshaw and Morgan, 1987; Townsend, 1989; Stitt, 1990). Thus a large proportion of the population, the majority of whom are women, are living in poverty because of benefit levels too low to provide adequate standards of nutrition, a spare pair of shoes, or enough warm clothing.

Findings that suggest benefit payments are so low as to constitute severe poverty are particularly revealing in comparison with research which suggests that women who leave relationships to become lone mothers on state benefit feel better off than before (Graham, 1987a; Maclean, 1987). This is despite having to manage on a lower income, and despite the meagre share most women receive on marital breakdown (Millar, 1989a; Eekelaar and Maclean, 1986; Maclean, 1987). One aspect of this is simply control: for the first time in the lives of many women, they are able to control outgoings and manage their income in ways which decrease some of the deprivations suffered (Graham, 1987a). However, the fact that women feel better off on a grindingly low income should not blind us to the very real nature of poverty for most women bringing up children alone.

Finally, resources are also acquired through intra-household transfers or the sharing of income and other goods and assets within the household, and this is a further way in which women might suffer poverty.

*Household transfers*

As already described, the transfer of resources between members of the same household is an important source of resources and there-fore an important aspect of poverty, particularly in relation to gender. The actual ways in which resources are distributed is crucial to women for two reasons: women's lower earnings in the paid labour market, and women's unpaid labour in the home which reduces their potential for earning outside the home. Although the large majority of adult women do have paid employment, for very many this is insufficient for economic survival: half of all British women working full time and 80 per cent of those working part time have an hourly rate of pay which is below the European Decency Threshold (Andrews and Jacobs, 1990). The vast majority of women with young children either do not have a paid job or have part-time employment, and as a result the ways in which resources are dis-tributed within the family can have a severe impact on their own experience of poverty and deprivation.

Having said this, one of the greatest difficulties lies in determin-ing how resources actually are distributed. As described earlier households act in a number of different and complex ways. The system adopted by a household at a moment in time is not static, and may change in response to circumstances. Equally, changing cir-cumstances may make the same system more or less equitable – for example, when women's housekeeping allowances remain constant despite increases in the size of the household, or in inflation (Kidd, 1989; Land, 1983). Trying to evolve a schema of money-manage-ment types, as some research has attempted to do (Zweig, 1961; Pahl, 1980; Land, 1983; Pahl, 1989) is difficult in the face of the real complexities in the way people actually handle money. Fluctuations in weekly and monthly income, changing expenses, different needs and different sources of money all mean that decisions about the same kind of expenditure may be handled in a number of different ways each time the expense is made. Clearly larger items – mort-gage payments, fuel bills, loan repayments for domestic items and so on – are more likely to be fixed, although this is not always the case. It is in the area of day-to-day purchases – such as food shop-ping, daily transport costs and children's lunch money, small items – such as getting a key cut, or shoes reheeled, and larger less frequent expenses, such as dental checks – which are the most complex to deal with. It is extremely difficult to reconcile these outgoings to a system type which reflects which partner makes the purchase, where the income came from, and finally, who uses the item most. The objective of such typologies is to relate power in households over the allocation of resources to different kinds of household. Is power and access to resources affected by occupational class, whether one or both partners are in employment, the level of income, the age of the partners, the presence of children, and so on?

Evidence does suggest women go without more often than men, that some women are denied access to resources and some go without voluntarily to increase that available for their partners and children (Brannen and Wilson, 1987; Glendinning and Millar, 1987; Daly, 1989). Women also go without when they are lone parents on a low income (Millar, 1989a; Craig and Glendinning, 1990). Women bringing up children alone will cut down on their own food to save money, and provide more for the children (Graham, 1986). In contrast, men will more often keep back some of their earnings, even in low-income households (Townsend, 1979; Millar and Glendinning, 1989; Pahl, 1989).

But it is more complex than this. As we have seen, some resources are apparently bought jointly, but consumption is not shared equally: the family car, heating for the home, and hot water, for example (Sinfield, 1986; Millar and Glendinning, 1987; Graham, 1984; Evason, 1980). There is also evidence to suggest that men and women hold different views over necessary expenditure, and the ways in which money can be saved – such as in the kinds of food bought (Pahl, 1985; 1980; Graham, 1987c; Charles and Kerr, 1988; Wilson, 1987b) and this pattern of consumption in low-income households makes women's task of making ends meet more difficult.

How, then, can women's access to resources be explained? Two reasons were suggested earlier for women's poverty within the household, where resources were not shared equally: women's lower earnings and women's responsibility for childcare which restricts their access to the labour market. These two are clearly intertwined – it is the discourse of women's work as wives and mothers which legitimates their low pay and poorer employment opportunities, and it is this same discourse – in which men are seen as the 'breadwinner' whose greater efforts outside the home need greater reward within the home – which legitimates an unequal division of resources.

Women carry out the vast proportion of unpaid labour in the home – domestic labour, childcare and the care of other dependants (Oakley, 1974; Malos, 1980), and even where men participate in this work, women remain largely responsible for ensuring that it gets done, the needs of different members of the household are met, children visit the dentist and there is a new roll of toilet paper in the bathroom: it is a system in which men may help, but women do.

This work is unpaid and it restricts women's opportunities for paid employment which would relieve them of their economic dependency, as well as contribute to the income of the household as a whole (Millar and Glendinning, 1989). Women are often only able to find employment which fits in with their domestic chores and as a result are restricted to part-time work, work which is local or near their children's schools, and work during anti-social hours when their partners are home to care for the children (Sharpe, 1984). As a result they are restricted to poorly paid employment with fewer opportunities either for promotion or job satisfaction. At the same time, their partners may oppose their employment unless the home environment does not suffer – that is, women's opportunities for paid employment are dependent on their ability to combine this with household duties (Sharpe, 1984).

The ideology of the male 'breadwinner' remains powerful despite the fact that women's earnings are now and always have been fundamental to the survival of many families (Land, 1981). This ideology contributes to the legitimation of men's control over household resources, greater share of food, and of 'higher status' food and drink, and men's ability to retain some of their earnings for their own consumption (Delphy, 1984; Charles and Kerr, 1988; Millar and Glendinning, 1989; Brannen and Moss, 1987; Pahl, 1989).

Further inequalities result from women's domestic work (Wilson, 1987a; Delphy, 1984; Brannen and Wilson, 1987). This labour not only restricts women's access to the labour market, but is also a resource: for example, women's labour caring for children during the hours that their father is out in paid work represents a saving of at least £50 a week to the household, whilst women's labour in shopping for food and its preparation and cooking is cheaper for the household than eating in cafés or buying precooked food.

However, a further effect of this in terms of household equality is that women's working hours – in paid and unpaid employment – occupy the majority of waking hours and consume vast amounts of energy, which reduces women's time and energy for leisure activities. If deprivation is to be counted as the inability to share in goods and activities taken for granted by the majority, women's restricted access to leisure as a result of the 'double burden' must be considered another inequality in intra-household transfers.

Thus women's access to household resources is crucial, for despite the importance of their own earnings to the household economy, these earnings alone are insufficient to keep women out of poverty. However, the complexity of methods of household management mean that we cannot simply look at his or her earnings to determine poverty. In particular, women contribute the majority of their earnings for household needs, and are more likely to spend their money on the household rather than on items for purely personal consumption, and so are more likely to experience deprivation in terms of their own needs. Although the assumptions underpinning the distribution of resources within the household are related to women's ideological position of economic dependency on men, the actual determination of who gets what and how money is spent is the result of the interplay of a variety of factors: state of household formation, amount of income, sources of income – whether in benefit or earnings – and the strategies adopted by household members in gaining access to different resources (Brannen and Wilson, 1987).

This underlines the fact that women are not, within this process of distribution within households, helpless victims who happily adopt whatever system is decreed by their male partner, or who are alone in going without to provide for others. Men in low income households will also go without, whilst women may use a variety of strategies to increase their own consumption or degree of choice in consumption. This is not to play down the importance of household divisions – disputes over money are a major trigger in domestic violence (Pahl, 1980). However, other aspects of the household which affect access to resources are also important, and these factors represent those which, like gender, are also important determinants of resources throughout the mechanisms of distribution in society.

## Conclusion

If the ways in which resources are acquired are analysed, women's poverty and deprivation clearly relate to the structuring of women's position in the labour market and the home. Women earn less than men, no matter how this is measured – in terms of pay, occupational benefits, or the hours they do in paid employment and domestic labour. These low earnings set up a powerful precedent for poverty in later life, poverty in motherhood, and the inaccessibility of some forms of wealth such as housing. The flip side of this picture is women's economic dependency on men, in relationships, as wives, partners and daughters, and the difficulties met by women outside the traditional heterosexual model on which both the 'breadwinner's wage' and social security payments are based. The model is further reflected in the taxation system – where, for example, the costs of childcare are not, in Britain, a tax-deductible expense.

The other component of women's poverty and deprivation is the way in which the economic value of women's contributions to the household and the economy – through caring work and domestic labour – fail to be recognized within households or by the social security system, as earning contributions towards future benefits such as sick pay or maternity pay.

The poverty experienced by some women within their sex – black women, women with a disability, older women and women who are lesbians – can be understood by this model of women as economic dependants, which is not only based on a heterosexual vision of family life, but one which is ethnocentric and takes no account of the different lives women of different races, abilities and sexuality lead. However, although other discourses of oppression mediate the experience of some women and bring their lives closer to those of men who share a structural disadvantage in the labour market, these act in addition to gender.

It is important to locate a discussion of the consequences of poverty in relation to gender within a framework which also incorporates other factors and their effect on health. Chapter 7 looks in more detail at these interrelationships. However, the consequences of poverty for all women are often severe, having an impact on every aspect of life, and in particular on both mental and physical health.

# CHAPTER 4

# MEASURING WOMEN'S HEALTH

This chapter and the ones which follow turn to look at the consequences of poverty and deprivation for women. In particular, these chapters explore women's health experience and the relationship between health and poverty. Does women's experience of being poor, of going short of food or warmth, or of living under the threat of poverty, add up to poorer health chances for women?

There is a large literature on inequalities in health which incorporates the issue of the impact of poverty on mortality risks and poor health experience. Indeed, the attempts of Seebohm Rowntree to discover a poverty line based on the level of resources necessary to maintain 'physical efficiency' were grounded on the notion that poverty leads to a deterioration in health and the attempt to devise a poverty line at the cut-off point where resources are no longer sufficient to permit this state of efficiency (Mack and Lansley, 1985). In Britain, as in other countries in both Northern and Southern hemispheres, the poor continue to suffer higher rates of mortality and higher levels of morbidity than the affluent. One of the largest pieces of research on the links between health and living standards focused on the relationship between occupational class and measures of mortality and morbidity. The Black Report, published in 1980, revealed a strong class association with both of these measures of health experience, such that those in the unskilled classes were more likely to die earlier and suffer poorer health during the course of their lives than those in professional and managerial classes. (Townsend and Davidson, 1982).

This pattern of poor health and lower life expectancy among

poorer occupational groups was uncovered in other studies, including research focusing on links between areas with high levels of deprivation and high levels of mortality and high scores on other health indicators, such as low birth weight (Townsend *et al.*, 1984; Townsend, Phillimore and Beattie, 1988), and research on premature death in poor and affluent areas (Phillimore, 1989). Studies also suggest a widening gap in rates of mortality, especially among adults (Whitehead, 1987; Smith, Bartley and Blane, 1990; Townsend, 1990e). Lower income groups are also less likely to survive cancer and coronary heart disease (OPCS, 1990b).

The Black Report identified poverty and deprivation as the major causes of inequalities in health between the highest and lowest occupational group, a finding confirming Rowntree's attempts to use a measure of health experience as an indicator of poverty (Black Report, 1980; Townsend and Davidson, 1982).

Inequalities in health have also been documented in relation to race, although the major sources of statistics on mortality and morbidity do not collect data on race or ethnic origin. There appears to be a complex relationship between race and poor health, and although much of the available evidence which demonstrates higher rates of mortality and illness refers to people born outside Britain, small-scale studies on the health of people from different ethnic groups have also highlighted the poorer health of some groups within the black population (Britton *et al.*, 1990; Whitehead, 1987; Grimsley and Bhat, 1988). The nature of the links between race and health is undoubtedly complex, and must take into account the relationship between class, deprivation, and discrimination and racism, as well as differentiating between both different ethnic groups and different kinds of health experience, including the relationship between health and the health services.

One central feature of this relationship between poor health, higher mortality risks and race is that which is measured, in part at least, by social class. Britain's ethnic and black population is disproportionately represented in the poorer social classes, and lower occupational groups; more black people are unemployed, particularly amongst the younger age groups, and more black households are living in poor-quality accommodation of all tenures (Bryan *et al.*, 1985; Thorogood, 1987; Grimsley and Bhat, 1988; Donovan, 1986). These are issues which are explored in more detail in Chapter 7.

Despite the large literature on inequalities in health, it is a literature which remains largely gender blind, with an overwhelming focus
on male mortality rates, and measures of morbidity (Arber, 1989,
1990a; Doyal, 1985; Phillimore, 1989). If this sounds familiar, that
is because it is: whilst the poverty women experience is obscured
by official preoccupation with household income, and household
measurement of the experience of deprivation, the relationship
between women's poverty and their health experience is similarly
obscured by the preoccupation with both male mortality and a
measurement of class based on male occupations and the household
as the unit of consumption.

Although most studies on inequalities in health do examine mortality and morbidity rates for women, the rationale often appears to
be to observe where they differ from male rates. Discussion of
inequalities in women's health experience is confined to a few pages
(Townsend and Davidson, 1982; Whitehead, 1987). The strength of
any association between social class and poor health for women is in
any case confused by the use of an occupational hierarchy devised
for the male labour market, which classifies women according to
different criteria, including their marital status.

Whilst previous chapters have looked at the difficulties involved
in defining poverty and measuring the experience of poverty and
deprivation from a feminist perspective, similar concerns arise in
the focus on women's health experience, and in the use of published
statistics in the area of health research. In addition, as in the understanding of poverty and gender, the association between health
and poverty for women invokes questions concerning the interplay
between health, gender and other factors: race, class, disability,
sexuality, and age.

One way of focusing this wide debate on factors determining
women's health, and the potential links between health, poverty
and gender, is by examining the apparent paradox in the question of women's health experience: that is, the difference between
the sexes in terms of life expectancy and levels of illness. Life
expectancy for both women and men has improved dramatically
over the past 100 years in all Western countries, and women
today can expect to live into their seventies and eighties. However,
whilst life expectancy has increased for both sexes, women's mortality has decreased at a faster rate than have mortality rates
for men, and life expectancy for a female child at birth is 77.6

years as opposed to a male life expectancy of 71.9 years (OPCS, 1986b).

Thus women in Britain and other Western countries live longer on average than men. The paradox of women's health is that, during their lives women also experience higher levels of illness than men: women are more likely to report themselves as sick in surveys relying on self-perception as well as those relying on consultation with the medical profession, absenteeism from paid employment and measures of limitation on normal activity (GHS, 1990; Verbrugge, 1986).

One way of exploring this apparent paradox is through the impact of poverty and deprivation on health. Previous chapters have argued that women's experience of poverty is obscured by studies in which poverty is measured by household income and household consumption, and have argued that gender-specific experiences of poverty have to be described in order to understand both the depth of poverty in Britain and other Western countries, and also the nature and origins of that poverty. Similarly, material and social deprivation can only be thoroughly comprehended in accounts which highlight women's specific experience.

Women's specific risk of poverty and deprivation stems from the structuring of women's economic dependency: within families and marriage, in the sexual division of labour and in social policy, which combine to create a gendered vulnerability to both poverty and deprivation. As a result, women are more prone to the experience of poverty during the course of their lives with consequent effects on health, and are more likely to suffer the ill effects of living with the threat of poverty.

Thus it may be that women live longer, but experience poorer health during their lives as a result of the way in which poverty affects their health. Clearly this is going to be a complex equation, where women's experience within the household is only one factor, and a formulation is needed which accounts for the extent to which women, men, and children within the same household might experience not only different levels of poverty or deprivation, but also different forms of health risk as a result. Other factors might also be drawn into the equation: biological or physiological differences between the sexes, different experience in paid employment risks, the impact of longevity on health, and, ultimately, the question of how health is being measured.

Most studies on inequalities in health start with mortality – a measure of early or premature death, and death at different stages of the life cycle – as a surrogate for a measure of health. This is not only an extreme and somewhat limited view of health, it is also an increasingly less informative one as mortality overall has decreased and life expectancy increased. Whilst recent research indicates a widening of inequalities in health over the past decades in Britain (Smith, 1990; Smith, Bartley and Blane, 1990; Whitehead, 1987), particularly in relation to social class, an overall decline in mortality has increased the need to find a measure of health capable of measuring a more positive or holistic definition of health, as well as one which will more clearly highlight where inequalities are experienced during the course of a lifetime (Blaxter, 1989).

This increased concern to measure the health of the living, and the use of measures reflecting self-perceived health demands the consideration of whether women and men attach fundamentally different meanings to the concept of health, when assessing their own health resources and state of health, their need for medical assistance and their ability to continue daily activities. And of course, as all women (and some men) know, the ability to stop either domestic labour or caring labour in order to take time off as 'ill' depends not only on perceived illness, but on other constraints as well. Jocelyn Cornwell, in her study of accounts of health in East London, found that paid employment and gender combined to structure responses to illness. Whilst the men in her study would tend to carry on working if they could, once they took time off from paid employment they would take to their beds and expect women's care. Women, however, are more likely to keep going, and cope with ill health and daily activities, either by taking non-prescribed medication or visiting their GP for help (Cornwell, 1984). Women's definitions of health reflect both this domestic role and the links between housework and health, so, for example, women are more likely than men to define health as the 'energy' needed to do the housework (Blaxter, 1990).

Sally Macintyre, writing in 1986, deplores the focus of the litera-ture on inequalities in health on continually proving that inequalities do exist, whilst there is too little research on what causes these inequalities (Macintyre, 1986; Blaxter, 1981). Despite some impor-tant studies on the impact of poor housing, specific structural defects such as damp, or the impact of poor nutrition on health, there is insufficient research on the ways in which these compound with each other to alter health chances, and too little on the relationship between health and poverty in terms of the factors which reproduce poor health.

To some extent this focus on reproducing the evidence which demonstrates the existence of inequalities in health in relation to social class, race and other factors is a necessity in a period of government cutbacks in income support, health services and other aspects of the Welfare State, and at a time when international restructuring of the labour market is likely to increase unemployment and low-status marginal employment without compensating support in terms of income maintenance above the barest of poverty lines. The need to continue to highlight the different health experience of different social classes in Britain was exemplified in the way in which the Black Report on Inequalities in Health was greeted in 1980 by the newly elected Conservative Government. In addition to the limited number of copies available and attempts to minimize publicity on its publication, the Foreword by the then Secretary of State, Patrick Jenkin, refused to endorse either the Group's conclusions as to the major causes of inequality in health experience or the Group's major proposals for reducing these inequalities. The need to monitor and highlight both the existence of the health divide and the structural causes of this also stems from debate within the academic community as to the statistical accuracy of the inequalities shown (see, for example, Illsley, 1986; 1987; Wilkinson, 1989; Townsend, 1990d).

The pages which follow are not, then, simply an account of women's health and inequalities in relation to gender, as a way of setting the record straight. It is also an account putting together the evidence which relates to the effects of the experience of poverty specifically from the perspective of women's health and using what we know about women's experience of poverty and deprivation. If poor housing means poor health, what is there about the lives of women and men which suggests poor housing will have an unequal impact on women's lives in comparison with the effects on men? Or that suggests that women's risks of experiencing poor housing are different? This is not an attempt to prioritize women's suffering or poor health over that of men, but to add to this process of understanding what it is precisely about poverty which is linked to poor health. Similarly, this is not an attempt to prioritize gender over and above class or race as factors in the construction of chances, opportunities and choices. For any individual their health experience, as with other things, will be the complex sum of such factors.

Finally, it is worth reflecting further on this paradox of women's health: the fact that women live longer yet appear to suffer poorer health during the course of the lifetime. Hart (1989) suggests that the way women's life expectancy has increased more rapidly than life expectancy for men over this century reflects women's natural superiority, which only becomes visible when living standards in general rise. Whilst both men and women have increased their life expectancies this century, mortality rates for women have fallen more rapidly, particularly at certain times during the century and amongst certain age groups (Beral, 1987). The best improvement was during the 1950s, amongst mortality rates for women under 35 years of age, whilst mortality rates for women over the age of 45 have not fallen as steeply as those for men. The apparent levelling off in the gap between women and men's mortality rates in later years may suggest new risks for women, such as those arising out of paid employment and occupational hazards, or changes in behaviour patterns, such as the narrowing gap between rates of smoking for each sex (Beral, 1987)

Hart (1989) suggests that a major reason why women have done considerably better than men in terms of increased longevity over the past hundred years is that as living standards have risen, women's access to scarce resources has also improved, and so have women's standards of nutrition. Hart draws on the work of McKeown, which links the decline in infectious diseases in the late nineteenth and early twentieth century to a decline in infective conditions, and to improved living standards and nutrition (McKeown, 1976). Hart argues that the impact of increasing prosperity is more significant for women, as women are denied adequate resources in poor communities or periods of history. It is through improved access to such resources, in particular better levels of nutrition, that the natural superiority of the female sex becomes visible. 'Perhaps', she argues, 'the female constitution is inherently stronger because the procreation role is more physiologically demanding' (Hart, 1989, p. 128). Women's social or economic status in poor societies elsewhere in the world appears to be linked to the gender difference in life expectancy and health experience. Women suffer poorer health and have higher levels of mortality in cultures where resources are scarce and women have a low status (Cortes-Majo *et al.*, 1990): one study of health in a developing country revealed malnutrition in over a fifth of all female children compared with less than 1 per cent of male children (Macormack, 1988). Such inequalities of sex relate to the distribution of resources: in the Punjab, male children are breast-fed longer, are older before being weaned, and receive more supplementary feeds (Macormack, 1988). In addition, the work women do in these societies adds to the toll on their health (Raikes, 1989; Macormack, 1988; Hart, 1989). The indicator most closely linked to infant mortality in developing countries is that of female literacy (UNDP, 1990), which may reflect women's higher social and economic status in these countries and higher nutrition in pregnancy and amongst breastfeeding mothers, rather than simply better knowledge of infant care.

The gap between the sexes is further extended by what men do with their unequal share of the resources, in particular the negative impact on health through the use of tobacco and alcohol (Hart, 1989). Other factors clearly feature, most obviously, perhaps, the development of more reliable contraception alongside economic change leading to smaller households, which resulted in a reduction of both the number of pregnancies and deliveries a woman would experience and of the number of abortions she might have. Given the rates of maternal mortality, the risks of abortion and the toll of repeated pregnancy and childrearing on women's health, these changes played a substantial role in improving women's life expectancy and health during their lives (Joyce and McCashin, 1982). In addition, Hart argues that women's exclusion from some occupational risks explains part of the gender gap, although the different way women and men resolve stress is seen as of greater significance. Women's greater use of psychotropic drugs and higher rates of depression, for example, suggests women's stress may result in behaviour or conditions which threaten day-to-day health rather than life itself, in comparison with higher rates of smoking, alcohol abuse and violence amongst men (Hart, 1989). The question of functional equivalence is important – does women's depression and use of psychotropic drugs represent a different response to the same stress (Smart, 1976). This would suggest that whilst behaviour is important, the reasons underlying behaviour might also constitute health effects and need separate examination.

However, women's life expectancy has risen by more than might be expected as a result of fewer children and better maternity services. And some if not all of the reduction in maternal mortality rates is the result of better standards of nutrition rather than better antenatal or hospital care, and so comes back to Hart's original thesis. This suggestion that women will fare better than men from an increase in standards of living as a result of an increase in their own levels of consumption which allows women's natural, physiological superiority to emerge, is clearly of interest in a discussion of the impact on women's health of poverty and deprivation. The previous chapters have argued that women fare worse in many poor households, either because they go without or they are denied a share in household resources. This is not a new suggestion, nor is the idea that this poor level of resources has a detrimental effect on health – both Boyd-Orr (1937) and Spring-Rice (1939) wrote over fifty years ago of the impact on women's health of their domestic role and position in the domestic economy (Phillimore, 1989).

In Hart's terms, the impact of poverty at the micro level, on the household, would indicate a greater contraction in women's access to resources, with implications for health and mortality, whilst women in more affluent households might be expected to demonstrate this natural superiority. Not only would we expect a class difference for both men and women in rates of mortality and morbidity, but also that the difference between the sexes reflects women's superiority in higher occupation groups. In fact, figures on self-reports of chronic ill health from the General Household Survey reveal that the sex ratio of chronic and severe chronic illness is widest in the lower occupational groups, and narrower amongst women in higher income groups. That is, whilst in all classes more women than men report chronic illness, the health gap between women and men is greatest in the lowest income group, and the ratio of women to men in unskilled occupations is greater than in the highest occupational group. This would indeed suggest that in the poorest households, women's health suffers more than that of men, whilst women's health status is more improved when resources are more plentiful, thus explaining how women's rates improve more than those for men as we go up the occupational class structure (GHS, 1990). Turning to mortality, health here for each sex is expressed in reverse – that is, women live longer and have lower mortality ratios than men. Again, there is a wider gap in mortality rates amongst women and men in the lowest income groups, whilst mortality rates are closer for women and men in the highest occupational group.

However, this line of thought can only be tested for women and men in two adult households, and it is precisely in the issue of women's social class and women's access to resources in such a household that the greatest difficulties lie.

A further factor is the way in which poverty and deprivation are experienced as periods within the course of a lifetime, whilst measurements of poverty are often based on current income rather than the history of poverty and deprivation over time. The study by Phillimore (1989) of premature mortality in North Tyneside found that a substantial number of the early deaths in middle-class and more affluent wards were 'new recruits', whose current living circumstances did not reflect their past experience. Similarly, health is measured mostly with indicators based on mortality or morbidity – measures such as low birth weight, self-perceived health status and absenteeism from paid employment (although this last has decreased in use as a result of changes in the payment and recording of sick leave). However, 'health' is also the sum of lifetime experience, and measures of the relationship between health and poverty which rely on such a 'snapshot' of both experiences are inevitably at best rough guides to the kind of relationship, and are suggestive rather than explanatory. The clearest links might be found between accidental death and material circumstances – mortality rates amongst young children indicate that factors such as living in close proximity to major roads and being without a safe place to play, for example, are most associated with accidents in this age group, and clearly a 'snapshot' approach to circumstances at the time of death is indicative of the material factors involved. However, the demands of caring for children and domestic responsibilities in circumstances of poverty are also important: in one study of low-income households, accidents in the home took place most often when mothers were having a 'time out', for example having a cigarette, as a way of coping with such demands (Graham, 1986; 1990). Factors such as a lack of alternative childcare and safe space to play are clearly important. At the other extreme lie mortality rates amongst the newborn, where factors such as low birth weight and pre-term delivery are important indicators of poor health, but of themselves do not explain how such children come to die in the first weeks or months of life, and a much longer term view is needed to examine the relationship between living circumstances and their impact on the health of both this generation and the next.

Such difficulties perhaps explain the preoccupation of research into inequalities in health with proving the existence and trends in the relationships and links with different measures of deprivation or material circumstances, and the lack of detailed study of how such factors as low occupational class or local authority housing contribute to poorer health. The relationship between poverty and poor health is complex, and difficulties of matching the experience of poverty over time with its effects are only just beginning to emerge.

## Measurements of health

At the centre of the literature on inequalities in health lies the fundamental problem of what is meant by health, how this varies across those very parameters by which inequalities are measured and how to reconcile the divide between positive concepts of health as more than an absence of illness, and the necessity of relying on the only regularly produced statistics which measure rates of death and sickness rather than health.

The most frequently used statistic in the field of health research is probably that of mortality: thus the health of countries, societies, cultures and people is compared by a measurement of death, often age and sex-standardized to reflect known differences in mortality at different stages of the life cycle or for each sex. It can then be seen in which country people die earliest, which has the greatest life expectancy or, conversely, the greatest risk of 'early' or 'premature' death.

Thus life expectancy can be compared across time, different countries, political systems and stages of development: in Britain in 1986, for example, life expectancy was 77.6 years for women, whilst in 1910–12 female life expectancy was 51.5 years (OPCS, 1990b). In Japan, women's life expectancy was 82.1, whereas in Ethiopia and Afghanistan it was 42 years on average for both sexes (UNDP, 1990). Similarly, mortality figures are used within countries to compare the risk of early death for different groups or subsections of the population, for example according to occupational class or socioeconomic status.

Mortality figures come, in Britain, from the information recorded on death certificates at the time of death, and so include data on sex, age, cause of death, area of residence and occupation at death or last recorded occupation. This information can be ordered to examine relationships between these different variables, for example, to look at mortality rates in different areas of the country, or for different occupations. One of the most frequent forms of interpretation is by social class, based on occupation at death or last recorded occupation. The data on age and sex is often used to produce what are termed standardized mortality ratios (SMRs) which remove bias in the figures as a result of an unusual population. For example, high mortality rates in an area with a disproportionate number of older people can be recalculated to take account of the age-profile of the population. Similarly, the greater life expectancy of women can be taken account of when comparing different occupations which have different sex ratios.

As with all statistics, the data is only as good as the information which is originally recorded, and mortality figures contain potential bias as a result of some of the ways data is collected. Phillimore (1989), in his study on premature mortality in two areas of North Tyneside, found that middle-class deaths were substantially more likely to have more than one description of cause of death than those in poorer areas – not because the causes of death in more affluent areas were more complex, but because such deaths seemed to require more explanation (Phillimore, 1989). Prior (1989) similarly found that middle-class deaths were more likely to go to the Coroner's office for investigation – as unusual or requiring greater levels of explanation than deaths in lower social classes.

Difficulties also arise with occupation, particularly where occupation may have changed in the last months of life as a result of poorer health or approaching retirement, and again the difficulty of matching social class and lifetime experiences to early mortality through a measure of last recorded occupation causes problems. For women, the issue of occupational class is extremely problematic, as we shall see later. The other set of indicators which act as a measurement of health are morbidity indicators. Morbidity refers simply to sickness, and as such indicators of morbidity tend to refer to states of ill health rather than a positive state of health. Regular sources of morbidity data include figures on absenteeism from paid employment, consultation with medical practitioners or admission to medical facilities, and self-reported illness, such as data collected in the General Household Survey which reports on chronic and acute illness.

Other indicators can also be used – for example, height, weight or Body Mass Index, which relates weight to height (Knight and Eldridge, 1984), birth weight and age at gestation, loss of teeth and the need for glasses. Blaxter (1989) divides measures of morbidity into three types – medical, based on clinical measurements and self-reports of clinically defined conditions; functional, based on limitations to activity; and subjective – based on self-perception. All three include some degree of subjectivity, and this is the greatest difficulty in the assessment of morbidity in relation to social or economic differences, in that different groups of the population might differ in their assessment of ill health, conditions and limitations to their activity.

As a result, measures of morbidity are not necessarily measuring like with like, and differences in perceptions of health and illness or in other constraints which affect behaviour when ill may account for differences in apparent morbidity. Measurements of inequalities in morbidity by class or gender, for example, may reflect differences not in illness but in perception of health and sickness, what is normal and abnormal health, and differences in the ability to take time off paid employment or domestic labour, to visit a doctor, and so on.

Readiness to report illness does appear to differ in relation to sex and class, as does health perception. Working-class women are more likely to see health in terms of the ability to get through the day, whilst middle-class women see health as fitness and the ability to cope with crises. These differences are linked to the different demands made on them as well as to different expectations of health in relation to experience of illness and disability at various levels (Calnan, 1987). People in lower socio-economic groups are more likely to view health as an absence of illness, compared with those in higher occupational groups, whose definition is framed more in terms of positive good health or vigour (Blaxter, 1989, Pill and Stott, 1982; Calnan, 1984). However, people with poor health measured according to medically defined conditions may still report themselves to be in good health (Blaxter, 1990. Cornwell, 1984; Macintyre, 1986): in other words, people from different social classes may have a different base line of health from which to measure a deviation or deterioration in health, with those in poorer social classes, who suffer poorer health as a norm, under-reporting poor health. Cornwell (1984) highlighted a further problem for research such as the General Household Survey: people have what she termed 'public' and 'private' accounts of health, and reveal only the public account in initial interviews.

One result of these conclusions is that measures of morbidity based on self-reports of illness are likely to seriously under-report clinically defined disease (Blaxter, 1990; Evandrou *et al.*, 1990), so that even on their own terms as a measure of illness, many morbidity instruments are inadequate. In addition, measures of morbidity mostly measure only the existence of illness or self-perception of illness, rather than the impact of that illness on the individual's life. This may vary in relation to gender, and one of the most frequently voiced explanations of women's higher levels of morbidity, and in particular higher levels of psychiatric illness, is the suggestion that women are more likely to see themselves as ill or consult a doctor than men at the same level of symptoms. However, in the General Household Survey, a large number of those who consult GPs also claim they do not suffer any of the kinds of ill-health listed in the same survey (Evandrou *et al.*, 1990).

A further important point is that even if we could be sure of measuring like with like, and that differences in measured morbidity do accurately reflect differences in sickness, these measurements remain locked within a medical definition of health as the absence of illness, rather than health as a positive state of well-being. It is nearly half a century since the World Health Organization produced their by-now famous definition of health as a positive construct, yet in the routinely available, regularly collected statistics used to measure health we remain dependent on figures of mortality and ill health.

## Women, health and social class

Women live longer than men, but are more likely to spend a large part of their lives in poorer health. The major tool of analysis which has been applied to rates of mortality and morbidity is that of social or occupational class – to what extent can this tool explain women's higher levels of morbidity and greater life expectancy? The relationship between health and social class has a large accompanying literature, and, as described above, focuses primarily on the relationship between occupational class and male mortality rates. Where women do enter the picture, they are invariably classified according to their husband's occupation, and not their own. Thus a complex picture is drawn where women who are single are described in terms of their own occupational status, married men are also described according to their own occupation, and married women – whether in paid employment or not – are referred to in terms of their partner's job.

There is, as part of this literature on health in relation to social class, a sustained critique of the nature of the relationship between occupational status and poor health. The question of whether mortality rates and the forms of measured morbidity available are truly representative of 'health', has been discussed above. There is the further issue of whether many different occupations can be ranked and grouped into six basic categories which accurately represent a complex range of differences in living circumstances, expectations, choices and opportunities, let alone risks associated with paid employment itself, and whether these aggregates of risk factors can represent differences in expectations of health.

However, the issue of inequalities in health in relation to gender has been as obscured as the relationship between gender and poverty. Official statistics on mortality rates and class have concentrated on male mortality, whilst women have been 'submerged' as a category (Arber, 1989, 1990a; 1990b; Doyal, 1985), presumed to have either the same relationship between class and death as men, or simply to matter less in terms of what female mortality rates might tell us about broader inequalities. This remained true up to the last Decennial Supplement covering 1979–83, where women were afforded a chapter of their own, covering mortality in the same depth as the chapter on men, in terms of classification of diseases, highlighting special areas of interest and change. However, the problem of measuring women's class position remained unresolved by this Supplement which was, anyway, unconvinced on the validity of grouping different occupations into larger social class groups, and which preferred instead for both sexes to highlight the mortality rates of different smaller specific occupational groups – textile workers for example.

However, it is not only in the realms of official statistics that women's health experience remains marginalized. For example, in 1990, one issue of Social Science and Medicine, a journal in which a number of feminist papers on women's health have been published in the past, was wholly taken up with a discussion of inequalities in health in Europe, without a single paper on women's health, with no mention of gender and with only scant mention of inequalities by sex, which looked solely at women's reproductive health (Social Science and Medicine, 1990, vol. 31, eds. Illsley and Svenssen).

Another publication in the same year, containing nineteen papers on health inequalities in Europe, included two papers on gender and health, and further references to rates of mortality and morbidity for women alongside those of men. Even so, and despite the high quality of those papers which did focus on women's health and gender differences, the overall perspective remains male dominated, with women's health of the tacked on, 'and women too', variety.

Thus there is a division between, on the one hand, a sustained critique of methods used to measure health and social class which argues that tools of analysis transferred from a study of male health to women's health simply will not do, and that women's health is marginalized in official statistics whilst, on the other hand, there remains the larger block of material – official statistics, and primary research studies – which treat women's health as a marginal issue. Whilst there is a growing literature from a feminist perspective on women's health and ways of measuring women's class position, this has yet to penetrate official statistics or, it seems, much of the male-dominated academic research on health inequalities.

## Women's mortality and social class

The relationship between social class and mortality for both women and men is documented in the major surveys of official data on mortality in recent years (Townsend and Davidson, 1982; White-head, 1987; Smith *et al.*, 1990).

Mortality figures are derived from the Decennial Supplements, which give a standardized mortality ratio (SMR) for social classes based on occupation recorded at death. The mortality rates derived from the last Decennial Supplement, for mortality in the years around the 1981 Census, are shown below for men, classified according to their own occupation at death, for all women, for married women, classified according to their husband's occupation, and for single women, classified according to their own occupation.

**Table 4.1:** Social Class and Mortality Amongst Adults, 1979–81 and 1982–83. (Standardized Mortality Ratios).

| Social Class | Men[1] | Married Women[2] | Single Women[1] | All Women[1,3] |
|---|---|---|---|---|
| I Professional | 66 | 75 | 75 | 69 |
| II Intermediate | 76 | 83 | 68 | 78 |
| IIIN Skilled Non-Manual | 94 ⎫ | | 80 | 87 |
| IIIM Skilled Manual | 106 ⎭ | 107 | 111 | 100 |
| IV Semi-skilled | 116 ⎫ | | 107 | 110 |
| V Unskilled | 165 ⎭ | 133 | 117 | 134 |
| RATIO OF CLASSES I & II TO CLASSES IV & V: | 1:2.5 | 1:1.8 | 1:1.6 | 1:1.94 |

1. OPCS (1986): Decennial Supplement, 1979–81 and 1982–83. Men aged 20–64, all women and single women aged 20–59.
2. Smith and Jacobson, 1989, Table 16, Married women aged 20–59.
3. Single women classified according to their own occupation, married women according to their husband's occupation.

For each of these different groupings there is a clear association between social class and mortality. Standardized mortality ratios (SMRs), which take account of age and sex differences of occupations, express the mortality rate of each group – in relation to an average figure of 100. Thus an SMR of below 100 indicates below average mortality, similarly an SMR of above 100 indicates a higher than average mortality for that group. Table 4.1 shows, therefore, that for both men and women of all marital states, higher social class is associated with a better chance of surviving beyond retirement age than exists for those in the lowest social classes. For men, for married women and for women as a group, the relationship is straightforward in that the SMR increases as social class descends. The strength of the relationship, or the gradient, between social class and mortality, is shown by the ratio of Classes I and II to Classes IV and V, which is greatest for male mortality, and least for married women classified according to their own occupations.

The relationship is more complex for single women, which may reflect a distinction between 'selection' factors in relation to marriage, combined with factors which make some career profiles more stressed for women and may lead to higher mortality from some conditions in particular.

Arber (1989) looking at figures relating to levels of morbidity and marital status found the opposite trend, that is, a stronger class gradient and a wider divide between ill-health amongst women in Class I when compared with women in Social Class V. This, she argued, could be the result of the selection factor in marriage: Women in Social Class I who have remained single may be more likely to have done so as a result of the 'career or family?' dilemma, and have chosen to follow a career rather than marry. On the other hand, single women in Social Class V appear more likely to be unmarried as a result of poor health or disability limiting their opportunities for marriage (Arber, 1989).

It may also be indicative of the problems of poverty faced by single women, as a result of low earnings, limited pensions and for many, sole responsibility for childcare. Thus the experience of single women in the poorest social class is materially different. Women in Class I may suffer the stresses of employment in professions dominated by men but are less likely to suffer poverty, whilst single women in the lowest social class are more likely to suffer poverty, having only one income, and the health effects of such poverty. This highlights an important complicating factor in the study of women's health: marital status, in combination with responsibility for children.

In the table, the SMRs for married women are higher than those for single women in Social Class II and in Classes IV and V, the semi-skilled and unskilled class. This is difficult to interpret because of the fundamental problem with the data – comparing mortality rates for one group of women according to the occupation of their partner, with mortality figures based on the women's own occupation means we are not comparing like with like.

The table also highlights another question in the interpretation of data on women's health. The SMRs for all women are higher than those for men in the two highest social classes, and the difference between the highest and lowest social class is much wider for men than it is for women. This suggests that perhaps there are greater differences in the health expectations and risk of early death for women in relation to social class, and what this particular variable attempts to convey, in terms of life experience and material conditions, is not a very good measure of inequalities for women.

Thus figures are complicated by the relationship between gender and social class, and whilst there is a difference in mortality for both men and women when the figures are related to social class, the gender difference between men and women is most marked in the unskilled social class, and least marked amongst the upper professional groups (Koskenuvo *et al.*, 1986). In addition, the gender gap differs by marital status, with greater gender differences in mortality rates in the no-longer married groups than amongst the married (Koskenuvo *et al.*, 1986).

This dilemma over measuring a woman's economic position and the resources she can hope to enjoy through the indirect and second hand status of male occupation makes the arguments relating to material causes of inequalities in health more complex, as it means that the links between class and health are only vaguely understood for over half of the population. A survey of premature death in North Tyneside showed how the health of women in middle-class areas was closely associated with their childhood health and circumstances, and also their own occupation and health hazards in the workplace (Phillimore, 1989). One of the key indicators of inequality and social class, infant mortality, perhaps highlights this argument most clearly. In studies comparing both international and national data, figures on infant mortality, birth weight and length of gestation, are seen as important indicators of the prosperity of a nation and of disparities between different social groups. The basis of social class allocation for the different measures is the occupation of the mother's husband. Typically, babies born to unmarried women have been left out of the figures, despite evidence that these women suffer poorer circumstances during the pregnancy and evidence linking this poverty and the stress of deprivation to low birth weight, pre-term delivery and perinatal mortality (Rutter and Quine, 1990; Pagel *et al.*, 1990). However, births to unmarried women, which represented in Britain in 1987 over 27 per cent of all births, are falling increasingly into two categories – those which are registered by two parents, and those registered by the mother alone. Clearly 'illegitimacy' itself is not necessarily directly related to lone parenthood and poverty, although for many women the arrival of a child will still herald income difficulties and the experience of poverty and deprivation.

Other evidence relating to congenital mortality, often associated with infant mortality, casts further doubt on the validity of using male occupation to rank figures of infant birth weight, pre-term delivery and mortality. There is a clear association between social class, using the occupation of the father, and the ratio of malformations at birth to live births. In 1977–79 the ratio varied between 73 per thousand for babies born in Social Class I to 180 per thousand in Social Class V. The same ratio exists when the data is reinterpreted using the mother's social class, although the gap between Social Class I and V narrows (OPCS, 1983). A large number of factors are associated with risks of congenital malformation, including the mother's age, hereditary factors, and standards of nutrition in pregnancy. As discussed in previous chapters, state support for pregnant women in maternity allowances is too low to allow women who have no other source of income to follow the diets recommended in antenatal care and by obstetricians, leaving poorer women particularly at risk. A further factor affecting women's risks of having a child suffering some kind of congenital abnormality relates to her levels of nutrition during early childhood and around puberty (Lovett *et al.*, 1990). Thus an insistence on father's occupational class does several things in the study of infant mortality: it removes over a quarter of all births from consideration, some of which are the most crucial in terms of the health impact of poverty, and it obscures the importance of the mother's health now and in earlier years.

Recalculating women's mortality rates using women's own occupations is also loaded with difficulties, and does not easily provide a solution. Problems arise in using an occupational stratification system created on the basis of male occupations, which leaves many of the jobs women do in positions in the structure which do not reflect the resources and risks associated with both the occupation and the rate of pay. The largest social class for women is the group III non-manual, which contains 39 per cent of all women in paid employment, whilst the largest single group for men is the group III Manual, containing over 36 per cent of all employed men. Women's occupations are concentrated in non-manual intermediate and skilled sectors, and women are more likely to be found in Classes II and III non-manual, which represent together virtually two-thirds of all employed women. Men's occupations are divided in two different areas of the hierarchy, with the majority – nearly 60 per cent – employed in skilled and unskilled manual work, and a further third employed in Social Classes I and II. Thus women's social class according to their own occupation places women higher in the occupational structure than men, though given women's lower average earnings and concentration in the lower tiers of organizational and occupational structures, this indicates a lack of coherence between social class, the Registrar General's occupational classification structure and economic circumstances, rather than women's higher socio-economic status.

Occupation at death or most recent occupation is also far less likely to be recorded for women than for men: the registrar's instructions allow women's occupations to be recorded only where they are in full-time paid employment and where a woman has had a paid job 'for most of her life'. It was estimated by the Decennial Supplement for 1979–83 that these restrictions 'may reduce the number of women for whom an occupation is recorded at death registration by a factor of around one-third of the total level possible' (OPCS, 1986b, p. 13). This reduction in the availability of data on women's occupations is unlikely to be evenly spread, and bias between which occupations are more likely to be recorded further distorts the data on women's mortality in relation to their own occupation (McDowell, 1983). In addition to these problems resulting from the recording of details at death, single women appear less likely to have an occupation recorded at census, which creates a further potential bias in the expression of mortality in relation to social class (Koskinnen, 1985, cited in Arber, 1989).

This structure is also entirely incapable of assigning women not in paid employment to a social class without reference to the occupation of their husband. In both sexes there is a group of people defined as 'unoccupied', who cannot be placed in the occupational or class hierarchy. This group, however, represents a much larger proportion of the female population than the male (38 per cent for women in 1981, compared with 3 per cent for men, OPCS, 1986b). The large majority of these women would no doubt admit to the job description, 'housewife', although this in itself may reflect more the limited employment opportunities for women after time out of the labour market to care for children, and the operation of unemployment and social security rules which restrict women's ability to claim unemployment benefit (Martin and Roberts, 1984; Dex, 1985; Pascall, 1986). However, the category 'housewife' has not found its way into the Registrar General's classification of occupations, and it is difficult to imagine how it might do so, despite attempts to find a location for domestic labour which has the same implications of material reward, occupational risk and access to resources as other occupational positions (Roberts and Barker, 1987).

In addition, in placing all women in the social class hierarchy on the basis of their own employment, we are failing to distinguish between women living alone and those who are married, and whose living standards may be different as a result. In terms of the impact of class on health, where in effect the relationship of material factors such as income adequacy, housing standards and so on are being related to the health experience, it is even more important to be sure all the variables which in sum might indicate the likelihood of poor income, deprivation in housing or environment, and so on, are being included. Not only is there a need to know the woman's household type, whether there are children and a partner, and what sex the partner is, but also it is necessary not to move from this to an assumption about access to resources and equality within the household. Thus some form of composite measure might be required in which household type and combined class is further differentiated according to division of resources within the household.

In addition, the issue of which women are in paid employment, and in full-time employment, is not necessarily distinct from the question of what jobs they have, how many hours they work and the effect of health on ability to participate in paid employment.

What is the effect on women's mortality rates if women's own occupation is used instead of that of their husband? Moser and Goldblatt (1985) recalculated OPCS Longitudinal data on women's mortality, finding that using women's own occupation rather than that of their husband produced a class relationship which was less marked: that is, when women are ranked according to their own occupation, there is a narrower divide between women in Class I and women in Social Class V. Whilst women with manual employment had higher rates of mortality than women in non-manual employment, the class gradient within the top three social classes and the gradient within the lower three social classes had disappeared (Moser and Goldblatt, 1985). This may simply reflect the fact that using the Registrar General's system of ranking occupations, which produces a distribution of women in employment in a narrow range of classes, does not accurately reflect the distribution of resources – income, other goods and services, time and status for example – which affect opportunities for health.

Other studies on women in employment have produced similar

findings. For example, a study of women in Scandinavia showed weaker occupational differences than mortality rates for men (Lynge, Andersen and Horte, 1989), although, as Arber (1989) points out, the difficulties over interpretation remain. Lynge's study related women's occupations to mortality, but could not take into account hours worked in paid employment and the hours worked outside of paid employment in domestic labour and childcare. Thus effects on health beyond paid employment are minimized in this formulation, whilst the effects of paid employment and the combination of both domestic labour and paid employment are minimized in using only husband's occupations for married women.

Alternative ways of trying to measure access to resources and risk factors for health have proved interesting. Car ownership, housing tenure and education have all demonstrated clear gradients in relation to mortality and morbidity in different studies. Tenure and area characteristics were revealed as strong indicators of early death in one study (Britton *et al.*, 1990). The study of health in the Northern region of Britain by Townsend, Phillimore and Beattie (1988) demonstrated that non car-ownership and local authority housing, for example, were significantly associated with higher levels of mortality. Goldblatt (1990) similarly linked car ownership and level of education to increased mortality, and in particular found being without access to a car a strong predictor of high mortality (Smith and Jacobson, 1989). The lower mortality rates of married women in paid employment, in comparison with both single women and married women without paid employment reflects the advantages of having two wage-earners in a household, even where women's earnings are low (Moser, Pugh and Goldblatt, 1987). Evidence suggesting lower mortality in households which own a car, are owner occupiers and have two earners, also suggests the need for a measure of socio-economic status which reflects these variables and the interrelationship between them (Moser, Pugh and Goldblatt, 1987).

There remain, however, difficulties in using such a system of indicators of material circumstances for both men and women, when the experience of each sex is different. The use of an indicator based on car ownership per household or of housing tenure still leaves the problem of conflating household experience with individual experience. Using a car as an indicator of resources more widely available to the household is, by definition, a measurement which

cannot differentiate between the individual members of the household, or take account of differential use of this resource (Sinfield,
1986; Deem, 1988; Grieco *et al.*, 1990).

Basing women's social class on a man's occupation is no longer
acceptable, if it ever was (Arber, 1989; Roberts, 1990), whilst using
the existing system of occupational classification, based on men's employment structure, results in an inaccurate expression of women's
hierarchies and access to resources (Hakim, 1979, Arber, 1989). It
is therefore inaccurate in what it conveys about women's health
experience (Moser and Goldblatt, 1985; Pugh and Moser, 1990;
Moser, Pugh and Goldblatt, 1987; Phillimore, 1989). Furthermore,
including women, classified by a mixture of their own employment
(single and no-longer married women) and their husband's occupation (married women), in a calculation of mortality rates across
class obscures class relationships for both men and women. Whilst
the argument here has focused on women's access to household
resources, the dilemma also relates to an accurate expression of
male resources, living standards and health experience. Women's
earnings are crucial in keeping a large number of households above
the poverty line (Land, 1981) and women's earnings often allow
men to keep more of their own income for their own consumption.
As a result, whilst figures of women's mortality in relation to occupational and social class indicate important differences in health
experience for women of different income levels, further delving is
also required to express the precise nature of this relationship
between poverty and poor health.

There are also marked gender differences in what people die
of, with some causes of death far more likely to affect men than
women. Although the ratio of male deaths to female deaths amongst
adults under retirement age is nearly three to one; men are over five
times as likely to die from violent causes of death, over 18 times as
likely to die from accidental poisoning, and nearly 6 times as likely
to die from alcohol related causes (Koskenuvo *et al.*, 1986).

However, these are the less common causes of mortality. Overall, causes of death for women and men are remarkably similar,
with both sexes sharing the same major causes of death: diseases of
the circulatory system, which accounted for 49 per cent of women's
mortality and 48 per cent of male mortality in 1984, cancer, which
accounted for 23 per cent of women's deaths and 25 per cent of
men's deaths, and diseases of respiratory system which produced 10

per cent of women's mortality compared with 12 per cent of male deaths in that year (Reid, 1989).

Within these conditions there is some variation – for example, circulatory disease accounts for similar levels of mortality amongst both women and men, but 31 per cent of male deaths were accounted for by ischaemic heart disease compared with 24 per cent of female deaths, and 15 per cent of female deaths were caused by cerebro-vascular disease or stroke, compared with 9 per cent of male deaths. Overall, however, the major causes of death were the same for each sex – nearly three quarters of both men and women died of cancer or diseases of the circulatory system (Reid, 1989).

Though both women and men die of the same kinds of conditions, and share the same major causes of death, the extent to which each sex suffers these types of condition varies. Men are more likely to suffer the principal fatal illnesses, and are more likely to die from these conditions (Verbrugge, 1986, Aggleton, 1990) – in other words, women and men suffer similar kinds of fatal illness and conditions, but women suffer such illness less often.

## Women's morbidity and social class

Interest in the measurement of morbidity has grown in recent years in response to decreases in mortality and increased life expectancy, and in response to growing unease about using death as a surrogate measure for health. Measures of morbidity refer to sickness, and as such, as discussed, remain locked within a medical framework. However, different ways of approaching the concept of morbidity incorporate different degrees of the subjective experience of health, and may lead to better understanding of social dimensions of the health experience.

A leading source of morbidity data in relation to social class has been the General Household Survey (GHS), according to which more women than men suffer chronic illness, women being slightly more likely to report a long-standing illness (GHS, 1990). Age is clearly important in relation to illnesses which increase later in life. The gap between the sexes is however most marked for older women, whilst rates were roughly equal for adults between the ages of 16 and 64, and rates for those aged 15 and under were reversed, with slightly more males reporting chronic illness or disability.

Limiting long-standing illness is the concept used by the GHS to measure severe chronic illness, those who suffer a long-standing illness and who have had their activities limited in the fortnight before the interview. For both sexes there has been a rise in recent years in the proportion suffering severe chronic illness, and again women are more likely to report on this measure in later life, with rates for adults under 64 being fairly close. As might be expected, rates rise for both sexes as age increases (GHS, 1990).

Acute sickness is defined by the GHS as 'having to cut down on any of the things you usually do (about the house/at work or in your free time) because of illness or injury' (GHS 1989, p. 28). As the GHS points out, responses to this type of question are determined by the kinds of activity required in paid or unpaid employment. The GHS suggests that this might result in under-reporting by those in less strenuous occupations, including higher occupational groups in non-manual employment. However, financial considerations which might limit time taken off paid employment are more likely to affect those without sick pay cover, including a large number of women in part-time employment, whilst women in full-time domestic labour have another set of constraints which operate against limiting activity in this way.

According to the GHS, in 1988 women had higher levels of acute sickness: having more days on average per year when their activities were restricted as a result of illness, with 14 per cent of women compared with 11 per cent of men reporting suffering acute sickness in the fortnight before the interview (GHS, 1990).

The GHS shows a relationship between social class and both long-standing illness and limiting long-standing illness, for both men and women. Thus women from unskilled and semi-skilled occupational groups are more likely in every age group to report chronic and severe chronic illness, with the greatest divide in terms of health being amongst women aged 45 to 64, where there were 43 per cent more women in manual classes suffering from severe chronic illness compared to women in the professional and non-manual occupations. The class divide overall was slightly greater for women than it was for men, for both chronic and severe chronic illness (GHS, 1990).

The class relationship for both women and men in relation to acute sickness was less straightforward than for chronic illness: in the age groups over 44 men appear more likely to suffer acute illness in the skilled, semi-skilled and unskilled manual classes, and to have more days when activity is restricted by acute illness. However, between 16 and 44 the rates for men in the professional class is slightly higher. Girls and young women up to the age of 16 are slightly more likely to experience restricted activity in the higher occupational groups, are equally likely to suffer acute illness in the age group 16–44, whilst over the age of 65 women in lower occupational groups suffer higher rates of acute illness. The class picture overall for women is less clear, and less one way, than it is for men.

In part, this is again a problem of statistics, and cannot be used to infer that social circumstances matter less in their impact on women's health, but rather that what is being measured is less related. Again, social class is measured here, for married women, in terms of their husband's job, with all of the problems that entails, figures refer only to actual reported illness, and there are likely to be differences in self-perception of ill health.

Whilst mortality ratios may be age-standardized and sex-standardized to take account of the fact that women live longer than men and mortality increases with age, the figures given in the GHS are simple totals of those reporting morbidity, without reference to the composition of that social class. Clearly, if social class four contains a larger proportion of older workers, given that both chronic and acute sickness rise with age, it would not be surprising to discover higher rates of morbidity in this class compared with Social Class I, and the class gradient would be an inaccurate reflection of the distribution of health.

Sara Arber (1990a; 1989) has taken GHS figures, averaged over three years, and converted these to a ratio on the basis of the age structure of each social class, as a means of taking account of age differences in social class structure. This produces a ratio similar to the SMR used for mortality, with 100 representing average levels of morbidity. Translating reported levels of limiting long-standing illness from the GHS into standardized limiting long-standing illness (SLLI) Arber found a mostly simple, indirect class gradient for men and for women, using the conventional approach, that is classifying married women according to their husband's occupation. So, under the conventional approach, women in the higher professional group had an SLLI of 63 compared with an SLLI of 127 for women in the unskilled group, virtually twice as much limiting long-standing illness amongst the lowest social group in comparison with the highest, a slightly narrower gap between women under this classification system than for men.

However, when women were reclassified according to their own current or last occupation, the relationship becomes less clear, with rates of chronic illness amongst lower professional women which are not only double those of the higher professional group, but also higher than both non-manual and manual skilled workers. The occupational classification based on past employment for some of these women may be quite dated, and may have less relevance to their current health than other factors, including household income, the employment of other members of the household and their own access to the resources of the household.

If instead only those women in current employment are classified according to their own occupation, the remainder being classified in the conventional way, the class relationship becomes less clear, with the highest rate of limiting long-standing illness reported amongst semi-skilled women, and again rates for lower professional women which are higher than those for the non-manual and manual skilled group.

As Arber points out, the class differences using both the conventional approach and standardized ratios of limiting long-standing illness (SLLIs) are very close to the Standardized Mortality Ratios for women and men in the 1979–83 Decennial Supplement (OPCS, 1986b). In addition, the lower SLLIs recorded for women working in unskilled occupations when classified according to their own occupations are similar to Moser and Goldblatt's findings (1985) of women's mortality using women's occupations.

But we are still left with the problem of confusing in one approach a number of different variables, for example, the need to take into account women's hours in paid employment and unpaid domestic labour, and the effect of these on health, in particular the cumulative effect of the total hours spent in labour of some kind, the stress of managing different jobs, and the potential for some hazards of work or home to accumulate and pose greater threat to health than each alone (Daykin, 1989). The issue of the healthy worker effect also remains, where those women whose own jobs are being used for stratification may represent a healthier section of the female workforce, or where women with poorer health are clustered at the foot of the occupational hierarchy as a result of the limitations their health places on the type of occupation they can obtain.

The relationship between health and employment status is itself complicated, and there is a relative lack of information and research on the links for women between employment, unemployment and health status. Research showing the differences in health indicates a link between mental health and employment, described by Brown and Harris (1978) as a protective effect, where paid work mitigates against depression amongst women.

The GHS analyses both chronic and acute sickness by economic activity status, using three categories of analysis: working, unemployed and economically inactive, which includes people who have retired, are not in paid employment as a result of sickness or disability, and those who are caring for others, or who work full-time in unpaid domestic labour – housewives.

Amongst women, both the unemployed and those defined as 'economically inactive' reported higher levels of chronic and acute illness than those in paid employment, although the gap between women in paid work and women who were economically inactive was narrower than the gap for men. Clearly, a number of those who are economically inactive are likely to be so as a result of poor health, and this partly explains the wider gap for men, fewer of whom are likely to be out of the labour market to care for others. However, the distinction between the status of unemployeds and that of sick or suffering a disability does not directly and simply relate to actual health and disability. Factors such as differences in the amount of benefit paid to the unemployed compared with sickness and disability benefits, the severity of disability tests, and the stigma attached to unemployment compared with that attached to poor health will affect both claiming behaviour and self-perception of status (Whiteside, 1988). Similarly, women's greater ineligibility for benefit and the ease of adopting the role of housewife will affect how women describe themselves in relation to the labour market (Martin and Roberts, 1984).

An alternative measure of morbidity which relies on subjective measures of illness combined with structural constraints which may affect behaviour is that of consultation with a medical professional, specifically with a GP. Use of all health care, including primary health care is affected by factors such as transport, the ability to take time off paid employment, the availability of others to care for dependants, and so on.

Women are more likely to visit their GP (GHS, 1990), and consult more often at every age (OPCS, 1986a; GHS, 1990), with the greatest gap in the ages 15 to 44. Whilst some of this consultation is in relation to contraception, ante-natal care and care after childbirth, these reasons have a very low rate of consultation and account for very few visits overall (OPCS, 1986a; GHS, 1981). Overall, rates of consultation are highest for working-class women, who are most likely to report visiting a GP in the previous two weeks and who have the greater average number of consultations per year (GHS, 1990).

One of the constraints on visiting a GP is paid employment, and being able to take time off to attend a surgery. The GHS shows more women in the economically inactive group consulting their GP compared with women in paid employment, although the gap between women in paid employment and those who are not is narrower than the gaps between men of different levels of economic activity (GHS, 1990). Again, the question of the so-called 'healthy worker effect' prevents us from concluding too simply that paid employment operates to protect health, whilst the much greater proportion of women in part-time paid employment means that some women may have more hours available in which to attend the GPs surgery. However the picture is again complicated by the fact that many of these women work part-time around childcare and caring for other dependants, and this restricts their ability to see a GP.

The 1981–2 survey on morbidity statistics from general practice gives considerable detail on consultations, calculated on the basis of social class for women using both the 'conventional' method, where married and cohabiting women are classified according to their partner's occupation, and non-traditional method, where married women are classified according to their own occupation, where they have one (OPCS, 1990a).

The study shows that, using this 'conventional' approach, women from Social Classes IV and V are more likely than women in Social Classes I and II to consult a GP, in particular for serious conditions, a definition which includes heart disease, Parkinson's disease, multiple sclerosis and ectopic pregnancy.

The divide between the higher and lower social classes is most marked in diseases of the circulatory system, where the standardized patient consulting ratio (SPCR) for women in Classes I and II is 16 points below the average of a hundred, and the SPCR for women in the lowest groups is 17 points over the average. Thus women in the lowest socio-economic groups are 46 per cent as likely to consult their GP for such conditions. Although the class gradient holds true for all consulting categories, other conditions where the gap is particularly marked include accidents, injuries and poisoning (a 35-point gap); mental illness (a 29-point gap) and diseases of the blood and blood forming organs, where women in socio-economic groups IV and V were more than twice as likely to be diagnosed by their GP.

The relationship between social class and consultation becomes less clear when the ratios for women are broken down into those for married and cohabiting women and those for non-married women (single, widowed and divorced), both groups stratified according to their own occupation. Married women under this approach show the same class gradient, although it is now less steep, and the picture for non-married women is mostly of a class gradient, with women in skilled non-manual employment having very similar levels of serious illness to professional women.

The greatest difference when women's class is recalculated according to their own occupation, is in diseases of the circulatory system, where the class divide is much wider for non-married women than for married women, classified according to their own occupation. Thus non-married women in the highest socio-economic group have an SCPR of 78, in comparison with women in unskilled occupations who have an SCPR of 133, a gap of 55 points. The gap for married women classified by their own occupation is much smaller, at 15 points, and is also narrower than the gap for women using the conventional method.

The problems of analysing women's class from either their partner's occupation or their own, and trying also to draw into the classification system adopted some measure of household income and avoid the pitfalls of an occupational hierarchy based on male occupations, has led many to use other variables as indicators of income and patterns of consumption. Housing tenure is a powerful indicator of variation in morbidity, as well as mortality.

Women living as owner-occupiers had lower than average consultation rates overall and in every category of condition, whilst women living as local authority tenants had higher than average rates of consultation in all categories except one: women living in council accommodation had lower rates of consultation than either women owner-occupiers or women in privately rented accommodation for neoplasms. In all other diagnostic categories, women in council houses were over-represented, the tenure divide being most marked between them and owner-occupiers in diseases of the digestive system, endocrine and related disorders and mental health problems. The consultation rate for women in local authority housing was nearly 25 per cent higher than the rate for women in owner-occupied housing.

Women in privately rented accommodation present a less clear-cut position, with low rates of consultation for some disorders, such as infectious diseases, and diseases of the nervous system, and higher than average rates for others – including neoplasms, endocrine disorders, and mental illness.

Some of the findings are surprising – whilst women in local authority housing have higher rates of respiratory illness than women in owner-occupied housing, women in privately rented accommodation also have lower than average rates. The association between poor housing and respiratory problems would infer that women housed in both local authority housing and private rented accommodation would have higher rates of consultation for such illness. However, the weight of findings in relation to women in privately rented accommodation is reduced by the fact that this group had the highest rate of non-consultation – which is partly associated with a greater degree of mobility amongst tenants in the private sector. Private rented accommodation also varies a good deal in terms of quality, and tenants at the more secure and better end of the privately rented market are also those least likely to move frequently. At the other end, women living in hostels and bed and breakfast accommodation, and women who are travellers, are less likely to be registered with a general practice (Victor, 1990, Cole-Hamilton *et al.*, 1988; Pahl and Vaile, 1988), and the health problems associated with poor quality privately rented housing may be partially obscured in this survey as a result.

Women's health varies, then, in response to a maze of interlocking variables: employment status and occupation, marital status, housing tenure, and responsibility for children or other dependants are all ways of reanalysing data on mortality and morbidity which suggest a hugely complex model of women's health. Whilst it is possible – and important – to use the data available from official sources to construct this model, this can only take us so far. The kinds of results this operation produces suggest that marriage improves women's health chances – but not as much as it does men's; paid employment also improves women's health chances – but it depends on the number of hours worked, the kind of job and health hazards at work, the pay and levels of support a woman can obtain from other members of the household or by buying domestic labour from outside; and having responsibility for children and other dependants produces a variety of effects – decreasing opportunities to take paid employment, increasing income needs, providing opportunities for satisfaction as well as sources of stress.

Whilst this data can be analysed further – to take account of women who are housewives as a result of poor health, or who are not married because of poor health, for example – the crucial factors of women's health experience appear to be their access to resources, and their work and the demands made on them. These factors are interlinked, and both relate to women's position of economic dependency: women's access to resources from the labour market, within the household and from social security systems. In other words, women's health is heavily dependent on the roles and labour they are called upon to perform, and the resources available to them for this work and for activities which could enhance their health (Millar and Glendinning, 1989; Popay and Jones, 1987). The health consequences of poverty and deprivation, therefore, require further delving into the distribution of resources such as food and housing, and the health impact of these on women.

# CHAPTER 5

# POVERTY AND WOMEN'S HEALTH

It is not difficult to imagine the ways in which poverty might affect health, both physical and mental well-being. Indeed, as the last chapter suggests, there is a powerful relationship between socio-economic status and poor health when measured by mortality and morbidity: people in lower occupational groups are more likely to die prematurely, to experience poorer health during their life-times, visit their GPs more often and their children are also more likely to die earlier and suffer poorer health than their counter-parts in higher occupational groups. Poor health chances amongst lower income groups extends to rates of recovery from illness as well – adults in lower occupational groups have a higher incidence of cancer and are less likely to survive cancer once diagnosed (OPCS, 1990b). This gap between the health experience of rich and poor has widened in the second part of this century, and in particular in the past few decades (Smith, Bartley and Blane, 1990; Whitehead, 1987; Hart, 1987; Townsend, 1990a). Whilst it remains problematic to measure health in such an indirect and medically oriented way, these statistics are telling evidence of the ways in which inequalities in living circumstances are reflected in inequali-ties in health.

However, although the existence of this relationship between occupational class and measures of health has been explored many times, the precise nature of the links between poverty and increased risks of mortality and morbidity has been indicated rather than proven (Macintyre, 1986; Townsend, 1990a). Despite the Black Report's call for more research on the material factors underlying higher mortality and morbidity amongst low income groups, funding has not been made available, and the structuralist arguments of the report have been neglected within social and government policy (Smith, Bartley and Blane, 1990). Those studies which have been carried out in this area have focused on the specific relationship between health and some forms of deprivation – for example, poor quality housing – and have begun to demonstrate more clearly the detail of the effect of poverty on health. This is a complex relationship, however, and the interconnections between the periods of time over which poverty is experienced, the different forms of deprivation which occur, and different patterns of health and illness are difficult to follow.

The issue for us here is that of gender – the ways in which women's experience of poverty specifically affects women's patterns of health. Previous chapters have argued that in poverty research the experience of women is obscured by a focus on men and the household. Chapter 4 argued that in the measurement of mortality and morbidity women's experience is again obscured. This has two dimensions: a focus on male mortality, and the use of a ranking structure based on male employment patterns and the male labour market. Women are again concealed within the household – through being classed according to their husband or partner's job, or according to a stratification system which does not reflect the gendered nature of the labour market and the different ranking of women's jobs. We need to open up the 'black box' of women's health experience (Arber, 1990a), alongside that of women's experience of poverty and deprivation.

This chapter, then, turns to look at the consequences of poverty: the effects of an inadequate income and other kinds of deprivation on people's lives and on their health – looking specifically at the ways in which the poverty and deprivation experienced by women affects their health. This entails drawing together different pieces of evidence on women's experience within the household, the impact on health of some kinds of deprivation, and evidence on the kinds of ill-health that women experience. That this has to be a kind of detective job speaks volumes for the predominantly male focus of research on inequalities in health.

Further complications arise in the consideration of what constitutes health, and how it is to be measured. Measures of mortality and morbidity are the most easily found, and are useful as indicators of relationships to explore in more depth. They cannot reflect health as a positive experience, or the many different facets of health which allow one to feel healthy despite or alongside major illness or serious conditions (Blaxter, 1990). Attempts to incorporate measures of health as a positive state focus on well-being but retain the dilemma over how to define this, and how to rank different perceptions of well-being when trying to distinguish between different levels of health in the population (Blaxter, 1990). Other scales such as the Nottingham Health Profile (Hunt and McEwan, 1980) try to incorporate an indicator of the impact of poor health on relationships and social activities – a measure closely associated with definitions of relative deprivation. As we have seen, both perceptions of health, and the extent to which poor health for any person is associated with a curtailment of employment (paid or unpaid) or social roles can be related to the very factors by which health appears to vary – social class, occupational status, race and gender.

The issue of how to define and measure health from a positive perspective, rather than one bounded by negative concepts of illness within a medical framework, is one not taken up by the feminist movement, although aspects of women's health have certainly been the focus of both the early women's movement and what is sometimes referred to as 'the second wave' of feminism. Feminist writing on women's health has tended to highlight some of women's experiences within the health service – specifically the experience of pregnancy and childbirth – as being healthy processes pathologized by the medical profession (Oakley, 1981; Ehrenreich and English, 1979). Others have written of women's treatment within psychiatry, women's higher rates of treatment for mental illness, and women's susceptibility to being labelled as mad (Chesler, 1974, Jordanova, 1981). There is a need for a model of women's health which is positively framed, incorporates physical and mental health, and women's economic and social status as part of the health experience. Aspects of health such as the ability to enjoy public space and public amenities without fear of harassment or violence are clearly important, as is the ability to enjoy private relationships without the fear of violence or abuse. It is important to frame a model of women's health which is both positive and wide ranging.

## Income and health

Using income as a starting point for an exploration of the relationship between poverty, deprivation and health appears straightforward, at least initially. Studies of the association between occupational or socio-economic status and mortality and morbidity lead us in that direction. Higher rates of mortality, greater risks of morbidity and early death amongst poorer occupational groups suggest a link between earnings and poor health. An assessment of the health risks of some occupations compared with others was the primary goal of the first calculations of different rates of occupational mortality (OPCS, 1986b), although the first Registrar General was concerned also with risks attendant on other factors, including sex, age, locality and the 'influence of civilization' (Farr, 1839, cited in OPCS, 1986b).

Income is, however, only a proxy measure of the amount and type of resources which can be acquired and which allow, enhance or re-duce health potential. Certainly, when the focus is on women, whose access to resources within the household cannot be determined by occupation alone, the problems associated with the use of occupa-tional class or status as a proxy measure for income which is in itself a proxy measure for access to resources are increased. The number of earners within a household is linked to premature mortality, with higher mortality in areas with a high proportion of households dependent on state income support, and lower mortality in areas with households with more than one earner (Phillimore, 1989).

Studies which have used indicators of deprivation rather than income-based measures of poverty have similarly found strong asso-ciations with increased mortality (Townsend, 1990e). Car owner-ship, for example, is linked both to low income and higher levels of premature death and chronic illness (Townsend, Davidson and Whitehead, 1988; Townsend, Phillimore and Beattie, 1988; Arber, 1989; Moser, Pugh and Goldblatt, 1987). One survey of living stan-dards in London, revealed rates of self-reported ill-health ten times as great amongst deprived households as amongst the least deprived, with the poorest being twice as likely to have suffered a recent illness and more than three times as likely to report a major health problem in the past year (Benzeval and Judge, 1990). The same survey revealed a strong and consistent association between material deprivation and premature death (Townsend, 1990b).

Other studies have shown how women in lower income groups suffer higher rates of specific diseases. The incidence of mortality from cervical cancer is greater amongst women in low-income groups, who are also less likely to be screened for this disease (Barker, 1990; Savage and George, 1989). The concentration of these preventable deaths from cervical cancer amongst poorer women relates both to low screening rates, and to the underlying causes of the cancer itself, which include structural factors such as poor diet, unhealthy living conditions and poverty (Hodgkinson, 1988; 1989) and risks associated with the occupations of partners (Robinson, 1982; General Municipal Boilermakers Union (GMB), 1987; OPCS, 1986b).

The links between income and poor health are also apparent in the poorer health experienced by some household types. Women caring alone for children are more likely to suffer poverty than two-parent households, and a greater proportion of lone mothers rely on state income support as their sole source of income (Millar, 1987; 1989a; Graham, 1986). Over half the lone mothers in one survey lived in households where income was below the minimum necessary to maintain the health of all members of the household (Graham, 1986). Perhaps not surprisingly, lone mothers report higher levels of illness than either women caring for children in a two-parent household or lone fathers: they suffer higher levels of disability, more acute and chronic illness and visit both their GPs and hospital more often (Ansen, 1988; Cox *et al.*, 1987; Blaxter, 1990; Graham, 1986).

Income is thus a measure of the resources which can be acquired and which in themselves enhance health, and it is these resources which must be examined in more detail to assess their impact on health. Income alone does not take account of the ways in which money is translated into other goods and the benefits and burdens of this translation are distributed. For example inflation has a greater impact on the poor (Fry and Pashardes, 1985; Institute of Fiscal Studies, 1986), and the failure of social security benefits to rise in line with either Retail Price Index inflation or the higher inflation experienced by the poor, affects the amount spent by poor households on food. When income is inadequate, the amount spent by households on different goods and services depends on the flexibility of that item, and food is, for most households, the item with the greatest elasticity (Cole-Hamilton and Lang, 1986; Daly, 1989).

Changes to social security payments have reduced the extent to which recipients can exercise choice over where cuts in expenditure can be made – for example, the deduction of rent and debt repayments before benefits are paid. It is these issues which mediate the links between health and poverty, in particular, the health experience of women whose access to resources is distinct from household patterns of consumption and whose lives are affected by deprivation in gender-specific ways. For this reason, the following sections examine different kinds of resources which are crucial in structuring health. However, whilst occupational class is used as a proxy for income, it is also used as a measure of risks attaching to the occupation and to employment status, whilst unemployment has implications not only for income levels and consumption but also for health in a more direct fashion.

## Paid employment

The relationship between the labour market, employment status and health most often focuses on male employment, and on unemployment as a factor contributing to higher levels of chronic illness, mental illness, premature mortality and suicide amongst men (Phillimore, 1989; Platt and Kreitman, 1984; Moser et al., 1984; Brenner, 1973). Unemployment for men is clearly associated with a substantially increased risk of early death and poor health, both physical and mental, whilst the health of the families of unemployed men is also poorer than where the man is employed (Fagin and Little, 1984; Moser et al., 1986). One question which arises is that of 'the healthy worker effect': are the unemployed also those in poorest health, who either cannot find employment or who are the first to lose their jobs when redundancies are made? Studies in periods or areas of high unemployment suggest that poor health is not the only reason for job loss where redundancies are widespread, and the effects of unemployment on health cannot be ruled out (Hunt et al., 1986; Platt, 1984; Platt and Kreitman, 1984; Smith, 1987). Similarly, the OPCS Longitudinal Study which traced the employment and health patterns of a sample of men 'seeking work' from the 1971 Census suggests health deteriorates as a result of unemployment as these were men distinguished as unemployed rather than sick in the Census, and as the mortality rates of the wives of the unemployed men were also higher than would be expected (Moser *et al.*, 1984; Whitehead, 1987).

The impact of unemployment on health is primarily associated with the loss of earnings and a reliance on state benefits which are inadequate to provide a level of living above or even at subsistence level (Townsend, 1989; Stitt, 1990). The majority of households where one or more adult is unemployed have inadequate diets, which are nutritionally poor, and which have an adverse effect on health (Lang, 1984; Cole-Hamilton and Lang, 1986). Cheaper sources of energy, such as bread, potatoes and cheap processed meat products do not provide sufficient nutrients to maintain health, and illness such as infectious diseases, diseases of the digestive system and circulatory system are more frequent amongst lower income groups (Cole-Hamilton and Lang, 1986; OPCS, 1990a; Daly, 1989). In addition, the stress of unemployment affects health, although the effects of the loss of status, the isolation of unemployment and the loss of a work routine are exacerbated by the stress of poverty, of reliance on a state benefit system and the stress of claiming benefits (Fagin and Little, 1984).

Unemployment is patterned by class, with high levels of un-employment amongst lower occupational classes, for both men and women (Arber, 1987). Gender and the sexually segregated labour market have created two models: whilst the one for men is more marked, with unskilled men seven times as likely to be unemployed as men in the highest occupational classes, women in unskilled occupations also suffer higher rates of unemployment (Arber, 1987). However, higher rates of mortality and morbidity amongst the un-employed persist even when the effect of their lower occupational class of the unemployed is taken into account (Moser *et al.*, 1984; Whitehead, 1987).

As the above account suggests, the association between unem-ployment and health for women is most often pursued through women's position within the unemployed household, where the male breadwinner is out of the labour market. The operation of social policy in the field of support to those out of the labour market means women are unlikely to retain paid employment themselves when their partner is unemployed, and one impact on women's health, in addition to the poverty and stress of coping on unemploy-ment benefit, is that of loss of her own status in paid work and her own source of income.

The links between unemployment, employment and poor health are not simple. Harsh working conditions in paid employment are linked to premature death (Phillimore, 1989), and the health hazards of paid employment contribute to higher mortality and morbidity in some occupations for both men and women. The health hazards of female employment are found in both skilled and unskilled occupations, and include injuries associated with repetitive operations, respiratory and skin diseases resulting from exposure to and use of chemicals, strain from poor seating and lighting, and the organization of office work, and the stress of discrimination and sexism in the workplace as well as sexual harassment (Pringle, 1988; Daykin, 1989; Stellman, 1977; Doyal, 1979). Women's role as providers of informal health care in the home (Graham, 1985; 1986) is replicated by an expectation of health maintenance activities in the workplace (Pringle, 1988; Daykin, 1990), and this too adds to the burden on women's own health (Oakley, 1986; Graham, 1986).

Occupational health and the risks associated with paid employment are typically framed in relation to the male labour market and male occupations (Daykin, 1989). As such, the focus is on dramatic injuries resulting from accidents, and severe chronic ill-health from a few well-known conditions such as asbestoses and pneumoconiosis (coal lung disease), rather than on injuries and diseases which result in a deterioration in health at a lower level (Lewin and Olesen, 1985a; Daykin, 1990). Some hazards to women in the workplace are exacerbated by domestic labour – for example, contact with the same chemicals, and injuries sustained in some forms of domestic labour (Daykin, 1989) whilst the literature on occupational health fails to take account of this cumulative effect for women in some kinds of employment.

In addition, the focus of the Health and Safety at Work Act, 1974 is on individual responsibility to protect one's own health in paid employment. This bias presents specific problems for women, a large number of whom are employed in small businesses, working part time, with no union representation and sometimes little contact with other employees. Such conditions combine with the underlying male bias to the definition of health hazards at work to make organization to highlight specific health problems in the workplace more difficult. Women's employment poses a number of health risks in direct association with the work itself and the way in which it is organized. Women employed in the National Health Service, for example, are in contact, often on a daily basis, with a number of hazardous chemicals, associated with both short-term health effects – such as nausea, eye irritation and headaches, and long-term problems including lung and heart disease, cancer and damage to the blood and bone marrow (GMB, 1987). Women working as cleaners are exposed not only to the chemicals used in cleaning but also to any health threat in the workplace where they are employed. In the engineering industry, for example, cleaners suffer serious threats to their health when working with solvents and degreasing agents; women cleaning offices are exposed to many of the same threats to health faced by clerical workers: chemicals from office equipment, poor air conditioning and lighting, for example (GMB, 1987; Stellman, 1977). A recent report on workers in the food industry, the majority of whom are women, highlighted the dangers arising from chemical additives, linked to symptoms ranging from eye irritation, nose bleeds and dermatitis to increased rates for serious conditions, including asthma, bronchitis and stomach cancer (*The Observer*, 1989).

In recent years some publicity around the issue of the effect on health of the new technology in offices has highlighted conditions such as repetitive strain injury (RSI) and eye strain as a result of prolonged use of VDUs, although the food and drink industry has the highest rate of tenosynovitis and RSI (GMB, 1987), in the kind of employment where women are the majority of the workforce: for example, packing foodstuffs in a production line. The increased interest in RSI in the last decade may have more to do with the growing number of men working with new office machinery. In fact, the focus on women's health in paid employment tends towards two obsessions – women's reproductive health and women's experience of role strain as a result of trying to be both a good wife and a good mother.

Women's reproductive nature was the central concern of legislation designed to restrict women's employment in certain industries and in shift work in the last century, although fear of women's sexuality also featured in debate over women working underground in the mines (Oakley, 1974). In recent times the overriding concern of both legislation and the unions has been to protect women's reproductive health and their unborn child. However, reproductive health is a concern for both men and women. Working with lead, for both men and women, was found to be linked to a higher rate of miscarriage, stillbirth and congenital malformations in the last century (GMB, 1987). Despite the way in which chemicals and other substances present a threat to the reproductive health of both women and men, much of the legislation focuses on women who are pregnant, ignoring also the fact that the greatest threat is posed at the time of conception and in the earliest weeks of the pregnancy, often when the woman does not know that she is pregnant (Lewin and Olesen, 1985a; Stellman, 1977; GMB, 1987). Whilst the issue of the threat to the embryo or foetus is important, the precise nature of the threat of many chemicals or workplace hazards is to a large extent unresolved. This area of women's reproductive health also illustrates women's invisibility in the literature of the health consequences of material factors, for, as Doyal points out (1988, unpublished), the failure to record women's occupations on death certificates for stillbirths means many of these links go unrecognized.

However, the dangers to women's own health as a result of both harmful working conditions and the stress of low earnings, unsatisfying work, and underutilization of skills should not go unrecognized (Lewin and Olesen, 1985a; Stellman, 1977; General Municipal Boilermakers Union, 1987).

The alternative vision of women's health in the workplace focuses on women's double burden and the toll this takes in terms of health, in particular the strain on mental health of trying to reconcile the image of the good mother with that of the good worker (Doyal, 1979). It is a vision which emphasizes the stress women experience trying to juggle home and work, and in particular the 'role conflict' women experience in being out in the public sphere of paid labour (Haavio-Mannila, 1986). There is some evidence to suggest that the strain of combining a job with caring for children and domestic labour does have a negative effect on health, for it is women who take responsibility for finding alternative childcare and who continue to manage the home, and carry out the domestic labour. (Sharpe, 1984; Brannen and Moss, 1987). In countries where the majority of women work outside the home and childcare is widely available – such as Sweden – the health of working women is better (Haavio-Mannila, 1986). This image of role strain amongst women in paid employment is, however, bound up with the issue of women's appropriateness in the workplace (Lewin and Olesen, 1985a; Arber, 1989; Arber, Gilbert and Dale, 1985), which allows material factors such as the inadequacy and cost of alternative childcare, poor public transport and women's low earnings to remain unexamined. Reports of increasing mortality amongst women for stress-related diseases imply women have joined the ranks of the stressed executive and are beginning to share the price he pays for that success (*The Guardian*, 1990) – and that this is a problem for women rather than for executives. The concept of the diseases of the rich has been discredited by evidence demonstrating that the affluent have higher mortality rates in only one major disease category – malignant melanoma caused by over-exposure to the sun (Whitehead, 1987). The stresses for women of paid employment are in fact more complex than the role strain or double burden theory suggests, and whilst many occupations carry hazards for women's health, paid employment for women also appears to increase well-being for some women.

Brown and Harris, in a survey of depressed women in Camberwell, London, found paid employment to be one of four factors which appeared to protect women from depression (Brown and Harris, 1978). Large-scale studies of mortality and morbidity amongst women suggest that both premature mortality and morbidity are higher amongst women who are full-time housewives than amongst women who are in paid employment (Haavio-Mannila, 1986; Passannante and Nathanson, 1985; Moser *et al.*, 1987; Beral, 1987). However, the precise nature of this relationship is less simple than the direct prescription 'paid employment protects health' would suggest. There are many reasons why paid employment might enhance both physical and mental health – increased opportunities for self-esteem and confidence were suggested by Brown and Harris in their study (1978). A more important factor for many women is the money earned – to offset either household or individually experienced deprivation. Greater opportunities for social contact, and for some women, the health resources of their place of employment may also be significant.

Paid employment can also have an adverse effect on health, both physical and mental. The 'de-skilling' effect of leaving the labour market to care for children or other dependants means that many women return to the labour market at a lower level than previous employment, and this is where they will stay, whether in full- or part-time employment (Martin and Roberts, 1984; Elias, 1988; Hunt, 1988a). A large number of those women in paid employment who have had time out will thus be working in jobs offering less satisfaction, lower pay, fewer opportunities for improvement and fewer benefits than earlier in their working history.

Given the likelihood that women who take on paid work do so in addition to an unchanging quantity of domestic labour, women in paid employment are also working in total a greater number of hours than either their partners or those women working full time in the home. Women also rely more on public transport (Grieco *et al.*, 1990), and are likely to have higher costs, both financial and time, in getting to and from paid employment. For many women, paid employment is only possible in the evenings, after the children have gone to bed and when their partner or other adult is available to take over the childcare or babysit, and this further limits the kinds of paid work available to women.

Given these factors, it is perhaps surprising that there can be any improvement in women's health when they take on paid employ-ment in addition to domestic and caring work. The fact that the health of women in paid work is better than women who are full-time housewives indicates perhaps the disadvantages in terms of health resources of staying at home, in a job which is unpaid, isolated and undervalued.

Women who are full-time housewives report higher levels of chronic illness, and poorer health overall (Arber, 1989; Beral, 1987; Blaxter, 1990) although women in full-time employment report more days of restricted activity (Arber, 1989). The issue is sorting out health and illness from the other factors – do women in full-time employment suffer poorer health than women in part-time employ-ment or full-time houswives, or simply have to take days of restric-ted activity whereas women in part-time employment and women who are housewives will have to keep going for longer? Or do women who suffer chronic illness tend not to have paid employ-ment, whilst the effect on health of full-time paid employment is on acute illness, rather than chronic symptoms? One problem in disentangling the effect of different factors is that there is no research on the 'healthy worker effect' which specifically looks at women's employment (Arber, 1989) and the findings in relation to men's employment cannot simply be lifted and transferred to women's jobs. Higher levels of chronic ill-health in particular amongst women without paid employment suggests poor health as a contributory factor preventing women from taking paid employ-ment (Arber *et al.*, 1985), especially where poor mental health might decrease women's opportunities for finding paid work. However, higher levels of acute illness amongst women in full-time employment in some studies suggest that paid work might produce more short-term illness as a result of the pressures arising for mothers in full-time paid employment, in the face of inadequate childcare provision, lack of support for working mothers and continued inequality in the division of labour in the home (Arber *et al.*, 1985; Beral, 1987). Much depends again on how health is being measured and the place of perceptions of health, and structural features of women's lives – that it may be easier to take time off from paid work rather than housework, for example. Higher levels of morbidity amongst women than men, for example, may reflect the greater proportion of men who are in paid employment and have recourse to workplace health services: women might have fewer choices of medical care and less preventive health care, and as a result both use state medical services more and suffer poorer health (Watkins, 1986).

In fact, despite the difficulties which arise when using social class for married women, this is a factor which offers some useful insights. Women in paid employment in unskilled and manual occupations have higher levels of ill health than women from the same class who are full-time housewives whilst the reverse is true for women in higher social classes, in that paid employment is linked to better health than that of women who do not work outside the home (Aggleton, 1990). Phillimore's research on early deaths in North Tyneside found that amongst the women in the poorer areas, more had had 'poor' or heavy jobs than women in more affluent areas, and that more had had insecure employment during their lives (Phillimore, 1989).

The General Household Survey gives data on employment status and levels of both chronic and acute illness, which indicates higher levels of severe chronic illness amongst women who are unemployed than women in paid employment, but lower than unemployed men. Similarly, women defined as 'economically inactive' have the highest levels of limiting long-standing illness – with over a third reporting such illness, but again this rate is lower for women than for men who are defined as 'economically inactive'. The major problem with these findings is that women are less likely to define themselves or be defined by others as unemployed, as a result of the operation of the social security system which militates against women signing on as unemployed, and encourages women to see themselves as 'housewives' rather than unemployed or sick.

Other studies have produced different findings. For example, Popay and Jones (1987) report more acute illness amongst unemployed women than men, which suggests that health should be distinguished more carefully along the lines of health status – which includes the kinds of ill health and disability related to lower rates of participation in paid labour – and health state, or short-term episodes of illness (Arber, 1990a). Acute illness, or poor health state, is likely to be more directly linked to employment, and the finding that both employed and unemployed women have poorer health states than their male counterparts suggests that both kinds of employment status have implications for health which do not correspond to those for men.

In fact, the links between employment and health for both women and men are complex, taking into account the impact of employment as well as unemployment on health, the extent to which ill health deters participation in paid employment, and also the difficulties in disentangling the timing of events. Phillimore (1989) found that unemployment appeared to exert a negative effect on health more rapidly amongst those in the poorer area of his study, illustrating the association between harsh working and living circumstances and other effects on health over and above unemployment itself. For women, this relationship between unemployment, employment and other living circumstances is further complicated by gender, in that women's position both in the labour market and in domestic labour is mediated by their sex. This suggests that the answer lies in a more complex approach to the question of paid employment, which takes account of the occupation and hours worked, and also of the material circumstances in which women attempt to carry out this 'juggling' act of home and paid work.

## Housing and the environment

The relationship between housing tenure and both mortality and morbidity is highly suggestive of the value of this indicator in relation to assessing the impact of poverty. Used as an indicator instead of social class, housing tenure is closely linked to both mortality (Phillimore, 1989; Townsend, Phillimore and Beattie,

1988; Arber, 1989; Fox and Goldblatt, 1982) and morbidity (OPCS, 1986a; OPCS, 1990a). Housing tenure is a powerful indicator of higher mortality for both women and men when used in conjunction with other indicators of area deprivation and poverty (Britton *et al.*, 1990). Given the difficulties described earlier of assigning women to social class based on occupation, housing tenure appears to offer an alternative that correlates more closely to women's health than to men's (Arber, 1989). Tenure is a longer-term indication of wealth and poverty than a snapshot of income in one period – it takes time to build up a deposit, and it takes regular secure employment to retain owner-occupied housing, whereas local authority and privately rented accommodation are less secure and require a lower capital outlay, even where a deposit is required. However, tenure alone is insufficient, as there are also substantial variations in housing standards within different tenure groups. For example, racism in the housing market not only restricts the entry of some groups to owner-occupied housing, but also operates to restrict the choice available, both through cost and the practice of vendors and estate agents.

The OPCS study on morbidity in general practice suggests that whilst consultation rates for different tenure groups are largely similar, in that for both women and men owner-occupiers have the lowest rates of consultation and those living in local authority housing have the highest, the significance of living in private rented accommodation is not equal for the health of both women and men (OPCS, 1990a). Women in privately rented accommodation have higher than average consultation rates for half of the disease categories, including rates of consultation for neoplasms which are not only higher than average, but also the highest of all tenures. Women in privately rented accommodation also have above average rates of consultation for mental disorders, and consultation rates which are again not only above average but also the highest for all tenures for problems concerning social and family problems.

Women living in privately rented accommodation are more likely to be living in the poorest quality housing, in a sector which contains the oldest housing stock, in poor repair (English House Condition Survey, 1986; Watson, 1988). Thus gender differences here reflect poverty associated not only with tenure but with quality differences within the tenure.

However, it is in local authority housing that both women and men suffer the poorest health, although again rates of consultation for women are higher than for men. To what extent does housing tenure reflect health opportunities? Housing is an important factor in determining health – and many of the conditions associated with poor housing show strong correlations with particular forms of ill-health.

The recently completed Health and Lifestyle Survey found strong links between housing lacking basic amenities and overcrowded accommodation and poor health, in particular higher rates of disease and disability amongst every age group, above average levels of illness and poor psycho-social health for women under the age of 60 (Blaxter, 1990). Similar findings from the survey of living standards in London revealed significant correlations between measures of housing deprivation, such as overcrowding and internal structural defects, and poor health (Benzeval and Judge, 1990).

Housing which is damp has been linked to increased levels of morbidity, in particular with asthma, respiratory disease, chest problems, depression, diarrhoea and vomiting (Hyndman, 1990; Strachan, 1986; Burr, 1986; Hunt *et al.*, 1986). Poor respiratory health in particular has been linked to damp, and to the mould created by damp (Byrne *et al.*, 1986; Keithley *et al.*, 1984; McCarthy *et al.*, 1985), and poor heating suffered by a large proportion of those in local authority housing. Other problems reported by local authority tenants include poor mental health, as a result of noise, damp, and having no safe space for children in which to play (Ineichen, 1986; Byrne *et al.*, 1986). Studies which have controlled for behavioural factors such as smoking and structural factors, such as social or occupational class of residents, show that the association between particular kinds of housing deprivation – damp and poor heating – and poor health remains (Hyndman, 1990).

This association between local authority housing and poor health can only deepen, as the sale of council houses over the past decade has exacerbated the plight of those left in the council sector by taking the better quality accommodation out of local authority hands (Forest and Murie, 1988).

One study which focused on two groups of residents in poor quality local authority housing, where one group suffered damp in addition to the other problems, found few differences in the health of the two groups, other than higher levels of poor mental health in the group living in damp accommodation, and higher levels of respiratory and infectious illness amongst the children (Martin *et al.*, 1987). A major finding of the study was rather the very poor health of both groups: the significance of damp in the housing of one group was less than the very poor condition of the accommodation of both local authority groups.

The difference between the health experience of women in different kinds of housing is highlighted by the OPCS survey on morbidity data from general practice. For some kinds of illness the gaps between women of different tenures were very wide indeed: women living in local authority housing had consultation rates for endocrine disorders which were 50 per cent higher than those for women in owner-occupied housing, whilst rates for mental disorders and diseases of the blood and digestive system were similarly high (OPCS, 1990a).

In addition, the difference in the rate of consultation of women in different housing tenures was wider than the gap for men for these illnesses. These gaps between consultation rates for each sex suggest that housing may have a more significant impact on consultation, and certain kinds of health, for women than for men, and suggest the strength of poor housing as an indicator of women's health. Why would this be the case?

Research on the outcome of pregnancy amongst homeless and poorly housed women suggests the considerable influence of inadequate or deficient accommodation on health. Women whose housing is poor have higher rates of miscarriage and infant mortality (Rutter and Quine, 1990). The most important factor appears to be the combination of poor-quality accommodation and poverty itself, where housing is an indicator of more widespread deprivation. A study of the outcome of pregnancy amongst homeless women living in hostel accommodation found similar levels of perinatal mortality and stillbirth amongst homeless women and women in the same area in poor quality local authority accommodation (Paterson and Roderick, 1990). Homeless women were more likely to have a child with a congenital abnormality; as a result of later booking-in at the antenatal clinic fewer had had a scan and blood tests where such problems may be picked up (Paterson and Roderick, 1990). The homeless have higher consultation rates for emergency and hospital treatment in comparison with local residents in the same area, and lower rates of consultation for primary health care (Victor, 1990). The combination of factors which leave women in accommodation for the homeless relate to poor health – poverty, financial difficulties and debt, domestic violence and abuse in their previous home and non-eligibility for both public housing and mortgage finance – which combine with health effects of such accommodation, and the obstacles which make primary health care less available to this group (Victor, 1990; Austerberry, Schott and Watson, 1984; Cole-Hamilton *et al.*, 1988).

A survey by the London Food Commission, the Maternity Alliance, and Shelter on the health of women and children in bed and breakfast hostels revealed considerable health problems amongst both groups, including high levels of depression, anxiety and stress, and poor quality diets which resulted in inadequate levels of nutrition for the majority (Cole-Hamilton *et al.*, 1988). Pregnant women in homeless accommodation were more likely to have their babies prematurely, and the babies were more often low birth weight. Trying to provide an adequate diet in such accommodation is immensely difficult. Often hostels have only one communal kitchen which is dirty and ill equipped, food cannot be left out, and without storage and a refrigerator buying and maintaining a store cupboard of the necessities for cooking is impossible. As a result people rely on cafés, take-away food and food which requires no preparation or storage – cakes, bread and biscuits for example. Not surprisingly, this takes a toll on the health of those who live in such conditions. The toll for women is exacerbated by the hardship of trying to care for children and provide safety, warmth, a stimulating environment and sufficient food to foster the development and health of the child.

The poor health of women in bed and breakfast accommodation is not isolated, but relates also to the health problems women experience when they are poor or deprived in other ways. Whilst hostels for the homeless suffer appalling problems of accommodation – non-existent or inadequate cooking facilities, nowhere to do washing, no play space and overcrowding – these are problems also found in all kinds of housing tenure. This combination of poverty and housing deprivation is illustrated powerfully by the health experience of women travellers. These women suffer higher rates of miscarriage, more of their children are born with a disability and more die in childhood, whilst the women themselves are substantially more likely to die prematurely (Daly, 1989).

Why does housing tenure link more closely to women's patterns of health than those of men? The actual health effects of poor quality housing – poor heating, high levels of noise, lack of space for children to play, and problems with damp – are all likely to have a greater impact on women's health. Whilst women carry the major responsibility for domestic labour, limitations in the working environment of the home add to the workload of women, whilst increasing the stress associated with trying to carry out the work to a high standard. Damp, in particular, makes the tasks of cleaning walls, worksurfaces and carpets more difficult, whilst maintaining the appearance and value of clothing is also harder. Damp clothing is also a risk to the health of the household, and increases the burden of women's health maintenance work (Graham, 1986).

Poor heating affects women more where they spend more hours at home – during the day, when they are not in full-time paid employment, and during the evenings, when women's leisure activities and childcare keeps them at home more than men (Deem, 1988; Graham, 1984). Fuel is one area where some low-income households can cut back on expenditure, although for many this may be restricted by the source and type of heating and method of payment. However, where there is flexibility, women are likely to cut back on their own expenditure of this resource, adding extra layers of clothing and going to bed early to save fuel costs (Daly, 1989). Women also describe saving fuel, or coping in the absence of money to pay for fuel, by putting children to bed early and keeping them in bed during the day to keep them warm (Daly, 1989). Again, women must balance conflicting goals in terms of health maintenance: the goal of keeping children warm might have to be set against child development. The cost is borne both by child, and the woman in guilt and worry.

Other problems affect women more than they do men, in the majority of homes. Being without hot water increases women's labour in caring for children and other dependants, and in doing the housework. It makes personal hygiene more difficult for both men and women, and this too has increased health implications for women, in the connections between cervical cancer and male hygiene (Smith, 1989; Robinson, 1982).

Other aspects of women's home life are affected by income and the amount of money available or set aside to furnish the home. Poverty may lead to either fewer of the labour-saving devices which make domestic labour easier, or poorer quality domestic appliances, which are harder to use or even unsafe. Second-hand cookers and heaters which have not been properly serviced are a hazard to all members of a household, but particularly so to those who use them more often, who are at home for longer periods, and who carry the greater burden of trying to care for children's safety.

The gap between the health experience measured by housing tenure is wider for women than for men, representing the substantial impact of housing deprivation on women's lives in association with women's domestic work and position within the privatized home. However, the impact of housing on health goes beyond the boundaries of the immediate accommodation. The wider influence of poor environment on health is also important. The survey on living standards in London showed how environmental factors such as excessive noise from transport or building work, litter and dirty streets, and isolation, were linked to poorer health (Benzeval and Judge, 1990). The significance of environment is mediated by gender: women suffer particular forms of environmental deprivation and this has a specific influence on their health.

Women's health is affected by a poor quality environment as a result of women's domestic labour and position within the home. Unsafe public space – for example, poor street lighting – constitutes deprivation in the environment for women, as does inadequate public transport and poor public amenities, such as community centres, libraries, nurseries and shopping facilities. Bleak housing estates with no play areas for children, nowhere to hang out washing, and shops which are poorly stocked and expensive contribute to women's isolation and poverty. The gendered dimension of the impact of such poverty on health is in relation to women's work in the home and their responsibility for childcare, which adds to the hours spent in such conditions and the stress which this work entails. A recent study of childhood mortality as a result of accidents highlights this stress: with mortality in relation to head injury, and most often as a result of road traffic accidents, clearly associated with deprivation and a lack of safe play facilities in the child's local area (Sharples *et al.*, 1990).

Race adds a further dimension to environmental deprivation, where women from some ethnic minority groups might have to go further to find shops selling food and other goods which they need, whilst racism makes the environment more dangerous.

One aspect of environmental health and the impact for women is illustrated by the higher levels of stillbirth and infant death in areas with a poor or polluted environment (Townsend, Simpson and Tibbs, 1984): for example, extremely high rates of miscarriage in Bratislavia, Czechoslovakia, described as 'an environmental disaster area' (Wright, 1990, p. 16) are revealing for what they indicate for the health of women themselves as well as the health prospects of future generations. The combination of poor diet and environmental deficiencies substantially increases the risk of malformation and poor childhood development (Wynn and Wynn, 1979).

### Nutrition and health

The most direct association between poverty and health is through food. Food is the major item of expenditure in poor households over which there can be some flexibility, in comparison to rent and housing costs and, to a lesser extent, fuel (Daly, 1989). In the Health and Lifestyle Survey poor diet was associated with low occupational class and with groups in local authority housing, whilst poverty in all age groups was significantly more likely to mean a diet which was deficient in important respects (Blaxter, 1990). A major review of research on the links between poverty and diet concluded that people on low incomes spent less on food, and had diets which were in danger of dropping below the recommended daily allowance (RDA) guidelines for some nutrients, and in particular are at greater risk of having diets which are too low in dietary fibre, vitamin C, folic acid, vitamin E and zinc (Cole-Hamilton and Lang, 1986). The problems are particularly severe for people dependent on state benefits, the real value of which has depreciated in recent years. Estimates of the portion of means-tested benefits designed to meet dietary needs suggest that the sum paid to households dependent on state benefit is too low to buy a diet sufficient in nutrients to meet RDA guidelines (Stitt, 1990; Cole-Hamilton and Lang, 1986). Changes to the payment of social security benefits in successive legislation in the late 1980s, and in particular in the 1986 Social Security Act, have intensified the difficulties of long-term claimants by the abolition of payments for special one-off needs, such as the replacement of domestic appliances, and replaced grants with loans for such items. The effect of this is to further reduce the amount of weekly benefit which can be spent on food. Households dependent on state benefit over a long period of time, therefore, have to make difficult decisions about what to spend money on, with resources necessary for the maintenance of health competing for limited funds. Thus, whilst poor households spend a far higher proportion of their income on food, and whilst they buy efficiently in terms of nutrition for each pound spent (Cole-Hamilton and Lang, 1986), the inadequacy of benefit levels leaves such households short of some nutritional needs.

The impact of poor nutrition on health is particularly clear-cut. Boyd-Orr, in 1937, observed the links between the poor diet of lower-income groups and their poorer health. For many women poverty meant going without themselves in order to provide for others (Spring-Rice 1939; Pember-Reeves, 1913), and their own health suffered as a result. Having too little to eat remains a strong indicator of poor health and higher levels of illness (Benzeval and Judge, 1990). Inadequate nutrition affects health in a number of ways, for example, in slow development amongst children (Boyd-Orr, 1937). Height is linked to diet, especially in childhood, where there are clear social class differences in children's height (Knight and Eldridge, 1984). Children and adults in poorer income groups suffer greater tooth decay and the loss of teeth in adulthood (Cole-Hamilton and Lang, 1986; Knight and Eldridge, 1984; Macintyre, 1986; GHS, 1989). Specific threats to health have also been linked to poor or inadequate diet – for example, cervical cancer (Barker, 1990). Doll and Peto (1981), in an influential review of the causes of cancer, attributed up to 80 per cent of cancer deaths to environmental and consumption factors, of which nearly half were attributable to diet. The significance of a poor diet on higher mortality rates for cancer for both women and men, and on survival rates after diagnosis, cannot be overestimated.

Whilst low-income households suffer poorer diets in general, certain groups within the population are at greater risk, either as a result of increased nutritional requirements or as a result of unequal distribution of resources within households, and sometimes both. Children and young adults have increased needs and in poor-income households are likely to suffer a diet which is deficient in some respect (Cole-Hamilton and Lang, 1986). Another group particularly at risk are women during pregnancy and breast-feeding. The amount paid in state maternity allowance is inadequate when compared with the cost of the diet recommended for women in pregnancy, and women who are wholly dependent on state benefit are unlikely to be able to provide a diet sufficient for a healthy pregnancy (Roll, 1986; Durward, 1984; Haines and De Looy, 1986; Cole-Hamilton and Lang, 1986).

A poor diet during pregnancy substantially increases the possibility of a poor outcome of pregnancy, and higher levels of congenital malformation amongst lower income groups might be the result of an inadequate diet during the antenatal period (Lovett *et al.*, 1990; Joffe, 1989). However, an inadequate diet casts a long shadow for women, and poverty in early childhood and puberty can also result in higher risks of a low birth-weight child or congenital malformation (Lovett *et al.*, 1990; Joffe, 1989). In addition, women whose diet is deficient at the time of conception have an increased risk of congenital malformation in their child (Wynn and Wynn, 1979). Inadequate nutrition for women at all ages implies a serious risk for their future children. As it is women who bear the burden of caring for a child or adult dependant with a disability (Smith and Jacobson, 1989), this has further implications for women's health in later years, over and above the emotional and physical cost to both parents of a child with special needs, in the face of inadequate financial or care support from public services. In one survey of health in families, children with a disability were concentrated in lone-parent households: to some extent the result of greater poverty suffered by lone mothers during pregnancy (Graham, 1986), this is also an indication of the greater burden – economic and emotional – carried by women trying to care for a child with a disability in circumstances of poverty. Overall, children with a disability are more likely to be born to parents in lower-income groups, and whilst this means the labour of providing and caring for such children is disproportionately carried by the poorest social class (Wynn and Wynn, 1979), it also means that poorer women carry more than their fair share of this struggle. The impact of caring labour on women's own health is revealed in the increased rates of morbidity amongst women caring for sick children (Popay and Jones, 1990; Osborn, 1983).

Although inadequate nutrition in pregnancy and during lactation pose a threat to the health of the child, the health of the woman is often at greater risk. Women during pregnancy and breastfeeding are estimated to require a further 800–1,500 calories to meet the nutritional needs of their bodies. When this increased intake of energy sources is not obtained, the woman's own health is likely to suffer.

Thus women in low-income households are more at risk of deficient nutrition as a result of increased needs at certain periods of their lives – puberty, pregnancy and breast-feeding in particular. Further risks may be created for women as a result of their position within the household and the sexual division of labour within the home. Women carry the major responsibility for food in the household, and this incorporates a number of tasks which are made more stressful and more arduous when money is short. Women plan shopping and weekly menus, and often are responsible for the major part, if not all, of the shopping. Women are also liable for the work involved in the preparation of food. Trying to provide food which is both nutritious and which the family will eat is accentuated by cash constraints. The price of different forms of food is often cited by those on low incomes as the most important factor determining what is bought, although value for money and food which is nutritious is also significant (Cole-Hamilton and Lang, 1986; Charles and Kerr, 1988). However, value for money is difficult to assess: whilst 'carcass' meat is healthier than processed meat such as beefburgers or sausages, the cost of a single beefburger is lower than a piece of meat. The cost of getting to different kinds of shops is also a factor determining the income available for food and choice of goods – processed food may be more readily available locally and be cheaper in terms of total expenditure.

Women may have the responsibility for providing food but this does not necessarily imply the power to decide what to buy. Within the household men retain considerable power over the translation of income into food – it is their tastes which are catered for. In this way, women and children are more likely to have low status food, and less of it (Charles and Kerr, 1988; Graham, 1987a). The implications for health are complex: Wilson (1987b) describes how men eat more, but eat more unhealthily. What is crucial is the combination of how much, how often and how good, and whilst men might consume food which provides essential nutrients in an 'uneconomical' fashion, by also consuming larger quantities, the overall total of these essential elements comes closer to minimum amounts than the diet of women which is poor in both quality and quantity.

A further problem arising from poor nutrition is that of obesity, as a result of too great an intake of cheaper foods which are high in sugar and refined calories, but which satisfy hunger. Between 8 and

15 per cent of adult women are obese (Wells, 1987; Gregory *et al.*, 1990). Over 15 per cent of women aged from 40 to 80, and nearly a quarter of all adult women in their 50s are obese (Wells, 1987). Obesity amongst women is related to class, with those in the lower occupational groups more likely to be overweight or obese (Knight and Eldridge, 1984). In the Health and Lifestyle Survey, over three times as many women from unskilled backgrounds were obese compared with women in the professional class (using husband's occupational class for married women: Blaxter, 1990). Women in poorer households are more likely to be overweight and experience greater difficulty in losing weight (Cole-Hamilton, 1987). Low-income households eat more of the cheap, filling foods, and more processed food, as a relatively inexpensive means of providing calories. In comparison, lower income households eat less cheese, vegetables, fruit, wholemeal bread, and high status sources of protein – carcass meat, fish and poultry (Cole-Hamilton and Lang, 1986). High-sugar and high-fat foods such as chips, cake and biscuits are often used by women to stave off hunger and meet food needs quickly. They are foods with little or no need of preparation and are a way of obtaining calories whilst seeing to other chores. Biscuits, cake and bread may meet needs quickly and are likely to be used to satisfy both children and adults, and give short-term pleasure, but they are foods which are low in dietary fibre and vitamins, and high in starch and fat – contributing to weight problems.

The health effects of such sources of energy, and inadequate levels of nutrition are not confined to weight problems and obesity, although this in itself poses a threat for women's health in terms of increased risks of breast cancer and recovery from breast cancer (Barker, 1990). The link between class, diet and breast cancer is, however, confusing. Women in higher occupational groups – according to their own or their partner's occupation – suffer higher rates of breast cancer and also a higher cancer mortality ratio from breast cancer – that is, women in Social Classes I and II are both more at risk of breast cancer and have a poorer survival rate after diagnosis (OPCS, 1986b; OPCS, 1990b, Phillimore, 1989). One factor which accounts in part for poorer survival rates among lower occupational classes (OPCS, 1990b) is later diagnosis and a lower rate of screening (Barker, 1990). This suggests that despite earlier detection of breast cancer amongst middle-class women, their prognosis is poor. This may reflect the low survival rate from breast cancer in general and the questionable value of mass screening as opposed to financing support for women once diagnosed, and action to reduce other structural effects also implicated (Barker, 1990). Increasingly factors such as stress, the timing of operations to remove the malignancy and supportive counselling are indicated in survival rates (Barker, 1990; Ramirez, 1989; Verreault and Brisson, 1990). Breast cancer is linked to a number of factors, of which a high-fat diet is only one, and is as yet only suggestive rather than conclusively proven (Beral, 1987). Other dietary factors include greater use of alcohol, whilst other demographic indicators of increased risk include an early menarche, or onset of menstruation, and having a first child in the mid- to late thirties. The greater risk of breast cancer for women in higher occupational groups may be partially explained by these factors, as the average age of having a first child is greater for professional women. Women who are teachers, for example, have very high rates of breast cancer (OPCS, 1986b). The incidence of breast cancer has been rising over the past century, in response to the later average age of women having their first child, women's greater longevity and changes to diet. The association between the contraceptive pill, introduced in the later years of the century, and increased risk of breast cancer suggests some link, although this might tie in with the increase in average age for first birth.

However, in other forms of cancer also associated with diet – for example, cancer of the colon – women in the higher occupational groups have higher rates of mortality (OPCS, 1986b). This raised mortality, reflects deaths amongst women as a result of dietary factors prior to the growth of knowledge about a healthy diet which has occurred in the past decade or so. Mortality rates in future years are likely to reflect the impact of this increased knowledge of healthy diet and the extent to which groups at different income levels can take advantage of better information to improve their health. Given what we know already about the diet of low-income households, focused on lower cost foods which are highly processed, high in saturated fats and low in nutrients, this pattern of higher mortality for some forms of cancer amongst women in high income groups may be reversed.

Poor diet is also linked to increased diseases of the circulatory system, including higher rates of coronary heart disease and stroke, and higher rates of diseases of the digestive system (Wells, 1987; Cole-Hamilton and Lang, 1986; NACNE, 1983; DHSS, 1984).

Consultation rates amongst women in higher income groups are considerably less for these diseases in comparison with women in the lower social classes. Consultation rates for women in the un-skilled and semi-skilled manual classes are 43 per cent higher than for women in professional and managerial classes for diseases of the circulatory system, and 28 per cent higher for diseases of the digestive system. A much smaller diagnostic group, which never-theless reveals substantial differences in consultation rates, is that of endocrine, nutritional and metabolic disorders, where women in the lower-income groups had consultation rates which were two-thirds greater than women in Social Classes I and II (OPCS, 1990a).

Some women on low incomes who are constrained both by in-come and tastes of other household members are more likely to find difficulty in losing weight (Cole-Hamilton and Lang, 1986), although for others poverty can prompt the onset of eating dis-orders, as women use the excuse of dieting to explain their lower food intake and skipping meals (Charles and Kerr, 1988). Women's eating patterns are influenced by a multitude of factors – images of attractiveness and the ideal of the feminine body, eating to keep down feelings of anger and powerlessness, and in response to stress (Orbach, 1986; Chernin, 1978). For women within poor households eating disorders take on a powerful new meaning, in terms of con-trol over intake and the imperative to deny oneself in conjunction with the need to control at least one aspect of life, and can lead to serious eating disorders. In the same way as women see smoking as something they do just for themselves, and as means of reducing stress or an alternative to expression frustration or anger (Jacobson, 1981; Graham, 1985), women can come to see denial of food as a way of exercising control over their lives in the absence of other avenues of power.

## Behaviour, health and poverty

One of the most frequently invoked explanations in relation to higher levels of mortality and morbidity amongst lower income groups is that of behaviour: that people in lower occupational classes suffer poorer health and shorter lives as a result of health threatening behaviour, specifically smoking, use of alcohol, poor diet and a lack of exercise. It is a view of inequalities in health, reinforced by government emphasis on health education and health promotion, in which the focus is on individual behaviour rather than the structural context of behaviour. Health promotion activities need rather to be viewed in the context of alternative forms of action open to governments to reduce consumption of health-damaging goods. For example, Maynard (1989) estimates that every year up to 100,000 people die 'prematurely' as a result of tobacco-related causes, and 40,000 die from diseases associated with alcohol (cited in Barker, 1990). Smoking is a contributory factor in at least 1 out of every 7 deaths amongst women under 75 (Wells, 1987). Despite these high levels of tobacco and alcohol-related mortality, and a target set by the World Health Organization of a 25 per cent reduction in alcohol consumption by the mid-1990s, the Conservative Government of the 1980s has made no move to reduce consumption of either tobacco or alcohol through the tax system. Behaviour is undoubtedly important in health – the crucial question is how behaviour relates to other aspects of experience. To what extent do women's higher levels of illness represent different kinds of behaviour in response to poverty and deprivation?

Tobacco companies in recent years have turned the force of their campaigns in two directions with implications for the smoking behaviour of two populations – people in the developing world and women (Barker, 1990). Primarily this is a response to the shrinkage in traditional markets, as the proportion of smokers in the West has declined, in particular amongst men, whilst the amount people smoke has also cut back (GHS, 1990) although the population of the developing world is increasingly involved in the production of cigarettes and tobacco as a cheap labour force, a factor increasing the drive by tobacco companies to raise tobacco consumption in such countries.

The greater targeting of women as smokers has meant tobacco companies in the USA breaking voluntary agreements not to advertise in magazines aimed at young women (Jacobson, 1986). The trend in women's consumption of tobacco is upward, with fewer women giving up smoking in comparison with men, more young women and girls starting to smoke in comparison with young men or boys, and women smoking more heavily (Wells, 1987; Smith and Jacobson, 1989; Jacobson, 1986). The health effects of smoking are well known: increased risks of lung disease and circulatory disease, with smokers having poorer lung function and a reduced resistance to illness (Blaxter, 1990). As more women smoke, there already are signs of a corresponding trend in tobacco related morbidity and mortality for women (Beral, 1987; Smith and Jacobson, 1989).

However, whilst the gender difference has narrowed, as women's smoking habits become closer to those of men, the class difference has widened, with those in higher occupational groups giving up smoking, and fewer starting to smoke, in comparison with those in the lower occupational groups (Blaxter, 1990). Women who are poor are also women who are most likely to smoke: women in low-income households, living with men who are unemployed, and lone mothers are more often smokers, who use tobacco for a variety of reasons which hinge on their role as mothers and their responsibility for domestic labour (Graham, 1987b). Women on low incomes describe smoking as a 'coping strategy', one of the few things they do for themselves, a form of leisure activity which allows them to relax, and to claim time for themselves. They also describe cigarettes as a reward for other ways in which they sacrifice their own needs or wants in order to make their income stretch further and to provide more for their children (Graham, 1987b). By placing women's smoking in this context of self-denial, responsibility for the care of children and the health of the family in the face of difficulties, it becomes an activity which protects the health and well-being of the family – smoking enables women on low incomes in particular to cope with the demands made on them and with their deprivation (Graham, 1987b). And, as with so many of women's health maintenance activities, does so at a cost to women's own health.

However, despite higher rates of smoking, this behaviour alone does not account for the difference in mortality rates between the poor and the affluent (Phillimore, 1989): when smoking rates for the social classes were reversed, as they were in the early part of this century with more smokers in the higher social classes, the mortality differential was no different: more of the poor died early (Smith, Bartley and Blane, 1990). The health risks of smoking are not experienced equally, and a poor environment and pollution both in the workplace and the home add to the likelihood of experiencing ill health (GMB, 1987; Phillimore, 1989). In addition, social circumstances affect the extent to which smoking decreases health resources, and the extent to which other positive forms of behaviour, such as exercise, can improve the health of smokers (Blaxter, 1990).

For women who smoke, the health risks are exacerbated by the nature of health hazards they encounter in their paid employment – in particular chemicals in some industries and occupations – and by their decreased likelihood of having other resources which improve health: a good diet, for example, or of experiencing an improvement in health as a result of taking part in exercise (Blaxter, 1990).

Alcohol has also been linked to a number of health problems, both physical and mental. In the Health and Lifestyle survey, heavy and moderate drinkers of both sexes had increased rates of health problems, including stomach trouble, problems associated with the liver, digestive problems and hypertension (Blaxter, 1990). Men are more likely to drink than women, and consume on average three or four times more than women do (Gregory *et al.*, 1990; GHS, 1990). Although a greater number of women do not drink at all (Blaxter, 1990), the use of alcohol is increasing amongst women, in particular amongst young women, who are drinking more often and more heavily than in the past, and health risks for women in relation to alcohol abuse are as a result increasing (Wells, 1987; McConville, 1983; GHS, 1990). In terms of overall numbers, alcohol abuse continues to represent a smaller threat to women's health than that of men: an estimated 1 per cent of all adult women drink at a level which is dangerous for their health (Wells, 1987; Blaxter, 1990), compared to 6 per cent of men. However, the sex ratio of men to women admitted to psychiatric care with a diagnosis related to alcohol is changing, and whilst men are still over-represented in the admission rates, the number of women in treatment has grown in the past decade (DOH, 1989).

Exercise is a further factor which affects health: exercise can decrease blood pressure, reduce obesity and links with breast cancer, heart disease, stroke and other obesity-related illness, and it can also slow down the rate of osteoporosis (Wells, 1987). People who exercise on a regular basis are fitter and report lower levels of psycho-social malaise than those who do not (Blaxter, 1990).

Despite an increase in some forms of exercise for women, most obviously the fitness boom of the 1980s and the growth of interest in female-dominated sports such as aerobics, women's participation in exercise is low, with less than half of all women taking part in any kind of exercise on a regular basis even in the younger age groups (Wells, 1987). Again, however, there is a class dimension to this experience, indicated by the fact that women in manual groups are least likely to take part in vigourous exercise. However, in addition to the fact that both women and men in higher occupational groups are more likely to take part in some form of exercise, fewer women than men in each class take part in vigourous exercise at a high or moderate level (Blaxter, 1990).

Women are restricted in their opportunities for activities away from home by poverty, and also by other aspects of their lives: childcare responsibility, lack of private transport, reduced levels of energy after the double burden of paid employment and unpaid domestic labour and feelings of what is 'appropriate' for women to do outside the home, feelings which are reinforced by men (Deem, 1988; Grieco *et al.*, 1990). The increase in exercise amongst women in the past decade has been largely amongst young single and child-less women, whilst women with children, working-class women and older women are less likely to take part in leisure activities, including exercise, away from the home (GHS, 1989).

How does this relate to poverty? In low-income households opportunities contract for either sex to take part in sport which requires participation fees, equipment or specialist. In addition, poorer areas have fewer leisure facilities whilst those who live in such areas are likely to be restricted in their travel by the cost of both private and public transport. Both men and women will be less able to pursue exercise outside the home, and for men this might constitute a greater deprivation relative to exercise enjoyed at times of higher income. However, for women, but not for men, lack of exercise is associated with another indicator of poverty: poor diet (Blaxter, 1990), suggesting women's openings for exercise are even more restricted as a result of low income.

Women do have very active lives however, and it is important to distinguish between exercise, as a leisure-based activity, and work which is of a physical nature, and which may confer some health advantage but may also deplete health. Women with children or other dependants have lives which make heavy demands on physical resources, and poverty increases these demands for women in par-ticular. Whilst repetitive domestic labour performed in isolation in the home without paid reward may disadvantage health, women who are poor experience greater demands on their energy. Again, the implications of women's greater reliance on public transport and walking mean opportunities for women are particularly limited.

Car ownership is used in some studies to indicate household

income or deprivation. It is an indicator which shows a stronger relationship for women's health than for that of men (Smith and Jacobson, 1989). Having access to a car is an indication of access to other resources, including employment and health care, and women's decreased access to a private car creates greater problems in attending for primary health care and hospital out-patient visits. There are also adverse health effects which are greater for women: isolation, particularly at night, and the 'wear and tear' of using buses all the time, particularly with children (Hamilton and Jenkins, 1989; Hamilton and Gregory, 1989).

Poor women have more health problems as do their children, they are more likely to seek help from social service offices, and will more often visit benefit offices and housing offices. These journeys must all be made in the cheapest way, often with one or more small children accompanying, and the problems of trying to entertain children whilst carrying out these tasks add to the cost for women (Daly, 1989). Poverty and deprivation lead women to substitute time for money, in order to survive: time spent in walking rather than using private or public transport, for example, or washing clothes by hand to save hot water and electricity. The cost, however, is paid also in depletion of resources which enable or enhance both physical and mental health: 'making meagre ends meet uses immense labour and energy' (Daly, 1989).

## Domestic labour

The final way in which the impact of poverty can be examined has been hinted at already in these pages – through women's domestic role. It is unlikely that women's health could ever be examined without reference to women's work as housewives, and mothers, and the demands of this unseen unpaid work. In the vast majority of households, women continue to bear the brunt of caring work and domestic labour, particularly after the arrival of children (Popay and Jones, 1987). Domestic labour and caring work exert a toll on women both in terms of the physical work and the mental strains of this status. 'What comes across most emphatically is the cost to their own health of protecting the health and well-being of their families' (Phillimore, 1989, p. 18).

There are a number of facets of this experience. One feature of women's health is their decreased ability to take care of their own health, as a result of the demands on their time (Popay and Jones, 1990; Gove *et al.*, 1973). Cornwell (1984) describes the links between women's responses to feelings of illness and their work in the home: 'the demands of employment are usually more contained, and more containable, than the demands of housework and childcare' (Cornwell, 1984, p. 139). As a result, women are less able to take time off in response to ill health, and will try to keep going, sometimes with the help of medicine, rather than take time out of their duties to get better. This may explain why women are more likely to visit GPs, in response to the need for something to help them cope and see them through an illness, and in particular might explain high consulting patterns for lone mothers (Popay and Jones, 1987). Both lone mothers and lone fathers suffer higher levels of chronic illness than people in a two-parent household, although lone mothers are most likely of all to report their health as poor (Popay and Jones, 1987; 1990). The problems associated with poverty, the pressure of the demands of childcare and the stress of managing alone are most acute for lone mothers, most of whom are in or on the margins of poverty (Popay and Jones, 1990; Millar, 1989a). Women isolated in the home, the way in which many with young children are, are also less likely to take advantage of preventive health services (Pill and Stott, 1985). This is a picture of women taking steps to cure health problems once they occur, rather than to maintain their own health through preventive health care, and it is a picture in which women's domestic work is central.

A major feature of women's domestic role is that of health maintenance (Oakley, 1987; Graham, 1985). This operates on a number of levels, from the provision of a healthy environment, healthy food, clean clothes and so on, to the reproduction of health behaviour, and mediator with health service and other agencies (Oakley, 1987; Graham, 1985). Land (1977) describes women as 'buffers' between the world and the other members of the household, absorbing the shocks, providing emotional support as well as managing the shortages by going without during times of deprivation. There are emotional and physical costs attached to this work, but for women on low incomes these costs are particularly high as a result of the greater shortage and higher levels of demands made on them, the stress of trying to be a good mother in the face of inadequate resources and the guilt attached to seeing children go without

(Daly, 1989; Glendinning and Craig, 1990). The guilt over failing to provide – whether it is the income to buy resources, a safe and warm home or new clothes and toys for children is experienced by parents of both sexes, but women, who spend longer hours with children in the home, in searching for bargains and watching their children play with others, experience this differently.

Children in poor households are significantly more likely to suffer poorer health than their counterparts in more affluent households (Townsend *et al.*, 1989; Cole-Hamilton and Lang, 1986), and again there are emotional costs attached to the experience of seeing a child's health suffer as a result of poor nutrition or housing, as well as the labour of caring for a sick child (Osborn, 1983; Butler and Golding, 1986).

The sheer volume of work attached to domestic labour inevitably climbs substantially with the arrival of children. Oakley estimated that women spend an average of 74 hours a week on housework, including both childcare and domestic labour (Oakley, 1976). More recently Popay and Jones (1987) estimate a weekly average of 24.1 hours a week for women without children, rising to 87 hours a week for women with children, and no paid employment; 75 hours a week for women in part-time employment and 64 hours a week for women in full-time employment. This represents, for women in both paid and unpaid employment a staggering 91 to 99 hours a week spent in work, over double the average working week of men in full-time employment, even including overtime. There is a direct relationship between the claims made on women as a result of their domestic role and the severity of their health problems (Popay and Jones, 1988).

Whilst there are strong implications for the quality of most women's lives, in circumstances where they spend an average fourteen hours a day in some form of employment, the other point to be made is that the difficulties of managing on a low income and of absorbing the demands made on them are clearly exacerbated for women. As Popay and Jones (1987) acknowledge, the arrival of children might also constitute an increased working week for men, who take on more overtime to meet the higher costs of children. This also has implications for health, and is clearly associated with higher morbidity and mortality amongst men in lower income groups. However, the qualitative experience arising from poverty is different for men and women, as a result of sex-segregated positions in both the home and the labour market. The difficulties of trying to carry out the tasks associated with motherhood, and caring for dependants, are exaggerated by the stress of poverty (Popay and Jones, 1990). For lone mothers, the impact of being in demand by children, combined with trying to manage on a low income and in conditions of deprivation constitute a serious cumulative threat to health, and the effects are measured in the higher rates of illness amongst women bringing up children alone. For married and co-habiting women, the demands of children are mediated by their relationship with another adult, who may act to increase or decrease the pressure of demands. For most women in two-parent families, the complexity of such demands and the decreased likelihood of experiencing poverty constitute a decreased health effect, and the rates of illness amongst women in two-parent households are lower (Popay and Jones, 1990). However, as Jessie Bernard wrote some years ago, there are in fact two marriages in the two-parent house-hold: his and hers (Bernard, 1972), and men inside a two-parent relationship have the best health of all. The impact of poverty, domestic labour and the demands of caring work are gender specific in their impact on women's health.

## Conclusion – poverty and health for women

The effects of deprivation on health are cumulative – mounting up over a lifetime (Phillimore, 1989). They also begin to have an effect even before birth. Children of low-income mothers are more likely to be born prematurely, suffer a disability, be of low birth weight, with implications for survival and future health, and have lower 'agpar' scores, which measure basic responses and health at birth (Lovett *et al.*, 1990; Rutter and Quine, 1990; Pagel *et al.*, 1990; Joffe, 1989; Cole-Hamilton and Lang, 1986). Women in low-income groups also have greater difficulty in conceiving (Howe *et al.*, 1985).

The nature of the links between poverty and poor obstetric out-come is directly through the health and conditions of the mother. Despite this, when low birth weight and infant mortality are used as measures of health inequalities in the population, in relation to socio-economic status, the occupation of the father is used. In-creasingly evidence suggests that the woman's standards of nutrition and experience of poverty, both during the pregnancy and during childhood are important indicators of future obstetric outcome.

The underlying causes of high rates of congenital malformation, miscarriage, low birth weight and high rates of perinatal mortality are tied to low income and inadequate resources. The risks of congenital malformations and miscarriage are higher when diet is poor, particularly when important trace elements are missing (Lovett *et al.*, 1990; Wynn and Wynn, 1979), although women in paid work in difficult conditions until late in the pregnancy also suffer an increased risk of pre-term delivery and low birth-weight babies – both factors significantly associated with perinatal mortality (Savel-Cubizolles and Kanuskin, 1982). There is a greater likelihood of having paid employment during the last months of pregnancy in relation to both class and race, and Afro-Caribbean women in particular are likely to work late in the pregnancy as a result of financial pressures. However, this is also likely to be work with the greatest effect on health, with heavy workloads in poor conditions, and this further increases the health risks for both mother and child (Thorogood, 1987).

Caring for others is stressful, and women's domestic role is a significant feature of women's health experience in poverty. The demands on women's time and emotional resources are boundless, and can appear infinite (Graham, 1985). As a result, women with children have poorer health than those who do not (Popay and Jones, 1988). Resolving competing demands will often result in a compromise in which the health of one member of the household is traded off against the health of another. As Graham writes, this may explain apparently illogical decisions, for example where the health of a new baby is set against the needs of other children – the decision to bottle-feed rather than breast-feed may be a logical resolution of competing demands from older children. However, the trade-off is most often accomplished at the cost of women's own health (Graham, 1985). The impact of poverty on such demands is quite simply to restrict the resources which would make such a trade-off or compromise less health threatening, and improve the material circumstances in which women perform these tasks.

Poverty makes demands on women's time and energy, both physical and emotional, and the draining effect of guilt and worry about meeting the needs of other members of the household, in particular the needs of children, creates a climate of health costs for women: stress, and anxiety, combined with a poor diet, lack of recreational exercise, health-damaging behaviour, housing and environmental hazards, the toll on health of both paid and unpaid labour, and fewer opportunities for positive experiences and pleasure. Poverty and its effects, particularly on their children, dominates the conversations of women struggling to survive on a low income (Daly, 1989).

The poor do not suffer different kinds of ill health but more of the same patterns of illness (Phillimore, 1989; Townsend, Phillimore and Beattie, 1988). Women do not die for different reasons from men, but suffer the same causes less often. However, it is the cumulative effect of poverty on health which is most noticeable: for those who are at greater risk of dying from heart disease, there are other increased risks: higher rates of suicide, diseases of the respiratory system, accident, violent death and so on (Macintyre, 1986). For women, the cumulative effect of living in poverty and deprivation mounts up an array of health hazards, which arise not only from the impact of poverty, and the gender specific experience of that poverty, but also the nature of the demands made on them in the midst of this deprivation. Such an accumulation of health hazards explains the poorer health of women at every age throughout adult life, and in every circumstance in comparison with men, whilst the impact of poverty explains the higher levels of mortality and morbidity amongst the poorest women in society – lone mothers and lone older women, in comparison with their married counterparts. For women, health experience is the sum of their caring work, paid and unpaid work, and the conditions under which they carry out this work. The myriad effect of poverty and deprivation on women's health is reflected not only in their poorer physical health, however, and the following chapter turns to consider the consequences of poverty for women's mental well-being.

# CHAPTER 6

# HIDDEN COSTS

## Women, Mental Health and Poverty

Throughout the Western world women are more likely than men to be treated for psychiatric disorders. Women are over-represented in figures for admissions to psychiatric hospitals, they are more frequently prescribed psychotropic drugs for depression and anxiety, and they are more often seen by their GP for what are termed 'minor' mental health problems. In addition, women are more often identified as psychiatrically ill in community surveys of random populations (Guttentag *et al.*, 1980; Brown and Harris, 1978; Chesler, 1974; Ricker and Carman, 1984).

However, this is no new epidemic. Seventeenth-century records suggest that women were more likely to seek help for what would now be termed psychiatric distress (MacDonald, 1981, cited in Porter, 1987), whilst since the development of 'mad-houses' and 'mad-doctors' in the nineteenth century women have formed the large majority of those incarcerated or treated for poor mental health, (Scull, 1979; Klerman and Weissman, 1980; Showalter, 1987).

Explanations of this apparent female vulnerability to mental disorder have been many and various. This chapter examines some of the theories of women's mental health in an attempt to unravel the relationship between this over-representation and women's experience of poverty and deprivation. If, as has been argued in previous chapters, women suffer disproportionately from poverty and deprivation, does this account, at least partially, for their higher rates of mental illness, and their apparent vulnerability to psychiatric disorder? A large part of women's higher levels of morbidity and health-service consultation is in relation to mental health problems, and the consequence of poverty and deprivation for mental health is significant in this exploration of the links between health and poverty. It is not difficult to imagine how the experience of poverty and deprivation might take a toll on mental well-being. Poor housing, an inadequate or erratic income, and poor nutrition all suggest levels of stress which may result in a threat to mental as well as physical health.

A structural account such as this would have to explain women's higher rates both across different countries and across time. Support for this comes from a number of sources. Porter (1987) described women's poor mental health in the seventeenth century as 'not surprising. They were bowed under by the weight of having to sustain multiple socio-economic functions – productive labour, running a household, raising a family. Moreover, the gynaecological problems of repeated dangerous childbirths eroded their health, both physical and mental.' (Porter, 1987, p. 104). Has the position of women changed, and if so, should one expect women today to enjoy better mental health? Certainly women have fewer children, and childbirth is now less of a threat to physical health than in the seventeenth century, when rates of maternal mortality were high. In addition, women's economic position has changed, as a result of shifts in the structure of labour in industrial capitalism. Women's contribution to the domestic economy altered: from being producers of goods for sale in their own right, women became primarily housewives, responsible for domestic work, and the care of children or other dependants. This domestic labour became increasingly invisible and unrecognized as economically productive, despite the actual value of what is created in terms of daily and long-term reproduction of labour (Delphy, 1984). The ideology of women as mothers and housewives took hold during the course of the move to industrial capitalist society (Pahl, 1989; Oakley, 1976) despite the necessity of women continuing to work in the labour market outside the home. However, some of the stresses Porter describes for women have not changed – women today are bowed under by the weight of having to sustain multiple socio-economic functions – unpaid productive labour in the home, employment outside the home, interspersed with periods out of the labour market, caring for dependants, often in isolating and difficult circumstances. In addition, the nature of some of the stresses has shifted – women's economic dependency as daughters, wives and mothers creates a vulnerability to poverty both inside and outside these traditional relationships.

Stereotypes of women's mental health highlight the depressed young woman at home all day with small children, or the isolated widow or the woman whose children have left home. Whilst not all women treated for psychiatric illness fit this pattern, a large majority do. This may simply reflect the reality that the years women spend in childrearing and after represent a major proportion of women's lives. This stereotype of women's mental health bears comparison with the stereotype of the woman who is poor: the lone mother struggling to survive on inadequate benefits (Millar, 1989a), the older woman whose widow's pension is insufficient for her needs (Groves, 1987; Walker, 1987) and women who are poor within the household where resources are not shared equally (Pahl, 1989; Glendinning and Millar, 1987). The suggestion that married women with paid employment outside the home are 'protected' from depression (Brown and Harris, 1978) may simply reflect the value of a woman's own earnings in helping to offset such poverty.

This chapter examines the evidence relating mental health to poverty in respect of material deprivation such as bad housing, and social deprivation such as isolation or loneliness. In doing this, the difficulties of defining mental illness require an evaluation of the various models of mental health, and a recognition of the cultural context in which mental illness is diagnosed. However, the overall goal of the chapter is not to explain women's higher rates of mental illness, but to analyse the extent to which poverty might explain depression and anxiety amongst some women.

In one sense the division of material in this chapter and the previous one on the basis of a division between physical and mental health is theoretically problematic. As discussed in Chapter 5, there are important links between the experience of poor physical health and poor mental health (Eastwood and Trevelyan, 1972; Smith and Jacobson, 1989), and in the causes of such illness. Many of those who suffer poor physical health will also suffer poor mental health, and to divide these two spheres of health is unfortunately to reinforce the division within the medical professions and in the medical model. The rationale for such a division here is partly to break up the material, and partly because of the need to highlight the problem of definition in relation to mental health in particular. Chapter 4 considered the question of measurements of health, and suggested that a feminist model of health might stress different aspects of the health experience for women. The question of mental health – what constitutes poor mental health and mental illness – is an important debate within the feminist critique of medicine, and one which requires further elaboration in this chapter.

In consequence, the following sections examine different ways in which women's mental health has been theorized, before looking at evidence which relates the experience of mental illness to poverty and deprivation. Other aspects of psychiatric illness are also important, however, and the over-representation of black and ethnic minority groups, as well as gay men and lesbians, and older people (Torkington, 1983; Bryan, Dadzie and Scafe, 1985; McNaught, 1988; Chesler, 1974) suggests that the operation of discrimination and oppression are also important contexts. These are taken up in detail in Chapter 7, although the discussion below on models of mental illness and links between poverty and psychiatric illness also highlights the kinds of relationship which exist between mental illness and other forms of oppressive discourse.

## Women and mental health treatment

Looking at the figures for treatment for psychiatric disorders in all settings, it is clear that women are more likely than men to be diagnosed as suffering from some form of mental health problem. Women's admissions to psychiatric hospitals in 1986 were 35 per cent higher than those of men (DOH, 1990). However, women also predominate in certain categories of illness. In particular, more than twice as many women are admitted each year for affective psychoses, neurotic disorders, and other depressive disorders. In contrast, women are admitted in roughly equal numbers for schizophrenic illnesses, whilst men outnumber women in diagnoses related to alcohol and drugs (DOH, 1990).

These are figures for total admissions, which include both new admissions and readmissions of people who have had a prior stay in hospital. When figures for new admissions alone are considered, whilst the difference becomes less marked, women's over-representation is still high, and the same diagnostic differences persist, with more women admitted for diagnoses relating to depression and anxiety (DOH, 1990).

This suggests that women are less likely to come into hospital, but once they have experienced a period of hospitalization may be less likely to remain outside without further periods of treatment in the institution. However, figures for in-patient treatment in psychiatric units and hospitals are notoriously difficult to unravel, and cannot be simply seen as indicators of the extent of an illness in the population. Admission policies have changed substantially in recent years, with increasing emphasis on care in the community for the mentally ill, reductions in the number of beds for psychiatric patients, and shorter average stays. It may be that the increasing number of total admissions simply reflects a core of patients who are continually discharged and readmitted – the 'revolving door' phenomenon – and shorter in-patient stays are reflected in an increase in total annual admissions.

If the trend of both all admissions and new admissions over time is examined, this would appear to be the case. Whilst new admissions dropped from over 57,000 to 51,000 between 1976 and 1986, total admissions increased by over 10 per cent. This, combined with a decrease in the average length of stay (DOH, 1989) suggests that some patients at least are finding it increasingly difficult to remain in the community – a finding which appears to bear out concerns over the current provision of community care support services. Thus high readmission rates may be indicative of the paucity of support services outside hospitals. Given the current policy of privatization of support services, combined with financial shortages, the pattern of discharge and readmission looks set to continue.

It is difficult to determine the reasons for the decline in new admissions – for example, whether this reflects fewer severe cases of psychiatric illness, or better primary care which prevents individuals reaching crisis point. Psychiatric treatment – in common with treatment for many physical health conditions – is determined not only, or even primarily, by level of need. Other factors are also important – the availability of beds, the availability of psychiatric personnel, either in hospital or in the community, the visibility of patients, the degree of tolerance extended both by society and the patient's immediate household, and differing ideas as to what constitutes psychiatric illness, what is treatable, and what are the best methods of treatment.

An intriguing factor in relation to figures for in-patient treatment is that the fall in new admissions is accounted for almost entirely by a reduction in the figures for women. In the ten years between 1976 and 1986 women's new admissions fell by 14 per cent, whilst those for men fell by only 3 per cent (DOH, 1990). One effect of this greater fall in new admission figures for women is that the gap between women and men in rates of treatment for both female dominated disorders – such as depression – and male dominated disorders – such as alcohol abuse – has narrowed slightly.

However the 10 per cent increase in figures for all admissions is accounted for mainly by an increase in male admissions – which rose by 16 per cent, compared with a rise in women's admissions of only 6 per cent.

The implications of these findings are interesting, although it is too early to be sure this is a genuine trend, and it is difficult to attribute the reasons for such changes. It may be that women's vulnerability to depression and anxiety is decreasing, whilst men are becoming more vulnerable. Certainly evidence suggests that women are more frequently turning to alcohol and drugs, and problems related to the use of these substances for women are increasing (McConville, 1983). Explanations for these trends can only be viewed in relation to broader models of women's mental health. Thus lower rates of hospitalization may be viewed variously as the result of a decrease in the factors precipitating either illness or hospitalization, such as stress; or a change in the way in which each sex deals with stress; or that drugs available combined with a policy of community care mean women are more likely to be treated outside of hospital, most particularly when they are responsible for the care of others. Women's domestic role is emphasized in the literature produced by pharmaceutical companies. Advertisements for drugs, for example, often portray women as being able to continue to function as a housewife with the aid of prescribed drugs (Jordanova, 1981; Doyal, 1979). The place of a discourse of feminity in which women's primary position is in the home, occupied in domestic labour, is also demonstrated when doctors and psychiatrists recommend women give up external interests – paid employment, for example – when they present with symptoms of depression and anxiety (Roberts, 1985; Barrett and Roberts, 1978).

Whether the explanation for this decrease in women's rates of hospitalization is seen as the result of women's fewer stresses (and possibly a triumph of women's liberation), or that stress for men is increasing, or that women are suffering more often at home than in hospital, and have become, statistically at least, more invisible, depends on the model of women's mental health which is adopted.

If poverty and deprivation can be related to psychiatric disorders, increases in the numbers of those in poverty in Britain would be reflected in higher rates of treatment for both men and women. This brings us back to the difficulty with using treatment rates – and particularly those for hospital treatment – as a measure of prevalence. Higher levels of poverty in the last decade are associated with government policy on restrictions in public expenditure and a shift to means-tested benefits. The same policy has reduced public expenditure on hospital care and given an impetus to programmes reducing the number of hospital beds for psychiatric care. At the same time an increase in psychiatric personnel working in the community and a move to locate outpatient psychiatric clinics in more accessible health centres has had some effect on the rates of hospitalization for different diagnoses.

Women are also over-represented in figures for other forms of treatment. Thus women are twice as likely to be prescribed psychotropic drugs such as tranquillisers and anti-depressants in both the United Kingdom and the United States (Belle and Goldman, 1980; Guttentag *et al.*, 1980; Cochrane, 1983). A similar picture is found in other European countries: women are over-represented in figures of psychotropic medication by between 40–45 per cent in Spain, Italy and Denmark; by up to 66 per cent in Belgium and Sweden; and 83 per cent in Switzerland (OHE, 1989). The figures of over-representation reflect similar levels of female poverty in these countries (Mitton *et al.*, 1983; Vogel *et al.*, 1988; Zopf, 1989).

Women are also the majority of those who are out-patients at psychiatric clinics in hospitals and health centres (Belle, 1980; Brown and Harris, 1978), and here too they are more likely to be diagnosed as suffering from depression (Klerman and Weissman, 1980; Dworkin and Adams, 1984; Belle and Goldman, 1980).

Community surveys have also revealed higher proportions of women with psychiatric symptoms (Srole *et al.*, 1961; Goldman and Ravid, 1980; Radloff, 1980; Dohrenwend and Dohrenwend, 1969). As what is defined as mental illness is not always treated, a large proportion of those classified in community surveys as exhibiting psychiatric symptoms may not have sought help (Chesler, 1974; Brown *et al.*, 1975; Brown and Harris, 1978). Those social factors which increase women's risk of suffering depression may also create difficulties which deter or prevent women from attending for treatment (Brown *et al.*, 1975), although conversely the stereotype of female mental health may mean women are more likely to seek professional help for problems they encounter.

Although community surveys are seen as indicative of the prevalence of psychiatric illness in the population, these concerns also suggest that they may not be an objective or accurate measure of true prevalence. Studies of random communities have some value, given the filters through which the individual must pass before receiving psychiatric treatment (Goldberg and Huxley, 1980) and the concern that hospital admission rates seriously under-represent the rates of mental illness in the wider population (Cochrane and Stopes-Roe, 1981). However, the methods used in these studies are problematic. In particular, assessment of psychiatric symptoms is usually made by clinicians – either practising or academic – and symptomology is constructed within a medical or psychiatric clinical framework. The concerns expressed by feminists over bias in the medical profession are therefore not eradicated in such surveys.

## Measuring mental illness

This highlights the vexed question of how mental illness can be measured, and the importance of definitions used. How is the dividing line between mental health, and mental illness to be decided?

Different conceptions of mental health approach this question differently. In social-psychiatric research, mental illness has often been defined simply as illness which the medical profession has decided to treat, either because this is seen as the most clear-cut definition of a case, whilst the meaning of mental illness is taken as unproblematic (for example, Faris and Dunham, 1939; Goldberg and Morrison, 1963; Hollingshead and Redlich, 1958; Miles, 1988), or because the study focuses on the experience of mental illness as it 'constitutes a social reality' (Miles, 1988, p. 14), and cases defined by the psychiatric profession represent this context. The support for such an approach is that these will be the most severe, though they may also be the most easily observed or the least powerful in society, and other factors may intervene to prevent some groups of people receiving treatment – for example the levels of support available within different communities (Dohrenwend and Dohrenwend, 1969; Cochrane, 1983).

Perhaps not surprisingly, the community survey has demonstrated a huge variation in levels of symptoms: different studies have found between 1 per cent and over 60 per cent of the population exhibiting psychiatric symptoms (Dohrenwend and Dohrenwend, 1969). Attempts to find the true level of incidence of mental illness in a population are clearly problematic. Although community surveys suggest that women do indeed have more symptoms than men, in particular for depression and anxiety-related illness (Goldman and Ravid, 1980; Gove and Tudor, 1973; Dohrenwend and Dohrenwend, 1969, 1974; Weissman and Klerman, 1977), the scales used by many of these surveys to assess levels of symptoms introduce a bias, in that questions focus more on symptoms associated with depression and anxiety, rather than symptoms reflecting illnesses which have a higher rate of treatment for men. In other words, community surveys do not tell us about true levels of mental illness as a whole in the community, but about levels of symptoms as assessed by the medical profession and which relate to specific illnesses where women are known to be more likely to be treated.

An additional criticism of such scales is that clinicians are more likely to see women as mentally ill in the first place. The well-known study by Broverman *et al.* (1970) described how practising clinicians in the field of mental health saw the mentally healthy man and woman in very different terms. Whilst the mentally healthy man was described in stereotypical traits such as self-confidence, independence, objectivity and aggression, the mentally healthy woman was described as being emotional, dependent, sneaky, illogical and given to crying easily. As Broverman wrote, such a description constitutes 'a powerful negative assessment of women' (Broverman *et al.*, 1970, p. 5). Perhaps the most compelling finding was that clinicians described the mentally healthy adult in terms of the male personality traits: in other words, women are caught in a double bind where to be a mentally healthy woman means remaining at a level of arrested development below the healthy adult, who is male. More recent studies have confirmed the idea that the mental health of women is seen in different terms (Rosenfeld, 1980; Jones and Cochrane; 1981).

Thus it is possible to argue that women's over-representation in both community surveys and in figures for treatment for psychiatric illness share a common starting point – the stereotypical image of women which is predominant in medical, and specifically psychiatric discourse. The issue of 'true prevalence' is a red herring in the assessment of mental illness in a given population, one which cannot be separated from the social and economic context in which mental health is assessed and defined.

According to one estimate, women have a one in eight chance, compared with a one in twelve chance for men, of being treated for psychiatric illness during their lifetime (Mind, 1980). Previous chapters have argued that women's risk of being in poverty or suffering deprivation over the course of their lives is similarly high. Many women will experience both poverty and mental illness, and many will suffer these experiences more than once during their lives. However, as with the issue of women's experience of poverty and deprivation, much depends on the definition of psychiatric illness and how models of mental illness conceptualize causes.

## Conceptualizing mental health

### *The medical model*

This term is used to reflect an approach to health in which the body is viewed as a machine, the sum of its parts, whilst disease is the malfunctioning of one or more of those parts. Health is simply the absence of disease, which is deciphered by observable symptoms. The advances of medical technology and scientific testing have meant an increasing number of conditions have been brought under the control of medicine or identified as appropriate arenas for the intervention of medical science.

The psychiatric model focuses on diseases of the mind or brain, whilst the role of the psychiatrist is to observe and decipher symptoms, and to treat the disorder, using primarily such methods as chemotherapy, psycho-surgery and electro-convulsive therapy.

The medical model focuses on the individual, rather than their environment, and the location of medical practice in the hospital or clinic consulting room, surrounded by the paraphernalia of the trade and the support services of the nursing staff, reinforces an individualistic preoccupation with the symptoms of disease, rather than the part played by external factors (Hart, 1985; Doyal, 1979). Similarly, medical tests focus on the individual and assert the superiority of diagnostic tests over the patient's experience of the condition. Diagnoses are divided into 'clinical depression' 'endogenous depression', 'affective psychoses' and so on, and are part of an international classification of diseases, which lends weight to the idea that psychiatric illness is a scientifically observed phenomenon which belongs within the medical framework. In fact, the International Classification of Diseases has changed many times over the years, and diagnostic categories are frequently redefined.

The operation of the psychiatric model in research practice results in a reliance on admission figures, for example, and focuses on diagnosed patients or cases. One effect of this focus on physiological change has been the attempt to locate in physical terms the area of malfunctioning, whilst a second result is the focus on physical cures, often forms of treatment developed prior to an understanding of why they work (Cochrane, 1983), or indeed, how effectiveness in such methods of treatment might be evaluated.

The role of the environment and social or external factors in provoking mental illness lies at the interstice of the medical model and other interpretations of mental illness. In the medical model, the physiological effects of stress are used to explain adverse mental health. Prolonged or repeated stress leaves the body in a state of constant arousal, causing both physical problems such as hypertension, cancer and heart disease, and mental health problems such as anxiety, depression, and even schizophrenia (Eyer and Sterling, 1977; Sterling and Eyer, 1981).

The fact that not all individuals in the same poor community or household suffer from mental illness is related to individual vulnerability, legitimating a focus on the individual rather than the system which results in the stress, and a similar focus on intervention through chemicals, electricity or surgery to enable the individual to cope (Hart, 1985; Navarro, 1976; Mitchell, 1984).

### The medical model and women's mental health

Women's higher rates of mental illness are therefore explained by women's unique biology. Women are seen as vulnerable to depression and anxiety as a result of their hormones. Such explanations have a long history – the 'floating' uterus for example was one of the early explanations of both physical illness and mental illnesses such as hysteria, whilst large numbers of women, particularly middle-class women, were viewed as intrinsically mentally ill (Douglas-Wood, 1974; Smith-Rosenberg, 1974; Showalter, 1987).

The evidence for women's biological susceptibility rests heavily on the apparent vulnerability of women to mental disorder at times of hormonal change. Thus the higher rates of women's illness during child-rearing years and later life are linked to post-natal depression, and the menopause. Disorders which have a relatively recent history – in terms of medical intervention – are also linked to women's biology. Pre-menstrual syndrome, for example, has been developed as a suitable case for treatment – to the profit of drugs companies and often to the detriment of women themselves as a result of treatment of unproven efficacy (Laws *et al.*, 1986). In addition, blaming women's behaviour on monthly hormonal imbalances serves to pathologize women's distress or anger, and denies any legitimate cause of such feelings.

The critique of this model is based on a rejection of such biological determinism, and that there are too many exceptions for the case to be regarded as proven. The over-representation of women is not equal in all societies – women in non-Western cultures, for example, do not appear to share this vulnerability (Dohrenwend and Dohrenwend, 1969), and also differences in rates of illness according to marital status appear more complex than a simple biological model can explain.

The position of women in the medical model and the sexist nature of the practice of medicine has been criticized (see, for example, Scully and Bart, 1983; Ehrenreich and English, 1979; Barrett and Roberts, 1978). Within the medical model, mental illness is emptied of its content and is seen as a purely physiological problem, resulting from physiological phenomena. The social context of the illness – differences relating to gender, social class, race, social isolation, isolation, for example – can only be explained through reference to genetic origins, which are unsatisfactory and disproved (Ingleby, 1981; Smart, 1976), or as secondary and less important factors – the trigger which causes the vulnerable person to become ill. The focus on the individual above all prevents those who suffer such illness from recognizing their common position and common causes beyond their own experience of illness to the wider context.

## The psychoanalytic model

The psychoanalytic model of mental disorder focuses on the processes of childhood development and the growth of the personality. Though traditionally located in opposition to the medical model (Cochrane, 1983), psychoanalytic theory shares some of its features. For example, although there are numerous variations of psychoanalytic theory today, the origins of psychoanalysis are individualistic, rather than structurally oriented – the focus is on the individual's personal history and growth, the developmental stages through which the individual must pass are physical stages of development (Hollingshead and Redlich, 1958), and the goal of the analysis is to restore the individual to conventional behaviour (Cochrane, 1983). The normal development of both sexes was described through a series of stages which must be successfully negotiated in order to attain maturity. The origins of mental illness – in particular neuroses – are seen to lie in childhood incidents, and relationships in the child's family. Here psychoanalytic theory links with models based on theories relating to the pathological family – problematic family relationships, bizarre and distorted inter-familial behaviour, and incidents such as child abuse and incest, family breakdown and lack of constancy (Lidz, 1975; Wynne and Singer, 1963; Laing and Esterson, 1970).

Whilst there is increasing evidence to support the idea that some forms of childhood experience – such as abuse or incest – have important effects on mental health (Kelly, 1988; Osborn, 1990), the individual focus of this model means the material context is overlooked and the effects on personal relationships of unemployment, overcrowding, poverty and poor environment are ignored.

## What do women want? Freud and women's mental health

Within the traditional psychoanalytic model women's greater vulnerability to mental illness is seen as the result of their difficult path to maturity. Freud's formulation of feminine development centred on the girl's anatomical deficiency: thus the little girl, on discovering she lacks a penis, faces a complex process of adjustment. This includes a transference of love-object from the same sex – her mother – to the opposite sex, her father, and a transference from a clitoral to vaginal sexuality. Women's ultimate fulfilment is through motherhood – where the woman accepts her castration, and the baby is seen as a substitute penis (Weisstein, 1970; Howell, 1981). Neo-Freudians have continued this emphasis on the mature woman's acceptance of her inadequate anatomy and her role as wife and mother (Erikson, 1965).

Feminist criticism has focused on Freud's construction of the feminine personality and women's roles – for example the emphasis on vaginal sexuality as the mature response (see, for example, Scully and Bart 1983); the emphasis on heterosexuality and mother-hood; and the individualism of Freudian theory – the failure to locate women's development and women's problems within the gendered environment (Chesler, 1974). But it also goes beyond that, to consider the way in which the discourse has operated to legitimate women's restricted access to the world beyond child-rearing and the home, women's secondary position in the labour market, and the lack of alternative childcare facilities.

Some feminists have tried to rehabilitate Freud's theories, or to develop the fundamental basis of psychoanalysis for use within a feminist dynamic (Mitchell, 1974; Eichenbaum and Orbach, 1983). Others have argued that Freud's theories were entrenched in the work of his followers without the reformulation he would have subjected them to had he lived (Howell, 1981).

## The social construction of mental illness

The starting point for models within this framework is a denial of the idea that there is an objectively determined state which con-stitutes 'mental illness'. Instead, the authors look to society to explain why some people have been seen at various times in history as the mentally ill.

Scheff (1966) argues that the mentally ill are simply those who have broken society's norms and who have been labelled as deviants. Scheff distinguishes between primary deviance – the behaviour which leads to being labelled as deviant – and secondary deviance –

which is that which occurs after being labelled, and which is caused by the labelling process. Thus the experience of being labelled as mentally ill, and institutionalized, reinforces the deviancy and is the cause of chronic mental disorder (Scheff, 1966) or 'institutional neurosis' (Barton, 1959). However, not all who deviate are equally likely to be seen as mentally ill – the rule-breaking of some groups is both more likely to be observed and more likely to be judged as deviancy, and this explains why working-class people are more often treated for mental illness (Scheff, 1966; Goffman, 1968).

The power of the medical profession to define and diagnose the mentally ill is central to the understanding developed by Szasz (1973). Mental illness is seen as a misnomer, being neither mental nor illness, but a valid and genuine reaction to what are termed 'problems in living' (Szasz, 1973). In this model, mental illness, for the individual, serves the function of defusing the pain and problems inherent in modern society. Szasz's model shares with Parsons the concept of the 'sick role' (Parsons, 1951), where the adoption of the sick role is an excuse for incapacity or the opportunity to abdicate responsibility.

The issue of the power of the psychiatric institution to determine who is seen as mentally ill is also central to models which focus on psychiatry as an institution of social control, particularly from a Marxist perspective. Here, the medical model rationalizes illness which is produced by the system, and by focusing on the individual, diverts attention from structural causes of illness arising from the organization of society (Navarro, 1976; Mitchell, 1984).

Thus the economic system creates stress through the alienation and burden of wage labour, lack of control over the production process, economic insecurity and the hazards to physical health which must be endured and which affect mental health.

> the work . . . is not part of his nature: and . . . consequently he does not fulfill himself in his work, but denies himself, has a feeling of misery rather than well-being, does not develop freely his mental and physical energies, but is physically exhausted and mentally debased . . .    (Marx, 1963, cited in Doyal, 1979, p. 74)

Scull (1979), analysing the growth of the asylum in nineteenth-century England, argues that the rise of industrial capitalism corresponds to the increasing regulation of the insane in the institution of the asylum, and suggests that the desire to segregate those who could not work from those who would not, formed part of this rationalization. The workhouse increasingly lost its inmates to the medical and psychiatric professions – the old, sick and mad were separated from the idle and feckless. At the same time, the goal of the institution was to restore health and sanity and to return the individual to the labour market.

Similarly, Foucault (1967) places the discourse of madness and unreason within the historical context in which it develops. Foucault emphasizes the importance of the historical process in understanding the present, and the need to look at the specific institutions or conditions in which the definition of sanity, and insanity, are developed. Discourses of madness are in this way related to the development of a public health movement within the context of the centralized state, and increasing regulation. The development of asylums during the nineteenth century is related to a similar transformation in means of surveillance and control, and in particular to the growth of the prison and criminal justice system.

## Women: depressed or oppressed?

If mental illness is a constructed discourse rather than an objectively measured state, as these models would suggest, the explanation of women's higher rates of treatment and higher levels of symptoms in the community must rest on how this discourse is structured: 'our very notion of what it means to be a woman is constituted in terms of typically female mental attributes, and hence sex-specific forms of abnormality' (Jordanova, 1981, p. 96).

Chesler's analyses of women and madness suggests that there is very little difference between women who are institutionalized as mad, and in need of treatment, and those who are not (Chesler, 1974). However, the discourse of 'femininity' means women are singled out for treatment where they do not fit the stereotype, and are only released from treatment when they do (Chesler, 1974; Smart, 1976; Jordanova, 1981). At the same time, the asylum might resemble only too closely the home for women, with the father/ psychiatrist in charge (Chesler, 1974). Foucault (1967) similarly saw madness as a return to infancy and the power of the father, though he did not in turn relate this to patriarchy, and failed to observe the female patient's place in this relationship. This sex/gender differentiation is however crucial: the stereotype of mental health is male, and that of mental illness is female (Broverman *et al.*, 1970; Chesler, 1974; Smith-Rosenberg, 1974). Given such an institutionalized version of women's health mental status, it is not surprising to discover more women both in treatment and in community surveys where the method of appraisal of 'caseness' is through reference to clinical thought. This stereotype is reinforced continually through medical training (Young, 1981; Women in Medicine Group, 1982) and medical literature (Scully and Bart, 1983; Lennane and Lennane, 1982); whilst the pharmaceutical industry represents women's depression and anxiety as an inability to cope with domestic labour (Doyal and Elston, 1983); men in the same literature are portrayed in pictures of dramatic acute illness which is 'transcended' by drugs (Jordanova, 1981).

The development during the nineteenth century of a psychiatric profession with a claim to cure was dependent on the captive population of middle-class women (Douglas-Wood, 1974; Smith-Rosenberg, 1974; Showalter, 1987) whilst psychiatry had a role to play in delineating appropriate behaviour for such women, and restricting their access to higher education, paid employment and the world beyond the drawing-room and good works. However, women are not simply the passive victims of male institutions: madness may be a rational response to the contradictions of women's lives, whilst in the nineteenth century (and no less today) women may have used their mental health in the attempt to regulate their sex lives (Chesler, 1974). Despite this, resorting to the psychiatric institution as a means of escape is a painful answer to a problem (Chesler, 1974), and lesser illnesses may not prevent the expectation that women will continue to perform their expected domestic duties (Jordanova, 1981).

## Material accounts of madness

This approach to an understanding of mental illness focuses on social factors and observable correlations between such variables as social class and psychiatric illness. Taking psychiatric illness as indicated either by figures for treatment or by the psychiatric questionnaire in untreated populations, the large majority of studies have demonstrated a disproportionate number of individuals suffering from mental illness in the lower social classes.

One of the first pieces of research to suggest this relationship between class and psychiatric disorder was carried out in 1855 in Massachusetts (Jarvis, 1855, cited in Hollingshead and Redlich, 1958). The study found 64 times as many asylum inmates from the 'pauper' classes as from other classes. Such findings were also observable in the asylums in England, although perhaps this is not surprising, given the structure of public health in the country at the time, where the majority of inmates to both Poor Law Hospitals and the asylum system were paupers (Taylor and Taylor, 1989). What is more questionable is whether they were insane – for example, unsupported women with children were more likely to be placed in both workhouse and asylum (Thane, 1978).

Studies of the relationship between social class and psychiatric disorder carried out during the middle years of this century demonstrated an inverse relationship between social class and mental illness, both in treatment statistics and in studies using untreated populations (Hollingshead and Redlich, 1958; Dunham, 1964; Myers and Bean, 1968; Cochrane and Stopes-Roe, 1981; Brown and Harris, 1978; Srole, Langner *et al.*, 1961).

These studies also attempted to identify the causes of this uneven distribution of psychiatric illness, and many considered the role played by the conditions of life in lower social classes – the environment, poor housing, unemployment and poverty.

The issue of causation was not easily resolved. The underlying question is that of social selection or 'drift' – to what extent do those who are mentally ill move down the social scale, or lose their jobs first in a recession, or move to poorer housing and suffer higher levels of stress as a result of their illness? The drift debate preoccupied social psychiatry over a number of decades, with conflicting results (Goldberg and Morrison, 1963; Turner and Wagenfeld, 1967; Harkey, Miles and Rushing, 1976; Kohn, 1972). However, the majority of these studies focused on male schizophrenics and women were generally excluded. Studies of male admission rates for schizophrenia would, by definition, be inconclusive on the role of social factors in the aetiology of the illness, as the social class of women – who represent half of those treated for the disorder – is problematic, and the part played by schizophrenia in a woman's occupational or social class position remains unexplored.

## The role of stress

The intermediary through which circumstances such as unemployment, poor housing, overcrowding are seen as affecting mental health is through stress. Studies on the physical effects of constant stress suggest a relationship between stress and physical conditions and diseases (Eyer and Sterling, 1977). The 'flight or fight' response has been identified as a component feature in a number of physical disorders, and stress-related mortality amongst the lower occupational groups is greater than amongst the professional and managerial classes (Townsend and Davidson, 1982; Townsend, Davidson and Whitehead, 1988). Similarly, stress is seen as an explanatory factor in the higher rates of mental illness amongst the lower social classes.

One indicator of the relationship between stress and poor mental health is seen in studies linking low social class with higher rates of suicide and self-harm, associated with poor housing, debt and money problems, and unemployment (Morgan *et al.*, 1975; Buglass, 1976). Whilst some research has suggested that it is the presence of positive events which protects the middle classes (Phillips, 1968), others have argued what is important is the degree of control the individual has over their life, and that stress is more threatening when combined with long-term events with little possibility of change (Davis and Low, 1989).

Some authors have translated this as the ability to cope and the acquisition of 'coping mechanisms' (Seligman, 1975; Selye, 1956). It is suggested that the circumstances of poverty and deprivation result in the transmission of apathy, underachievement – theories which come close to the 'culture of poverty' and dependency theories heavily criticized for being individualistic and 'victim-blaming' (see, for example, Lewis, 1964).

Thus the influence of stress, whilst important, is complex. The impact is seen as depending variously on long-term and short-term stresses, the effect of positive stresses to compensate for intermediary variables such as social support, the issue of power and powerlessness, and, for some commentators at least, learned responses to stress, learned helplessness and coping mechanisms. How do these ideas relate to the over-representation of women in the figures for the mentally ill? Is it that women are less able to cope with the stress and strains of poverty? Or is the answer rooted in women's greater feelings of powerlessness, stemming from the position of women in Western economies, and their lesser actual power? Do women suffer higher levels of poverty or suffer this in ways which are specific to their experience as women? For, if poverty is implicated in the aetiology of mental illness, why are there not the same high levels of depression and anxiety amongst men in the same poor households?

## Women and stress

The potential sources of stress in women's lives, however, are wider than the traditional measurements of stress would imply. Stress inventories used in psychiatric research do not include stresses which are specific to women, nor do they weight separately for men and women events which appear likely to have a different impact on each sex (Makosky, 1980, 1982), in the same way as deprivation indices have obscured the particular experience of women. For example, the stress inventory developed by Srole, Langner *et al.* (1961), which has been widely used since then (Cochrane, 1983), asks questions of all participants on pregnancy and gives respondents an equal stress score, whether the respondent is male and describing the pregnancy of his partner, or is female and describing events which happened directly to her. Similarly stresses such as sexual harassment, sexual attack and rape are not included, despite the obvious stress to women experiencing such abuse. More minor stresses such as changes in childcare arrangements, which have a greater effect on women given the structure of responsibility for children in society, are also rarely included (Makosky, 1982). Thus studies measuring stress inventories against mental health are likely to underestimate women's levels of stress, and as a result suggest women's mental health problems are less founded in circumstances and events than those of men. Stresses such as oppression and discrimination, the isolation of domestic labour and women's fixed roles (Oakley, 1974; Gove and Tudor, 1973) and women's treatment by the medical profession (Barrett and Roberts, 1978; Roberts, 1985; Doyal and Elston, 1983) are never incorporated.

**Women, mental health and poverty**

To what extent, then, does the evidence suggest that, for some women at least, their mental health problems are caused by the experience of poverty and deprivation? The rest of this chapter explores both official statistics and small-scale research, including a qualitiative study of thirty women who were psychiatric patients in Bristol, to look at income and aspects of deprivation – housing, the environment, physical health and social isolation. The complex and interlocking effects of the experience of poverty and deprivation, in the past, the present and the threat of poverty again in the future, highlight the impact of poverty on mental health.

One way of examining these consequences is through reference to the statistics for those in treatment: are there more poor women in psychiatric treatment? Published data on patients in psychiatric hospitals in Britain does not give social class or standardized ratios for patients as a proportion of people in the class. The General Household Survey does ask questions about class, but has not often taken data on the type of illness. The latest survey of GPs in Britain does give an indication of one level of morbidity figures – those based on consultation. Table 6.1 reveals that women in the lower occupational groups, using the 'conventional' method of assigning married women to their husband's occupational class, are over a third more likely to consult a GP for mental health problems than women in Classes I and II (OPCS, 1990a), and there is a clear

**Table 6.1:** Standardized consultation ratios in general practice: mental health disorders

| Social Class | All Women | Married | Single, Widowed and Divorced |
|---|---|---|---|
| Classes I and II | 84 | 81 | 84 |
| Class III N | 97 | 102 | 104 |
| Class III M | 112 | 109 | 103 |
| Classes IV and V | 113 | 113 | 111 |

*Source*: OPCS 1990a Morbidity Statistics From General Practice. All women classified according to their husband's occupation in column 1, and their own occupation in columns 2 and 3.

inverse class relationship: the rate of women consulting increases with each step down the occupational hierarchy. The same inverse relationship between class and mental health is found for all women, whether categorized by their own occupation or not, and whether married on non-married, with the widest class gap amongst married women classified by their own occupation. Interestingly, the OPCS data shows higher consultation rates for men than women in all but the largest class for men, Social Class III Manual. When the figures for men are broken down by marital status, there is a very high consultation rate amongst widowed and divorced men, and men living alone, which suggests that some of this higher consultation is due to greater effects on mental health of the end of a marital relationship. However, for both sexes, the class relationship suggests an important link with resources.

These figures tell us about those women who consult their GP for problems which she or he identifies as psychiatric, which clearly means that women who would identify themselves as having poor mental health but who do not seek help from the medical profession are not included. The figures also suffer from problems identified earlier in relation to the use of an occupational class structure based on male employment – the fact that the vast majority of women's jobs are clustered in two categories. In addition, the supplementary classification used in the study to denote problems which GPs could not fit into the international classification system of diseases includes consultations for economic problems, poverty, poor housing and problems in caring for dependants, such as a sick person or ageing parent. The extent to which GPs might classify the problems of women in poverty as 'supplementary', and those of women in high-income households as genuine mental health problems, suggests that the figures here might underestimate, if anything, the strength of this class relationship.

The question can be approached differently by asking if women who are in psychiatric treatment are more likely to be in or on the margins of poverty than the population in general (Belle, 1982; Payne, 1987). The over-representation of poor women in treatment is highlighted in the greater numbers of women from those house-holds which are more often on a low income. So, for example, women bringing up children alone have higher rates of treatment for depression and anxiety than women in two-parent households (Osborn, 1983; Belle, 1980; Daly, 1989) as do older women, divorced women, widows, and women from ethnic minority groups (Belle 1982; Pearlin and Johnson, 1977; Radloff, 1975; Guttentag *et al.*, 1980; Makosky, 1982; Gove, 1973).

Surveys based on a sample of women in the population have similarly found more working-class women amongst figures both for treated and untreated psychiatric illness. The major study in Britain by Brown and Harris in Camberwell, London (1978) found a higher prevalence of depression amongst women from unskilled and manual backgrounds in comparison with women from higher social classes (Brown and Harris, 1978). Once again the issue of social class is problematic: this study resolved the issue by using husband or father's occupation wherever possible, including in one instance using the occupation of an ex-husband for a divorced woman. They wrote that, 'it matters remarkably little which of the various alternative measures are employed – they give essentially the same result.' (Brown and Harris, 1978, p. 151).

Despite reservations about this approach, their findings are interesting for the links made between depression and women's lives. Brown and Harris identified two reasons for poorer mental health amongst working-class women: that these women suffered more of the stressful life events and conditions which took a toll on mental well-being, and that these women were more often vulnerable to depression as a result of four factors: loss of mother in childhood, lack of paid employment outside the home, lack of a close confiding relationship, and having three or more young children at home (Brown and Harris, 1978).

Women in lower income groups suffer more stressful events more often: problems with debt, eviction, unemployment, illness, and having to deal with state agencies are more common occurrences amongst poor households, as a result of low income. Poor physical health, for example, is related to poverty as we have seen in the previous chapter, and the stress of dealing with both acute and chronic or ongoing poor health takes a toll also on mental health. The impact on women's mental health is particularly severe, as a result of the burden of caring for sick dependants, trying to cope with housework, caring work and often paid employment as well in the face of her own poor physical health. Equally important is the stress of worrying about the health of others. Land (1977) describes women as the buffers of the household, absorbing shortages and providing emotional support. Graham (1987b; 1990) similarly describes the work women do in the home as health maintenance work, which maintains and promotes the health of the household often at the expense of the woman's own health. In the last chapter the effects of this compromise were examined in relation to physical health – the impact on physical resources of poor nutrition, inadequate heating, damp housing and so on. However, the influence on women's mental health is equally strong.

Much of the research in this area of stress and mental health has focused on events which damage mental health, as a result of the stress they create. Events are most often seen as discrete – eviction rather than ongoing housing problems, bereavement rather than prolonged or permanent poor health or disability, an unwanted pregnancy, rather than the stress of coping with an added child in a poor household, the arrest of a member of the household, rather than the stress of living with a partner or child in prison, on remand, or having to pay a fine to the courts. Events such as these are seen as stressful in their immediate and short-lived impact on mental well-being – and this impact is seen as quantifiable. In this way, re-searchers compiled lists of stressful events and attempted to tie them in to the onset of depression or anxiety attacks.

The other way in which the trials of life obstruct mental well-being is through ongoing conditions of life – poverty, poor-quality housing, which is damp or overcrowded, for example, living in a poor neighbourhood, surrounded by run-down buildings, with in-adequate amenities, unsafe streets, and so on. Conditions such as these are implicated also in poor mental health as a result of the negative effect such material circumstances may have. The stress of living constantly in damp or dirty accommodation, of worrying about children's safety when there is nowhere for them to play, or of having your nerves stretched to the limits with noisy, cooped-up, frustrated children trapped in a small high-rise flat, for example, sug-gests powerful explanations for higher rates of depression amongst women without paid employment (Brown and Harris, 1978; Osborn, 1983; Radloff, 1980), or women living with small children in local authority flats (Fanning, 1967). Going out becomes a nightmare, especially with babies and toddlers, where pushchairs or prams must be negotiated down numerous stairs, where there is no lift or the lift no longer works (Matrix, 1984).

It is these events and conditions which are the key to the relation-ship between poverty and poor mental health, whilst gender affects the way such events and conditions make their impact on the lives of the poor. Many events turn into poor conditions later: the loss of paid employment, for example, is a stressful event which becomes a stressful condition – being without paid work and being in poverty. Makosky (1980) argues that the stress of events is greatest when they are recent. However, this association is difficult to unravel – the impact of unemployment may lead to more observable stress (Brenner, 1973; Platt and Kreitmann, 1984) whereas the longer term consequences of being without paid work and struggling to survive on a poverty income result in a less visible reaction – poorer health which will be evident in years to come and a greater risk of premature death (Phillimore, 1989; Fox and Goldblatt, 1982).

## Housing and the environment

A number of studies have highlighted the part played by poor housing and the environment in the onset of poor mental health, in particular depression and anxiety. The early studies of structural associations with mental health such as the work of Faris and Dunham in Chicago (1939) and of Hare in Bristol (1956) demonstrated the over-representation amongst admissions to psychiatric hospital of those living in poorer areas of the city. This precise impact of poor housing has been studied in many ways.

Overcrowding has been linked to poor mental health in several studies (for example, Gove *et al.*, 1979; see Cochrane, 1983; Gabe and Williams, 1986), although other studies have found little relationship between density of accommodation – persons per room – and higher symptom levels, or higher symptoms also in under-occupied accommodation (Gabe and Williams, 1986). The survey of women in psychiatric treatment in Bristol found they were more likely to be living in circumstances of overcrowding, often as a result of having had to move to temporary accommodation which was inadequate for their needs, and which they had occupied for some months, despite describing it as temporary (Payne, 1987).

Studies which have found a higher rate of mental health problems amongst people in local-authority housing suggest a strong link between poor housing and psychiatric distress. One way in which this has been measured is in studies concentrating on high-rise accommodation. Higher levels of mental illness amongst residents of the higher floors of tower blocks, in comparison with those lower down, suggests that housing type can exert a particular influence over and above other forms of deprivation (Fanning, 1967; Gilloran, 1968; Ineichen and Hooper, 1974; Ineichen, 1986). The study by Ineichen and Hooper in Bristol found a higher level of neurotic symptoms associated with high-rise accommodation in comparison with households of similar composition and social circumstances in ground-level accommodation. The association is not identical for each sex, and perhaps not surprisingly studies have found the strongest relationship between high-rise accommodation and poor mental health for women, with better than average mental health amongst men who lived in high-rise flats (Gillis, 1977). The crucial factor which distinguishes these diverse reactions is gender, and women's domestic labour. Women who are caring for young children in poor accommodation suffer this for longer periods of time, and also suffer more from the greatest problems for those with young children and domestic responsibilities: lack of safe super-vised play space, difficulties in getting out, carrying shopping and so on. Women at home with young children suffer immense problems with isolation (Oakley, 1976; Sharpe, 1984) – problems which are exacerbated by the design of modern estates and tower blocks which have no gardens, no street and no similar informal communal space where friendships are formed and sustained.

Other problems associated with local-authority housing are the state of repair and difficulties in getting problems resolved, de-creased mobility and poor public space. The Bristol survey of women in psychiatric treatment found fewer women in local auth-ority housing, but those who were suffered more problems in their housing than owner-occupiers. Two-thirds of the council tenants suffered damp housing, and the majority had limited or no space for their children to play (Payne, 1987).

Clearly, poor housing is rarely suffered in isolation, and those whose accommodation is poor are also significantly more likely to suffer deprivation in other ways. The study by Hunt *et al.* of the health of the inhabitants of poor-quality tenement flats in Edin-burgh focused on two groups of the population – those in damp housing and those whose housing, while poor, did not suffer from damp (Hunt *et al.*, 1986). They found surprisingly high levels of morbidity and poor health in both groups, but found that women in the damp housing reported greater emotional distress, and that the children in the damp housing had significantly poorer health. Women's work in damp housing is made more difficult, and gives rise to greater stress. Domestic labour in housing marked by damp, which invades furniture, clothing, discolours wallpaper and paint-work and leaves the air musty and fetid is not only more difficult in physical terms, but is also more stressful. Housework offers little by way of reward: it is unpaid, unstructured, performed in isolation, and satisfaction from the outcome of the job itself is an important source of reward for those who do it. As a result, cleaning and other household chores in circumstances where even this short-lived satis-faction of a clean and tidy house is denied create additional stress for the woman who has to do this work.

Poor-quality housing also affects the health of children, and damp accommodation in particular was linked in Hunt's study to higher rates of respiratory problems, bronchitis, asthma, other allergic reactions, vomiting and diarrhoea (Hunt *et al.*, 1986). The study of women in Bristol found that over two-thirds of those in both privately rented and local authority housing suffered problems with damp, with consequences for both the women's own health and that of their children. The impact of poor housing is related to employment status and gender: poor housing shows the strongest association with mental health amongst those who spend longest at home – women with small children who do not have a paid employment, unemployed men and women, older people who have retired (Ineichen and Hooper, 1974; Blackman *et al.*, 1989).

The impact of poor-quality housing was one aspect of a study of poor health in two areas of poor housing in West Belfast (Blackman *et al.*, 1989). Although housing deprivation was marked, so too was deprivation: 96 per cent of the adults in one of the areas, the Divis Flats, were in or on the margins of poverty, and 82 per cent of the second group, living in the Twinbrook area, seen locally as rep-resenting better housing and a better environment. Levels of ill health were high in both areas, and women suffered poorer health than men in both areas.

In terms of mental health, women in both areas suffered poorer mental health than men, and women in the Divis Flats – the poorest area – suffered the poorest mental health of all: 56 per cent of women in this complex reported mental health problems – 50 per cent more than the men. The gap between women and men in the Twinbrook area was greater, with over three times as many women reporting poor mental health, although overall the rates were lower for both sexes (Blackman *et al.*, 1989). In the study as a whole nearly half the women suffered from symptoms of depression, compared with 28 per cent of the men. Again, levels were higher amongst women in the Divis Flats than anywhere else, with 70 per cent of these women reporting symptoms. These are levels of mental ill health substantially greater than for the population as a whole, and indicate quite strongly the impact on mental health of poor housing experienced alongside other forms of deprivation. Both groups suffered high levels of poverty and higher than average levels of poor mental health, but the additional factor of poor housing appears to greatly increase the likelihood of experiencing poor mental health. That women suffer levels of mental illness which are substantially above those for men in both areas indicates, once more, the greater impact on women of deprivation in general, and in housing in particular.

An additional feature of the group living in the Divis Flats was the greater number of lone parent households, who are more likely to suffer poverty and suffer higher rates of mental ill health (Popay and Jones, 1987). The links between income and poor housing were also marked in the study of women in Bristol, which found that women in the poorest households were most likely to report difficulties, such as damp, structural problems and poor repair, in all housing tenures (Payne, 1987).

Another report of research in the Divis Flats complex similarly found higher levels of poverty and deprivation, unemployment and poor housing amongst the inhabitants (Sluka, 1989). More than 70 per cent of households studied were found to contain at least one person suffering from some kind of mental health problem: depression, insomnia, bad nerves, or dependence on alcohol or tranquillizers. Women reported symptoms more often than men, and were more likely to be taking psychotropic drugs, in particular tranquillizers. The housing problems – poor quality accommodation, in poor repair, with damp, mould and mildew, broken elevators, overcrowding and inadequate waste disposal – carried difficulties for women, and were combined with the experience of isolation and feelings of powerlessness to alter the circumstances of disadvantage which were also crucial (Sluka, 1989).

However, women and men in both studies suffered also from harassment and oppression – deprivation in relation to the political conditions in which they lived (Sluka, 1989). The stress of poverty and poor housing in these studies is intensified by abuse and intimidation from both loyalists and the armed forces (Sluka, 1989).

The environment in which housing is located and in which the household or individual spends their time is a further form of deprivation in which the stress falls differently on women. The design of public space, transport policy and women's domestic labour are structured by discourses in which women are the adjuncts of men (Matrix, 1984). The stress of design which adds to women's vulnerability to attack, public transport which is irregular, expensive and inadequately policed, poor street lighting, amenities which are dominated by men means that many women are afraid to go out at night and often during the day as well (Jones *et al.*, 1986). Such fears are not unrealistic – women who are poor also suffer higher rates of crime and violence against the person, as do ethnic minority and black women, and both crime itself and the stress of living under the threat of crime add to women's mental health problems (Belle, 1984; Jones *et al.*, 1986).


## Physical health

Poor physical health – both frequent illness and chronic or on-going health problems – are frequently found alongside poor mental health (Eastwood and Trevelyan, 1972). The effects of stress are not confined to mental health, and a number of illnesses and conditions are associated with stress, including tuberculosis, heart disease, skin disease, transient diabetes and leukemia in children (Makosky, 1980; Eyer and Sterling, 1977). The effect stress has is to produce an internal reaction which prepares the body to deal with the source of stress – what is often known as the 'flight or fight' response. Stress provokes physiological and psychological arousal which enables us to react to threats to health or well-being. Whilst this response is valuable in some circumstances, continuous stress results in health-damaging reactions: stress invokes a faster heart beat, an increase in blood pressure, increased release of hormones and a change in metabolic rate, and the body in total is affected (Eyer and Sterling, 1977).

People in lower income groups and those suffering poverty are more likely to suffer premature death than those in more affluent social classes (Townsend and Davidson,1982; Whitehead, 1987; Smith, Bartley and Blane, 1990). An effect of this is to greatly increase the likelihood of suffering bereavement, especially at an early age. Women and men in lower income groups are more likely to suffer the death of a baby or child, are more likely to be widowed at a young age. Bereavement is a major stress factor, a life event closely associated with increased risks of depression and anxiety (Reese, 1982). Women are more likely to suffer the loss of a partner, as a result of women's greater longevity, and poor women are substantially more likely to suffer the loss of people close to them. Brown and Harris (1978) found that women whose mother had died in their childhood were more vulnerable to depression in later years, a vulnerability factor which is linked to poverty and social class, in the higher mortality rate of women from lower income unskilled backgrounds.

## Poverty and managing a low income

*The stress of poverty itself is in trying to manage on a low income and the greater likelihood of experiencing the events and conditions which lead to stress. The finding that poor women are particularly vulnerable to poor mental health (Belle, 1982; Radloff, 1975; Guttentag, Salasin and Belle, 1980; Daly, 1989) suggests the greater impact of poverty on women. Poverty has been linked to poor mental health at different stages of the life cycle – disadvantaged women report greater depression in later years and at the menopause, and at younger ages, with young children (Osborn, 1983; Graham, 1986; Davis and Low, 1989). Life circumstances are a powerful predictor of mental health (Reese, 1982). The Bristol study of women who were psychiatric outpatients found that a substantial majority of the women lived in households in or on the margins of poverty, whilst a number of those women in apparently more affluent households did not know how much their partner earned, and were unlikely to be sharing equally in the resources of that household (Payne, 1987). Whilst women as a group suffer more poverty, and a greater threat of poverty, during their lives, women also suffer higher levels of poor mental health than men in the same household. To some extent this reflects this hidden poverty: some women going without to decrease the shortage others experience;

and to some extent this reflects households where resources are denied women. However, it is equally true to say that not all poor women suffer depression, even if, as in some surveys as least, the vast majority do (Blackman *et al.*, 1989).

A crucial feature distinguishing the experience of poverty for women and men is that of domestic labour. Women in poor households take the responsibility for managing (Pahl, 1989) and making meagre ends meet (Daly, 1989). The contagion effect observed by Makosky (1980), where women are more likely to report as stressful events incidents where someone else was the central character, relates to women's role as 'buffers', absorbing the shocks and emotional needs of others (Land, 1977). Belle *et al.* (1980) note that whilst married women have better mental health than women who are separated, widowed and divorced, the mental health of those without children is better than those who have children. Whilst this reflects the isolation of many women at home with young children and the decreased likelihood of such women having paid employment, which offers protection against poor mental health (Brown and Harris, 1978; Radloff, 1975), the greater poverty of households with children combined with the responsibility of caring for the needs of children are the factors which combine to mitigate against good mental health for many women.

Women who were psychiatric patients in the Bristol study were likely to talk of the stress of managing on their income, in particular where money was tight. Lone mothers described going without, to make sure the children were fed properly, going without heat after the child is in bed, and buying their own clothes second-hand in order that their child might have new clothes (Payne, 1987). This putting of children's needs first was seen by these women as a natural solution to money problems, but one which had costs for themselves and which did not entirely resolve the difficulties of trying to manage on a low income.

Women in two-adult housholds also described worrying over their income and having to make ends meet – an illustration perhaps of the extent to which the work of being a good manager and a good wife and mother dominates women's lives, and women's feelings of well-being. It is unsurprising therefore that women who do have to manage on impossibly low incomes should report a high level of anxiety about this task.

Women in poverty suffer extremely high levels of stress simply from the difficulty of managing on a low income, negotiating between conflicting demands and needs of different members of the household, and the worry and guilt when ends won't meet, as they invariably won't (Evason, 1980; Glendinning and Craig, 1990; Craig and Glendinning, 1990; Daly, 1989). Women's health maintenance work explains the intensity of this: the conversations of poor women are dominated by worries of the impact of poverty particularly on their children (Graham, 1986; Oakley, 1986; Daly, 1989), and for women this domestic role places them in a unique position of work and worry.

## Social deprivation and isolation

Attempts to measure social deprivation as a separate, if related, phenomenon have focused on a lack of integration into the community, rights in paid employment, deprivation of family activity, forms of recreational deprivation, and educational deprivation (Benzeval and Judge, 1990; Townsend, 1990b). Specific forms of social deprivation in relation to race and racism are subsumed under the heading of community participation, whilst women's experience of social deprivation in relation to fear of violence is also assumed in this heading, as being 'relatively unsafe in surrounding streets' (Benzeval and Judge, 1990, Annex 1). Discrimination in paid employment on the grounds of race, sex, age, disability or sexual orientation is also listed as a form of social deprivation.

However, there is no further account of women's experience of social deprivation specifically in relation to gender. Women, particularly when alone, have more restricted access to some public spaces – pubs, clubs and bars for example – whilst women are also deprived in circumstances where their housing prevents the building up of the kinds of social relationships which are open to women. These informal relationships in the community can be crucial to women who are otherwise isolated in the home – lone older women and young mothers, in particular, and housing construction such as flats may act to reinforce women's isolation. This may be a further factor in the health differences between women in paid employment, who suffer less from isolation, and those at home all day.

## The nature of women's mental illness

Poverty accounts for a proportion of psychiatric illness, and women are uniquely placed to experience stress resulting from poverty and deprivation. Are lower rates for men simply the result of less stress, or also of stress which is experienced differently? Klerman and Weissman (1980) argue that it is women's 'maladaptive role' which leads to depression in the face of difficulties in life, whilst others have argued that women are socialized into learned helplessness and behaviour which is inward, and which turns anger and frustration into depression. Radloff (1975; 1980) argues that women suffer greater learned helplessness as a result of stereotypical conditioning during childhood, but that their difficulties are also structural, and result from the greater number of stressful events and conditions women have to deal with in their lives.

The question of the extent to which women are able to control their lives is a related issue. Makosky (1980) argues that women are less able to control the events which have a significant negative impact on the lives, and their mental health. The sources of women's poverty and deprivation are economic dependency on men and the State, interlocked with their secondary position in the labour market. Women who are dependent on resources within the household have less control over their lives than single women who are earners, and also in comparison with the men on whom they depend economically. And whilst all of those who are dependent on state benefit have little or no control over their income and increasingly have little control over how it is spent, as more deductions are made at source, women in households which are dependent on state benefit are less likely to be the named claimant, and have less control over this meagre income than their partners.

The picture which emerges of the consequences of poverty and deprivation for women's mental health is of women's increased risk of being depressed and suffering anxiety as a result of the struggle to make ends meet. Whilst physical health is affected by poverty and deprivation, there are also strong links with problems of mental well-being. Undoubtedly the difficulty of defining and measuring mental health means that it is difficult to be certain what is being measured – women's greater likelihood of turning frustration and anger caused by stress inwards rather than outwards, women's greater chance of being seen as mentally ill when they are poor, and struggling to survive, or women's greater poverty? In many respects this dilemma is irrelevant – it is certain that the women who go to their GPs, see a psychiatrist, take psychotropic drugs or simply suffer on their own are unhappy, and that of the numbers of women who are defined in some way, by themselves or others, as depressed and neurotic, a large proportion are also suffering poverty and deprivation in a variety of ways. And whilst some of the women who are seen as mentally ill enjoy an affluent lifestyle, the common economic dependency they share with others of their sex will, for a number of women at least, account for their poor mental health: these women fear poverty in the future, as a result of old age, widowhood, separation and divorce.

# CHAPTER 7

# OPPRESSION, HEALTH AND POVERTY

This book focuses on the interplay between gender, poverty and health. As suggested earlier, both health and poverty are related to factors other than or in addition to that of gender. All women are not equally vulnerable to poverty and deprivation, and all men are not equally protected from such an experience. Whilst gender is a central factor in the determination of risk factors, there are others which are just as important.

Racism and discrimination in Britain and other Western countries result in a greater exposure to structural disadvantage – people and households from ethnic minority backgrounds are more likely to be in low-income occupations, to suffer material deprivation such as poor quality housing and to suffer unemployment (Thorogood, 1987; Zopf, 1989; Doyal, 1985; Bryan et al., 1985). They are also more likely to suffer abuse, racial attack and harassment by both white society and state institutions such as the health and social services (Doyal, 1985; Bryan et al., 1985; Fisher et al., 1986; Cook and Watt, 1987; Donovan, 1986). Similarly, gay men and lesbians are more likely to suffer unemployment, discrimination in the labour and housing market and also harassment, abuse and attack (Galloway, 1983; Altman, 1989; Boogaard, 1989; Taylor, 1986; Focas, 1989). In both instances, structural disadvantage – poor housing, poverty, unemployment and increased reliance on inadequate state benefits – is related to and exacerbated by forms of oppression and prejudice.

To some extent there are parallels with an analysis of the relationship between health, poverty and gender. Women as a sex suffer material deprivation which is related to and exacerbated by their position in the labour market and the home, and which is supported by both material and ideological structures. There are also other similarities – in particular, the need to emphasize the way neither women nor black and ethnic minority populations nor people with a disability are simply passive victims (Cook and Watt, 1987; Donovan, 1986; Ernst and Goodison, 1981; Lonsdale, 1990). Cultural and informal sources of support, more organized support such as self-help groups and political struggle are ways in which minority and oppressed groups of people fight back.

It is also important not to be too simplistic in the ways in which the more detailed experience of such groups is discussed. This point relates not only to the need to distinguish carefully between groups of different ethnicity, whose culture and experience varies substantially, but also groups with different kinds of disability, or between gay men and lesbians. There is a political sense to a unification of such groups who are discriminated against or oppressed on the grounds of their ethnicity, culture, age, disability or sexuality, and referring to the experience of black people or people with a disability as a single group emphasizes the basis of that oppression. However, in trying to distinguish the links between health and poverty and factors such as race and gender, it is crucial to retain both of these perspectives – based in the larger sense on oppression, and in the more detailed sense on a precise description of experiences of health and illness, in the labour market, and so on.

## Poverty, health and race

One of the greatest difficulties in assessing the extent to which people from particular ethnic groups differ in their health experience, and the relationship of this to other factors such as poverty and occupation, lies with the availability of data. Much of the data on occupational class, for example, is based on a match of the occupations of those who have died in the years around the ten-yearly census with occupational groups in the census itself. In this way, mortality rates for different occupations and social classes can be calculated. Despite problems in this method of assessing health (see Chapter 4) the data is valuable in many respects.

However, race has not in the past been one of the census questions and data on the mortality of different ethnic groups is based on immigrants rather than those born in Britain. Increasingly this is a reflection of only a very small group of the ethnic minority population, and whilst it demonstrates some kind of relationship between race and health it is difficult to determine the causal links. The gap in data on the health of ethnic minority groups is reflected in the relative lack of detailed discussion in the major accounts of inequalities in health (Townsend and Davidson, 1982; Whitehead, 1987; Smith and Jacobson, 1989; Fox, 1989; Illsley and Svensson, 1990). Small-scale studies and data on health amongst the immigrant population collectively begin to indicate a picture of health in which some ethnic groups have higher mortality rates for some diseases, and that this pattern of increased vulnerability is related to increased risks of poverty as well as specific risks from illness such as sickle cell disease or thalassemia, and is also related to racism within the health services at a number of levels (McNaught, 1988; Bryan, Dadzie and Scafe, 1985; Torkington, 1983; Marmot *et al.*, 1984; Fenton, 1986; Donovan, 1986).

This patterning of health is complicated and there are substantial variations in the health of different ethnic groups. For example, in comparison with mortality rates for people born in England and Wales, people from the Indian subcontinent have higher rates of mortality from ischaemic heart disease and tuberculosis, higher rates of maternal mortality, and lower rates of mortality for various cancers. People from Africa and the Caribbean have higher rates of maternal mortality and hypertension and stroke, and are also more likely to die early of liver cancer, and tuberculosis. All immigrant groups have higher mortality rates for violence and accidents, and lower rates for chronic bronchitis (Marmot *et al.*, 1984).

A more recent study confirms these findings. More than half of early deaths (here defined as under the age of 50) amongst men from the Indian subcontinent resulted from circulatory diseases, and in particular ischaemic heart disease, compared with only a third for all deaths. Amongst women from the Indian subcontinent, the major cause of death was neoplasm, whilst women from Scotland, Ireland, Africa and the Caribbean had higher than average mortality related to external causes such as accidents and violence (Balarajan and Bulusu, 1990). Women from the Indian subcontinent, Africa, the Caribbean and Mediterranean countries also had higher mortality rates for circulatory disease and digestive diseases (Balarajan and

Bulusu, 1990). Overall, mortality rates for women under retirement age from the Indian subcontinent, Caribbean and African Commonwealth, Scotland and Ireland were all higher than average in comparison with England and Wales as a whole (Balarajan and Bulusu, 1990).

Infant mortality rates are also higher amongst children born to women from Africa, the Caribbean and the Indian subcontinent (Britton *et al.*, 1990), although again the picture is complex. In comparison with the United Kingdom, rates of infant mortality are higher for women from Pakistan, the Caribbean, India, Eire and West Africa, although women from Bangladesh and East Africa have lower rates than women from the United Kingdom (Balarajan and Raleigh, 1990). Children born to women from Pakistan and the Caribbean also have higher rates of postneonatal mortality, whilst for perinatal mortality all immigrant groups have higher rates than women from the United Kingdom, with the rate for women from Pakistan over 80 per cent greater than that for women born in the United Kingdom (Balarajan and Raleigh, 1990). Thus some groups of women born outside the United Kingdom are more likely to suffer the loss of a child in the first weeks and months of its life.

Figures for infant mortality in the United Kingdom are inversely related to the social class of the father: that is, that women whose partner is in an unskilled occupation are up to 80 per cent more likely to lose their baby in the first year of life. The study by Balarajan and Raleigh similarly found substantial class differences within the figures for infant mortality amongst children born to women from India, Pakistan, the Caribbean and Africa. For example, women from India whose partner was in a Social Class V occupation were more than twice as likely to lose their child in the first year of life than where the father was in a professional occupation (Balarajan and Raleigh, 1990). However, the problems of measuring social class for women and their children are substantial. The class gradient was not smooth in each case: women from the Caribbean whose partner's job was classified as skilled non-manual were over three times as likely to lose their baby as women whose partner held an unskilled manual job. This is perhaps an indication of the complexity of measurement using such blunt tools as country of birth (but not occupation) for the woman and occupation (but not country of birth) for the man.

Local studies of infant mortality which offer evidence in relation to ethnic group rather than country of birth also show higher levels of infant mortality, low birth weight and still birth amongst minority and black women (Terry *et al.*, 1980; Whitehead, 1987; Butler and Golding, 1986).

When differences are measured by morbidity figures, such as health-service consultation rates, people born outside the United Kingdom appear to have more health problems. Figures for consultation in general practice show that women from the Caribbean have a higher consultation rate than either men from the Caribbean or women born in the United Kingdom, whilst women from the Indian subcontinent have higher consultation rates in comparison with women born in the United Kingdom but lower than the consultation rate for men from the Indian subcontinent (OPCS, 1990a). The differences between ethnic groups are most marked in the consultation rates for serious diseases such as tuberculosis and cancer, with women from the Caribbean and Indian subcontinent over 50 per cent more likely to consult their GP for serious illnesses in comparison with women born in the UK (OPCS, 1990a).

However, there is some indication that even these high rates of consultation may not represent need, and that people from different ethnic groups may underutilize the health services (Fenton, 1986; Donovan, 1986). Racism within the health services and policy planning adds to cultural and language barriers to make women likely to use services less, whilst the concentration of black and ethnic groups in poorer inner-city areas means that they not only suffer more from environmental and housing deprivation, but also from the poor quality and underfinancing of health practices in such areas (Doyal, 1985; Torkington, 1983; Fenton, 1986).

The impact of this is perhaps most clearly illustrated in relation to infant mortality and antenatal care. Despite high levels of attendance for antenatal care and lower than average rates of smoking during pregnancy, women from ethnic minority groups are more likely to have low birth-weight babies, more pre-term babies and a longer delay in the period immediately after the birth before the baby establishes regular breathing (Butler and Golding, 1986; Osborn and Butler, 1985). Women from ethnic minority groups are also more likely to have poorer care during their pregnancy – more of them receive antenatal care from a GP without obstetric qualification and more suffer 'mistakes' in their obstetric care during labour (Grimsley and Bhat, 1988; Osborn and Butler, 1985).

It is not only a question of the care received from the health services, however. Health relates also to poverty and the experience of deprivation. Both women and men from ethnic minorities have poorer jobs, with lower pay and worse conditions of employment, and suffer higher rates of unemployment (Cook and Watt, 1987; Thorogood, 1987; Westwood and Bhachu, 1988). Black women in America are substantially more likely to be poor than white women – 86 per cent of young black female householders in the USA in 1983 were on or below the poverty line, and at every age and level of education there were more black women in poverty than white (Zopf, 1989). The relationship between race and poverty cannot be simply tacked on to that of gender, and the complexity of differences means that the poverty experienced by black women and their vulnerability to poverty is not simply an extension to a gendered experience.

A major cause of poverty for both black and white women is their access to and position in the labour market. A sexual division of labour, in which women's income and commitment to paid work is seen as secondary to the 'breadwinner's' income, means women's jobs are poorly paid, with fewer benefits, less security and fewer opportunities for promotion or satisfaction (Martin and Roberts, 1984; Dex, 1985; Hunt, 1988a). However, the position of ethnic minority women in the labour market is essentially different, and reflects a different history, in particular the history of British colonialism and oppression in developing countries, and the growth of international capitalism (Thorogood, 1987): 'Black and white women in British society do share some common experiences but they are also divided by racism . . . racism and sexism complicate women's relationship to class and poverty' (Cook and Watt, 1987, p. 54).

The majority of ethnic minority women are employed in jobs with lower pay than white women, as well as poorer working conditions, poorer hours, and little job security (Thorogood, 1987; Cook and Watt, 1987; Bryan *et al.*, 1985). However, there are also important differences within different ethnic groups which suggest a different experience of and vulnerability to poverty and which are also important for the direct impact of occupation on health.

Afro-Caribbean women are more likely to head households and bring children up as single-parent householders, reflecting the value of economic independence as well as the impact of a different political history, of slavery, colonialism and imperial capitalism

(Thorogood, 1987; Bryan *et al.*, 1985; Fisher *et al.*, 1986). Whilst for many women who are lone parents the only solution to their poverty may be remarriage or a new relationship (Millar, 1989a) this does not guarantee freedom from deprivation, because resources are not always shared within households (Pahl, 1989; 1980; Land, 1983; Brannen and Wilson, 1987). The low earnings of ethnic minority men means that black women are less likely to be in positions of economic dependency, and have always been more likely to be in paid employment and to depend on their own earnings (Cook and Watt, 1987). In addition, women from the Caribbean employed in Britain are likely to be sending money home – either to support other family members or to be saved towards financing their travel to the United Kingdom (Thorogood, 1987; Bryan *et al.*, 1985).

Poverty within black households is fundamentally different – not only in relation to the greater economic independence of some black women, particularly Afro-Caribbean women, but also in relation to a culturally specific sharing of resources, as for example, within the Rastafarian culture (Cook and Watt, 1987).

Traditional poverty research not only obscures the experience of women and the importance of gender: it also obscures the association between poverty and race. Lists of the causes of poverty cite access to the labour market and caring for dependants as major explanations of poverty. Whilst this is valid, it understates the complexity of this relationship between the labour market and caring work, and this understatement obscures the complexity in particular for black and ethnic minority women. In the United Kingdom, as migrant labour and UK-born, black and ethnic minority women have occupied the lowest strata of the labour market, in much the same way as women have been employed in their countries of origin (Westwood and Bhachu, 1988; Cook and Watt, 1987; Mitter, 1986).

However, black and ethnic minority women may have more in common with black men than with white women, throughout both the developed and developing world. The growth of international capitalism has meant that increasingly there are commonalities amongst women, and in particular ethnic minority women in Britain and women in the developing world, which are related to both gender and race.

Women in developing countries also suffer poverty and deprivation, and although this picture is complex, the ways in which women in such countries experience poverty are important aspects of an understanding of poverty for ethnic minority and black women in the Northern hemisphere also. Throughout both developing and developed countries women perform the vast majority of domestic chores – labour which in both North and South is unpaid and invisible. It is also labour which is counted as non-productive in development surveys and in estimates of the country's economic structure (Karlekar, 1982; Rogers, 1980). World-wide, up to one quarter of all women are neither housewives nor in paid employment, but are engaged in productive labour on behalf of the household, often at home, often in sporadic forms of work: one estimate suggests that nearly half of the female labour force in rural India is in fact in the unpaid labour force, and is invisible (Karlekar, 1982).

However, this invisible labour is both time-consuming and arduous. One study of Bangladesh estimated women spent between 10 and 14 hours each day in productive work, including income-generating and expenditure-saving labour, in comparison with 10 or 11 hours spent by men (Rogers, 1980). Another study in Java estimated women's hours in productive labour at over 11 hours, whilst men spent an average of 8.7 hours a day in such work (Rogers, 1980).

The invisible productive labour women engage in is also crucial to the survival of the household. In most instances this is labour which transforms products into the means of existence: turning crops into edible foodstuffs involves vast amounts of time and work, both in the preparation of food from grain, and in the cooking of the food. Water collection is an activity which throughout the world is mostly performed by women, and again is essential to the household's survival. Similarly, fuel collection – which is becoming increasingly time-consuming as a result of deforestation in many parts of the world – is female work which is crucial, yet invisible (Rogers, 1980; Taylor, 1985). It is not only that this labour and the 'use-values' it creates (Delphy, 1984) should be recognized, but also that if total hours in productive labour are related to resources acquired, the vast majority of women world-wide are clearly poor (Scott, 1984). In performing this labour, women are reducing the poverty and deprivation of others, whilst increasing their own economic dependence on others whose labour is rewarded, either in the outside labour market, or as farmers engaged in the trade of produce.

Women in developing countries who are engaged in paid employment, however, are not necessarily economically independent or more free than their sisters in unpaid labour (Mitter, 1986; Gulati, 1982). The vast majority of women in paid work in many countries live in poor households, and their earnings are simply absorbed in the relief of that poverty (Karlekar, 1982). Paid employment of itself does not change the asymmetry of household relationships, whilst gender itself is an insufficient explanation of the economic status of individuals: as Karlekar points out in her study of women sweepers in Delhi, women also exploit other women, and women's position is determined as much by class as by gender (Karlekar, 1982). Resources within the home are not necessarily shared, whether the household is affluent or poor. Men and boys are likely to receive more of the food of the household, for example (Macormack, 1988; French, 1985; Gulati, 1982), whilst boys are less likely than girls to be expected to perform the domestic labour of the household (Gulati, 1982). In India, men spend 70 per cent of their wages on themselves, whilst virtually all of women's wages goes to the household and the children (French, 1985). Women's paid work is also often carried out in the home, particularly in countries where ideologies of seclusion create a discourse in which women's presence and their productive labour becomes even more invisible (Afshar and Agarwal, 1989).

Capitalist expansion in developing countries has created an expansion in the female labour market. However, within this market women have remained 'submerged' with female employment more often located in marginal and casual work, and in the home (Mitter, 1986). One effect of the changing industrial map was the loss of much of women's traditional employment – as women's productive labour was replaced by machinery and in turn men were trained to use this machinery (Karlekar, 1982).

Another development of industrial capitalism in recent years is that of 'free trade zones', where developing countries draw foreign investment and international companies by attractive packages – low taxes, low wages, relaxed laws, for example in relation to safety of the workforce, fewer currency controls and anti-strike legislation (Taylor, 1985). Women form the majority workforce in free-trade zones, particularly young women: up to 85 per cent of employees in some free-trade zones are women under 24 (Taylor, 1985). However, employment in such zones constitutes work in the secondary labour market – poorly paid, with little or no union representation, no job security, a high turnover and, not surprisingly, given little control over safety measures, a high health risk (Taylor, 1985).

The health effects of women's poverty in developing countries are stark: over half-a-million women die each year in childbirth in Africa and Asia, and an estimated 25 million women a year suffer illness as a result of pregnancy and childbirth (Taylor, 1985). Life expectancy for women is low in the poorest countries – in Sierra Leone the female child has a life expectancy at birth of 33.5 years, in Gambia it is 35 years, and in Afghanistan it is 37.3 years (Women, A World Report, 1985). Although in most countries life expectancy for women is greater than for men, this is not the case for every age group, with far higher mortality rates amongst women of childbearing age as a result of the demands made on women's health by repeated pregnancy and childbirth. In comparison with a maternal mortality rate of 11.6 deaths per 100,000 live births in the United Kingdom in 1980, Ecuador had a rate of 198.5 (Women, A World Report, 1985). Nutritional anaemia from inadequate diets is the norm amongst pregnant women in many countries: in Gambia, for example, 80 per cent of pregnant women suffered anaemia through poor diet, whilst similarly high rates are also found amongst non-pregnant women – many of whom would be breastfeeding, and have higher nutritional requirements (Women, A World Report, 1985). One study in Gambia found that women in their last three months of pregnancy actually lost weight, whilst poor women in India put on only 1.5 kilograms during pregnancy in comparison with 12.5 kilograms put on by wealthier women in that country (Taylor, 1985).

Although health in pregnancy and childbirth is a crucial determinant of women's life chances and health experience in many countries, women also suffer more frequently from other forms of sickness – parasites and diarrhoea, for example, and more from industrial diseases and accidents (Taylor, 1985). Health threats arise in many female occupations: in the electronics industry, for example, hazards connected with dangerous chemicals and also eye-strain affects the health of women workers; similarly, in the textile and garment industry dyes, cloth dusts and the working environment collectively contribute to the poor health and higher mortality of women in this industry (Mitter, 1986).

The health effects of occupation amongst women who are homeworkers are less visible than for other women. However, the insecurity of the work, the lack of control over the allocation of work, the appalling rates of pay and long hours needed, and the isolation in which the work is performed for many women have substantial effects on health, in addition to the poverty associated with this form of production (Hakim, 1987; Brown, 1974; Mitter, 1986).

Although the term 'homeworker' is more difficult to define in developing countries, women in both these countries and in the United Kingdom and the developed world, are overwhelmingly female and exploited. Black women are also substantially more likely to work at home in this way, partly because of racism and the structure of the labour market outside the home which makes finding paid employment in the primary sector more difficult, and partly because homeworking offers for many women a safer environment. This applies most notably to Asian women, who experience perhaps the greatest difficulty in finding paid employment outside the home because of lower rates of literacy and less familiarity with the English language. However, there are also reasons why women would prefer or seek homeworking or employment in a family business, not only in response to ideologies of seclusion and exclusion (Afshar and Agarwal, 1989) which restrict women's participation outside the home, but also because such employment within their own home or family minimizes the experience of racism in employment (Westwood and Bhachu, 1988). In reality, work experience for black women is complicated – and this complexity of their relationship to the labour market incorporates resistance. Black women are not passive victims of either racism or patriarchal control by their male relatives and partners (Westwood and Bhachu, 1988; Cook and Watt, 1987).

The consequences for health of poverty amongst black women are mediated both by gender and race, but the relationship is more complex than a simple addition of risk factors, and there are important differences in some of the ways in which resources are allocated within the labour market and the home for black women. The health impact of this particular relationship to the labour market and to poverty may have more to do with class, and the structural disadvantage stemming from racism and the economics of capitalism, than with gender. However, there are specifically gendered differences even where both men and women suffer poverty – for example, the increased likelihood that black women will work in the final months of pregnancy as a result of poverty wages and less maternity benefits has important consequences for their health.

Many of the relationships described here are as important for black women – the links between poor nutrition and poor housing and increased levels of illness remain central to an understanding of the links between poverty and health, although there may be differences. For example, poor housing is likely to exert a greater health effect for women working at home in paid employment, and so poor housing amongst those groups with a higher number of women who are homeworkers suggests a greater health risk for those women. Cultural differences in relation to diet may improve nutrition from one perspective – such as a greater emphasis in the diet on fresh vegetables – whilst the fortification of foodstuffs typically eaten by the white UK population and not by black households will mean poverty has a more severe impact on standards of nutrition and health. Thus whilst gender is still a variable of use – and differences in consumption and experience in relation to sex are important – race and racism exert other influences on health opportunities which require separate evaluation.

### Disability and age

There is a clear association between disability and poverty, with substantially increased risks of poverty amongst people with a disability. Lower rates of employment and decreased access to the labour market combine with inadequate state benefits and provision for people with a disability to create and perpetuate poverty (Townsend, 1979; Walker and Townsend, 1981; Walker, 1987; Lonsdale, 1990). There is however a causal aspect to the relationship between poverty and disability which should also be explored. Babies with congenital malformations are more often born to women from lower-income groups (OPCS, 1983), and factors such as poor nutrition during pregnancy are associated both with a higher rate of children with a disability and with poverty as a cause of poor nutrition (Wynn and Wynn, 1979; Lovett *et al.*, 1990). As a result, low-income groups bear a disproportionate share of the work of bringing up children with disabilities. However, they do so in circumstances of poverty as a result of the operation of social security and the inadequacy of benefits for either children or adults with a disability (Lonsdale, 1990).

Other disabilities occur during the course of a lifetime and, although more boys are born with a disability than girls (Hart, 1989), women form the majority of the population with a disability (Lonsdale, 1990), a reflection of the impact of disability in later life and women's greater longevity (Victor, 1989). This association between disability and the ageing process means that amongst the very old a substantial number of the population suffer some form of disability. However, despite women's greater life expectancy and the greater number of women amongst the very old, women are also more likely than men of the same age to suffer a disability, partly because some conditions, such as arthritis, are more likely to affect women than men (Walker, 1987).

Both disability and old age are associated, however, with poverty. Women with a disability are particularly likely to suffer poverty as a result of their greater dependence on benefits not linked to National Insurance contributions, and which are paid at a lower rate. Thus women are more likely to receive the Severe Disability Allowance and men to receive benefits related to industrial injury and war disablement (Lonsdale, 1990). In addition, women who suffer a disability are less likely to take part in rehabilitation programmes, which are largely male oriented. Lonsdale (1990) cites one study where women made up a mere 12 per cent of those in rehabilitation programmes, which are most likely to be offering occupational rehabilitation for young men with spinal injuries.

Whilst gender intersects with disability to create a double jeopardy, rates of disability are also higher amongst ethnic minority groups: Afro-Caribbean households suffer a higher rate of disability than white households or Indian households (Lonsdale, 1990).

People with a disability – at all ages – are also likely to have greater needs, which are mostly unmet by the social security system. Needing to have heating on for longer periods, requiring special transport or taxis rather than buses, having to replace clothes which wear out more quickly, or having more washing as a result of incontinence means that the cost of living is greater, whilst people with a disability are more likely to be amongst the poorest in the country. Figures from the Households Below Average Income tables of 1987/88 show a disproportionate number of households in the lowest income group headed by someone with a disability.

Managing on a low income is made more difficult by the fact that these increased costs are not met by the benefits system. Changes to social security payments have removed or eroded the added-on value of payments to meet these extra needs – for example, the disability premium which is added to income support payments was £15.40 for a single person or for a household with a child with a disability in 1990–91. This is to meet the extra heating, diet, washing, travel costs of people who might require bedding and clothing to be washed every day, and dried in time to be replaced, who might need heating on throughout the day, and who rely on special transport or taxis to carry out even everyday tasks. Special clothing, footwear and other needs are also to be met from this premium, which hardly compensates for the low level of basic benefit, and certainly is unlikely to provide for future income needs. People with a disability are not only likely to be in low-income groups as a result of restricted access to the labour market; this in turn affects poverty in old age, for these are groups who will be dependent on means-tested benefits over retirement age also.

Wealth accumulation – in the form of owner-occupied housing as well as private pension plans – is virtually impossible for women with a disability who are not in the labour market, and this also increases their likelihood of poverty in later life. Age itself is significantly associated with poverty for women in particular, as a result of increased life expectancy and decreased years in the labour market, through which future prosperity is bought. This too has changed in the recent past and, as discussed in Chapter 3, women's opportunities to purchase an occupational pension through the State Earnings Related Pension scheme (SERPs) have been reduced with the substantial contraction in that scheme. Women's ability to rely on the pension bought by their partner's paid employment increases once more their economic dependency and their vulnerability to poverty outside this relationship, and future years are likely to see a growing number of women reliant on means-tested support in their old age and surviving on the barest of poverty lines.

The impact of these factors on health is again complex – disability often predetermines responses to health questions and suggests that the task of unravelling the relationship between poor health and poverty for people with a disability is not only difficult, but also of limited value. Overall, however, the role of gender is related to the impact of this combination of disability and poverty: women with a disability are more likely to be poor, and to be poorer, than men, as a result of the operation of a discourse of femininity in which women are seen as having a secondary connection to the labour market –

through a male 'breadwinner'. Thus gender operates to protect the income of a man with a disability more than that of a woman, and whilst both sexes are poor this is an experience mediated by gender.

## Health, poverty and sexuality

The final way in which the experience of poverty and deprivation, and its consequences for health, varies is in relation to sexuality. Here again a number of different dimensions combine – the experience of both gay men and lesbians is of oppression: in the labour market and paid employment, in the criminal justice system, and in the law (Galloway, 1983; Weeks, 1985; Taylor, 1986). Increased risk of violent attack on the streets combines with decreased police protection to create quite specific health effects for both gay men and lesbians (Boogaard, 1989; Focas, 1989).

However, discrimination and heterosexism in the workplace mean gay men and lesbians are more likely to occupy lower-paid employment, be passed over for promotion and to lose the paid employment they have. The presentation of AIDs and HIV-related disorders in the media as a gay plague has increased both violent attack and discrimination in places of work and leisure, whilst discrimination within the health and allied services operates at an individual level and at the level of policy to deny resources and services to those who need them (Aggleton and Homans, 1988).

Deprivation in housing is the most marked example of this discrimination: the owner-occupied housing market has become more difficult for gay men to enter as a result of AIDs test requirements by building societies and life assurance companies. At the same time, discriminatory principles in the public sector exclude non-heterosexual couples from council housing, on the basis that local authorities are not required to house 'single' people, a category which for most local authorities includes couples of the same sex. For those who have managed to buy into the owner-occupied sector in advance of AIDs testing, the loss of paid employment, particularly after being diagnosed as HIV-positive or as having the AIDs complex, is likely to lead to difficulty in paying mortgage costs, and loss of housing, with few other options open.

Looking at the specific experience of women, lesbians suffer particular forms of discrimination in employment: specifically forms of sexual harassment related to both their gender and their sexuality (Taylor, 1986; Pringle, 1988). In the criminal justice system, lesbians have been subjected to specific forms of abuse again related to gender as well as their sexuality – bodysearches, for example, and questioning on their sex lives (Galloway, 1983). Other studies have shown how the fear of harassment and assault on public transport operates to limit both the use of public transport by lesbians, and to force lesbians to modify their behaviour in a way not expected of heterosexual couples (Focas, 1989).

A further form of discrimination relates to the use of reproductive technology, where lesbians wishing to have children are denied access to health service artificial-insemination-by-donor programmes, and are more likely to turn to friends and contacts. The health risks of donor insemination which result from the spread of AIDs and HIV disorders means again that there are health implications for all women who choose to have children this way, but that these are increased where women do not have access to artificial-insemination programmes where some form of testing is at least possible.

The effect of discrimination in the labour market and in the operation of social policy is an increased risk of poverty: a greater risk of unemployment, greater difficulty in providing for old age as a result of heterosexist assumptions in the operation of insurance and occupational pension schemes, and more difficulty in accumulating wealth in this form and in owner-occupied housing. In addition, lesbians are likely to suffer other kinds of deprivation, such as violence on the street and the increased fear of violence.

The health consequences of these experiences cannot be overestimated: harassment and violence, the failure of services to provide for specific needs combines with the stress of suffering discrimination and heterosexist abuse, and of being unable to lead the life others take for granted – such as the open expression of affection in public. These are effects specifically related to sexuality which add onto the health consequences of poverty and deprivation. However, once more the impact for women is different, and whilst lesbians share many of the same experiences of oppression with gay men, their experience is also mediated by gender. So, for example, they share with all women the risk of sexual attack, low pay, sexual harassment, the failure of the social security system to adequately provide for women with children, and so on.

## Conclusion

World-wide, what makes women poor, and what makes women ill? These are the themes of this book, which has focused on women in developed countries and more specifically, on women in Britain. However, can the answers to these themes in relation to Britain and the West be extracted to explain in the wider sense why women suffer higher rates of illness, and suffer more poverty, than their male counterparts. And can a model be constructed which allows for the intersection of different factors of oppression, which does not prioritize gender over race, class or other forms of oppression but which explores gender as one facet of experience which is mediated by these other dimensions?

## Women and poverty

Women are poor as a result of economic dependency needs which are not met. They are vulnerable to poverty even in affluent homes because resources are not shared equally within the household. They are vulnerable to poverty throughout their lives as a result of the assumption in the labour market and in government policy in the vast majority of countries that women are economically supported by a male breadwinner, whose earnings are sufficient to provide for the needs of the household and who is the person to whom support should be directed if these earnings are not adequate.
Women, then, are poor because they are paid less than men, receive fewer advantages such as an occupational pension, sick pay, and other occupational benefits. Women are less able to take paid employment as a result of the corollary of this discourse of economic dependency – women's private work in the home. Women perform the vast majority of the world's domestic and caring labour – providing food, a task which includes buying foodstuffs, or growing crops, and turning this into food for consumption. Women do the work which sustains life – whether it is fetching water, washing clothes, cleaning the home, or providing a hygienic, safe environment. Women do the caring work, the work which reproduces the next generation and which extends beyond pregnancy and childbirth, to caring for the new infant, and educating the child in the skills of life.

The location of women in the labour market, in the provision of government income support systems, and in development projects (Rogers, 1980; Karlekar, 1982) is as secondary employees, primary homemakers, who are supported by men.

Women who cannot rely on male earnings will be poor where they cannot take paid employment themselves – if they are too old to find work in a labour market which does not want older workers, if they have small children in a society where childcare is seen as women's work and alternative care is either non-existent or too expensive to be bought out of women's earnings, if they have other dependants who must be cared for where no other care is available, and if they are not able to find paid employment in a labour market which does not need women's work or where ideologies of seclusion or exclusion prevent women entering the public world of employment outside the home.

Women will also be poor when they are in paid employment and the pay is too low for their needs, and poor in households where neither partner can earn enough to maintain an income above the barest minimum. Women are also poor in comparison with men when their pay is below the earnings of men, and when they cannot provide for their old age or sickness because they are not eligible for occupational schemes, or paid maternity leave to have children, or paid parental leave to care for sick children.

## Women and health

The health consequences of poverty for all people are enormous, and people from low-income backgrounds are more likely at every age to die in comparison with their better-off counterparts. However, it has been argued here that the health consequences for women might explain the apparent paradox in women's health: that women live longer than men but, no matter how it is measured, suffer more health problems and illness than men during the course of their lives. To some extent this reflects greater longevity, but it also reflects women's poorer health, both physical and mental, and their greater likelihood of suffering a disability.

The ways in which poverty and deprivation interact with women's experience as women, and with other aspects of their experience – as black women and women of colour, women with a disability, older women, women who are lesbians and women of working-class backgrounds – are numerous, complex and impossible to rank or prioritize. What this book has tried to do is to explore further the nature of women's poverty, and the nature of women's health risks, to assess the consequences for women's health, and women's lives, of suffering poverty and deprivation. This is not to argue that men do not also suffer poverty, or that the health risks for men are not also great. The high rates of premature mortality amongst lower class men testify to the severe cost to men's health of inadequate income, housing deprivation, occupational risk and stress, and so on.

Whilst the health consequences of poverty for both sexes are serious, ultimately the experience of women differs from that of men in substantial respects, as a result of women's position in the labour market and in the home. It is this positioning, and the work women are called upon to do, and the care women give, which structures women's patterns of health – in response to other components of their lives, such as age or disability, and in response to the material resources they have with which to carry out this work and meet these demands. Women's lives are, at the end of the day, made up of caring work, of secondary employment in the labour market, of economic dependence and vulnerabilty, and of social deprivation. Against this are, without doubt, the pleasures of caring, and the strength women draw from their children, partners and from each other. It is these complex set of factors influencing women's lives which must be thought through in order to understand not only the health experience of women, but also the continued and widening inqualities in health which exist today in both the developed and developing world.

# BIBLIOGRAPHY

Abbott, P. and Payne, G. (eds.) (1990), *New Directions in the Sociology of Health* (London: Falmer Press)

Afshar, H. and Agarwal, B. (eds.) (1989), *Women, Poverty and Ideology in Asia* (London: Macmillan)

Aggleton, P. (1990), *Health* (London: RKP)

Aggleton, P. and Homans, H. (eds.) (1988), *Social Aspects of Aids* (London: Falmer Press)

Alcock, P. (1987), *Poverty and State Support* (London: Longman)

Allen, S. and Wolkowitz, C. (1987), *Homeworking* (Basingstoke: Macmillan Education)

Altman, D. (ed.) (1989), *Homosexuality? Which Homosexuality?* International Conference on Gay and Lesbian Studies (London: GMP)

Andrews, K and Jacobs, J. (1990), *Punishing the Poor: Poverty under Thatcher* (London: Macmillan)

Ansen, O. (1988), 'Living arrangements and women's health', *Social Science and Medicine*, vol. 26, pp. 201–8

Arber, S. (1987), 'Social class, non-employment and chronic illness: Continuing the inequalities in health debate', *British Medical Journal*, 294, pp. 1069–73

Arber, S. (1989), 'Gender and class inequalities in health: Understanding the differentials', in J. Fox (ed.), *Health Inequalities in European Countries* (Aldershot: Gower)

Arber, S. (1990a), 'Opening the "Black Box": Inequalities in women's health', in P. Abbott and G. Payne (eds.), *New Directions in the Sociology of Health* (London: Falmer Press)

Arber, S. (1990b), 'Revealing women's health: Re-analysing the General Household Survey', in H. Roberts (1990), *Women's Health Counts* (London: Routledge)

Arber, S., Gilbert, N. and Dale, A. (1985), 'Paid employment and women's health: A benefit or source of role strain?', *Sociology of Health and Illness*, 7, pp. 375–400

Atkinson, A.B. (1985), *How Should We Measure Poverty: Some conceptual issues*, Discussion Paper no. 82, Symposium on statistics for the Measurement of Poverty (ESRC)

Atkinson, A.B. (1989), *Poverty and Social Security* (Hemel Hempstead: Harvester Wheatsheaf)

Austerberry, H., Schott, K. and Watson, S. (1984), *Homeless in London 1971–81* (London: ICERD)

Bagilhole, B. (1986), *Invisible Workers: Women's experience of outworking in Nottinghamshire* (Nottingham: University of Nottingham)

Balarajan, R. and Bulusu, L. (1990), 'Mortality among immigrants in England and Wales, 1979–83', in M. Britton (ed.), *Mortality and Geography: A review in the mid-1980s* (London: HMSO)

Balarajan, R. and Raleigh, V. S. (1990), 'Variations in perinatal, neonatal, postneonatal and infant mortality by mother's country of birth', in M. Britton (ed.), *Mortality and Geography: A review in the mid-1980s* (London: HMSO)

Barker, W. (1990), 'Women and cancer', *Empowerment*, 1, 4, Spring 1990

Barrett, M. and Roberts, H. (1978), 'Doctors and their patients: The social control of women in general practice', in C. Smart and B. Smart (eds.), *Women, Sexuality and Social Control* (London: RKP)

Baron, R.D. and Norris, G.M. (1976), 'Sexual divisions and the dual labour market', in D.L. Barker and S. Allen (eds.), *Dependence and Exploitation in Work and Marriage* (London: Longman)

Barton, R. (1959), *Institutional Neurosis* (Bristol: John Wright)

Bebbington, A.C. (1988), 'The expectation of life without disability in England and Wales', *Social Science and Medicine*, 27, pp. 321–6

Beechey, V. (1987), *Unequal Work* (London: Verso)

Beechey, V. and Whitelegg, E. (1986), *Women in Britain Today* (Milton Keynes: Open University Press)

Belle, D. (1980), 'Who uses mental health facilties?', in M. Guttentag *et al.* (eds.), *The Mental Health of Women* (New York: Academic Press)

Belle, D. (1984), 'Inequality and mental health: Low income and minority women', in L.E. Waler (ed.), *Women and Mental Health Policy* (London: Sage)

Belle, D. (ed.) (1982), *Lives in Stress: Women and depression* (Beverly Hills: Sage)

Belle, D. and Goldman, N. (1980), 'Patterns of diagnoses received by men and women', in M.Guttentag *et al.* (eds.), *The Mental Health of Women* (New York: Academic Press)

Benzeval, M. and Judge, K. (1990), *Deprivation, Health and Inequality*, paper presented to Social Policy Association Annual Conference, July 1990, Bath

Beral, V. (1985), 'Long-term effects of childbearing on health', *Journal of Epidemiology and Community Health*, 37, pp. 313–46

Beral, V. (1987), 'Have the changes in women's employment affected their health?', in H. Graheme (ed.), *Women, Health and Work* (London: Women's Medical Federation)

Bereria, L. (ed.) (1982), *Women and Development: The sexual division of labour in rural societies* (New York: Praeger)

Bereria, L. and Stimpson, C. (eds.) (1987), *Women, Households and the Economy* (New York: Rutgers University Press)

Bernard, J. (1972), *The Future of Marriage* (New York: World Publications)

Berthoud, R. (1989), *Credit, Debt and Poverty* (London: HMSO)

Beveridge, W. (1942), *Social Insurance and Allied Services* (London: HMSO)

Bhat, A., Carr-Hill, R. and Ohri, S. (eds.) (1988), *Britain's Black Population* (Aldershot: Gower)

Binney, V., Harkell, G. and Nixon, J. (1981), *Leaving Violent Men: A study of refuges and housing for battered women* (London: Women's Aid Federation)

Black Report (1980), report on the working party on inequalities in health, chaired by Sir Douglas Black (London: DHSS)

Blackman, T., Evason, E., Melaugh, M. and Woods, R. (1989), 'Housing and health: A case study of two areas in West Belfast', *Journal of Social Policy*, 18, 1–26

Blaxter, M. (1981), *The Health of the Children* (London: Heinemann)

Blaxter, M. (1983), 'The causes of disease: Women talking', *Social Science and Medicine*, 17, pp. 59–69

Blaxter, M. (1987), 'Evidence in inequality in health from a National Survey', *The Lancet*, ii, pp. 30–3

Blaxter, M. (1989), 'A comparison of measures of inequality in morbidity', in J. Fox (ed.), *Health Inequalities in European Countries* (Aldershot: Gower)

Blaxter, M. (1990), *Health and Lifestyles* (London: Routledge)

Boogaard, H. Van (1989), 'Blood furious underneath the skin', in D. Altman (ed.) (1989), *Homosexuality? Which Homosexuality?*, International Conference on Gay and Lesbian Studies (London: GMP)

Booth, C. (1969), *Life and Labour of the People in London* (London: Hutchinson)

Booth, M. and Beral, V. (1989), 'Cervical cancer deaths in young women', *The Lancet*, 616

Boserup, E. (1986), *Women's Role in Economic Development* (Aldershot: Gower)

Boyd-Orr, J. (1937), *Food, Health and Income* (London: Macmillan)

Bradshaw, J. (1989), *Lone Parents: Policy in the doldrums* (London: Family Policy Studies Centre)

Bradshaw, J. and Morgan, J. (1987), *Budgeting on Benefit* (London: Family Policy Studies Centre)

Brannen, J. (1987), *Taking Maternity Leave: The employment decisions of women with young children* (London: Thomas Coram Research Unit)

Brannen, J. and Moss, P. (1987), 'Dual Earner Households: Women's financial contributions after the birth of the first child', in J. Brannen and G. Wilson (eds.), *Give and Take in Families: Studies in resource distribution* (London: Allen and Unwin)

Brannen, J. and Wilson, G. (eds.) (1987), *Give and Take in Families: Studies in resource distribution* (London: Allen and Unwin)

Brenner, M. (1973), *Mental Illness and the Economy* (Cambridge, Mass.: Harvard University Press)

Britton, M, (ed.) (1990), *Mortality and Geography: A review in the mid-1980s* (London: HMSO)

Britton, M., Fox, A.J., Goldblatt, P., Jones, D.R. and Rosata, M. (1990), 'The influence of socio-economic and environmental factors on geographic variation in mortality', in M. Britton (ed.), *Mortality and Geography: A review in the mid-1980s* (London: HMSO)

Broverman, I.K., Broverman, D., Clarkson, F. Rosenkrantz, P. and Vogel, S. (1970), 'Sex role stereotypes and clinical judgements of mental health', *Journal of Consulting and Clinical Psychology*, 34, pp. 1–7

Brown, G.W., Bhrolchain, M.N. and Harris, T. (1975), 'Social class and psychiatric disturbance among women in an urban population', *Sociology*, 9, pp. 225–48

Brown, G.W. and Harris, T. (1978), *Social Origins of Depression: A study of psychiatric disorder in women* (London: Tavistock)

Brown, J.C. (ed.) (1984), *Anti-Poverty Policy in the European Community* (London: Policy Studies Institute)

Brown, M. (1974), *Sweated Labour: A study of homework*, Low Pay Pamplet no. 1 (London: Low Pay Unit)

Bryan, B., Dadzie, A. and Scafe, S. (1985), *The Heart of the Race* (London: Virago)

Brydon, L. and Chant, S. (1989), *Women in the Third World* (Aldershot: Elgar)

Bryson, L. (1988), 'Women as welfare recipients: Women, poverty and the State', in B. Cass and C.V. Baldock (eds.), *Women, Social Welfare and the State* (Sydney: Unwin Hyman)

Buglass, D. (1976), 'The relation of social class to the characteristics and treatment of parasuicide', *Social Psychiatry*, 11, pp. 107–19

Burr, M.L. (1986), 'Damp housing and respiratory disease', paper presented at the Conference of Unhealthy Housing, University of Warwick.

Butler, N.R. and Golding, J. (1986), *From Birth to Five: A study of the health and behaviour of Britain's five-year-olds* (Pergamon Press)

Byrne, D., Harrison, S.P., Keithley, J. and McCarthy, P. (1986), *Housing and Health: The relationship between housing conditions and the health of council tenants* (Aldershot: Gower)

Callender, C. (1987), 'Redundancy, unemployment and poverty', in C. Glendinning and J. Millar (eds.), *Women and Poverty in Britain* (Brighton: Wheatsheaf)

Calnan, M. (1984), 'The health belief model and participation in programmes for the early detection of breast cancer: A comparative analysis', *Social Science and Medicine*, 19, pp. 823–30

Calnan, M. (1987), *Health and Illness: The lay perspective* (London: Tavistock)

Calnan, M. and Johnson, B. (1985), 'Health, health risks and inequalities: An exploratory survey', *Sociology of Health and Illness*, 7, pp. 55–75

Carr-Hill, R. (1987), 'The inequalities in health debate: A critical review of the issues', *Journal of Social Policy*, 16, pp. 509–42

Cass, B. (1988), 'Redistribution to children and to mothers: A history of child endowment and family allowances', in B. Cass and C.V. Baldock (eds.), *Women, Social Welfare and the State* (Sydney: Unwin Hyman)

Central Statistical Office (1990), *Annual Abstract of Statistics* (London: HMSO)

Challis, L. and Hutchins, J. (1990), *The New Occupational Welfare*, paper presented to Social Policy Association Annual Conference, July 1990, Bath

Charles, N. and Kerr, M. (1987), 'Just the way it is: Gender and age differences in family food consumption', in J. Brannen and G. Wilson (eds.), *Give and Take in Families: Studies in resource distribution* (London: Allen and Unwin)

Charles, N. and Kerr, M. (1988), *Women, Food and Families* (Manchester: Manchester University Press)

Chernin, K. (1978), *Womansize: The tyranny of slenderness* (London: Women's Press)

Chesler, P. (1974), *Women and Madness* (London: Allen Lane)

Clark, W.A.V., Freeman, H.E., Kane, R. and Lewis, C.E. (1987), 'The influence of domestic position on health status', *Social Science and Medicine*, vol. 24, pp., 501–6

Cochrane, R. (1983), *The Social Creation of Mental Illness* (London: Longman)

Cochrane, R. and Stopes-Roe, M. (1981), 'Women, marriage, employment and mental health', *British Journal of Psychiatry*, 139, pp. 373–81

Coie-Hamilton, I. (1987), 'Food and poverty in the 1980s', *Radical Community Medicine*, pp. 37–39

Cole-Hamilton, I. and Lang, T. (1986), *Tightening Belts* (London: The London Food Commission Promotions Ltd)

Cole-Hamilton, I., Durward, L. and Conway, J. (1988), *Prescription for Poor Health: The health crisis for homeless families* (London: London Food Commission, Maternity Alliance, SHAC and Shelter)

Cook, D.A.G. and Morgan, H.G. (1982), 'Families in High-Rise Flats', *British Medical Journal*, pp. 284, 846

Cook, J. and Watt, S. (1987), 'Racism, women and poverty', in C. Glendinning and J. Millar (eds.), *Women and Poverty in Britain* (Brighton: Wheatsheaf)

Cornwell, J. (1984), *Hard-Earned Lives: Accounts of health and illness from East London* (London: Tavistock)

Cortes-Majo, M., Garcia-Gil, C. and Viciana, F. (1990), 'The role of the social condition of women in the decline of maternal and female mortality', *International Journal of Health Services*, 20, pp. 315–28

Cox, B., Blaxter, M. *et al.* (1987), *The Health and Lifestyle Survey* (London: Health Promotion Research Trust)

Cox, G. (1989), *Working Women: A study of pay and hours* (Greater Manchester: Greater Manchester Low Pay Unit)

Craig, G. and Glendinning, C. (1990), 'Parenting in poverty', *Community Care*, 13 March 1990, pp. 24–7

Daly, M. (1989), *Women and Poverty* (Dublin: Attic Press)

Daniel, W. (1980), *Maternity Rights: The experience of women* (London: Policy Studies Institute)

Davis, D.L. and Low, S.M. (1989), *Gender, Health and Illness: The case of nerves* (New York: Hemisphere)

Daykin, N. (1989), *Unhealthy Transitions: Young women, health and work in the 1980s* (Bristol: University of Bristol PhD thesis)

Daykin, N. (1990), Health and work in the 1990s: Towards a new perspective', in P. Abbott and G. Payne (eds.), *New Directions in the Sociology of Health* (London: Falmer Press)

Deem, R. (1988), *All Work and No Play: The sociology of leisure* (Milton Keynes: Open University Press)

Delphy, C. (1984), *Close to Home: A materialist analysis of women's oppression* (London: Hutchinson)

Dennet, J. (ed.) (1982), *Europe Against Poverty: The European poverty programme 1975–80* (London: Bedford Square Press)

Department of Employment (1990), *Family Expenditure Survey 1988* (London: HMSO)

Department of Employment (1990), *New Earnings Survey* (London: HMSO)

Department of Health (1989), *Income Support Statistics, Annual Enquiry, 1988* (London: HMSO)

Department of Health (1990), *Health and Personal Social Services Statistics for England* (London: HMSO)

Department of Health and Social Security (1984), *Committee on Medical Aspects on Diet and Cardio-vascular Disease* (London: HMSO)

Department of Health and Social Security (1988), *Households Below Average Income 1981–85* (London: HMSO)

Department of Health and Social Security (1988), *Low Income Families Statistics, 1985* (London: HMSO)

Department of Social Security (1989), *Social Security Statistics, 1989* (London: HMSO)

Department of Social Security (1990), *Households Below Average Income, 1981–87: A statistical analysis* (London: Government Statistical Services)

Dex, S. (1984), *Women's Work Histories: An analysis of the women and employment survey* (London: Department of Employment)

Dex, S. (1985), *The Sexual Division of Work: Conceptual revolutions in the social sciences* (Hemel Hempstead: Harvester Wheatsheaf)

Dohrenwend, B.P. and Dohrenwend, B.S. (1969), *Social Status and Psychological Disorder* (New York: John Wiley)

Dohrenwend, B.P. and Dohrenwend, B.S. (1974), *Stressful Life Events: Their nature and effects* (New York: John Wiley)

Doll, R. and Peto, R. (1981), *The Causes of Cancer* (Oxford: Oxford University Press)

Donovan, J. (1986), *We Don't Buy Sickness: It just comes* (Aldershot: Gower)

Douglas-Wood, A. (1974), 'The fashionable diseases: Women's complaints and their treatment in nineteenth-century America', in M. Hartman and L. Banner (eds.), *Clio's Consciousness Raised* (New York: Harper and Row)

Dowling, S. (1983), *Health for a Change: The provision of preventive health care in pregnancy and early adulthood* (London: Child Poverty Action Group)

Doyal, L. (1979), *The Political Economy of Health* (London: Pluto)

Doyal, L. (1985), 'Women and the National Health Service: The carers and the careless', in E. Lewin and V. Oleson (eds.) (1985), *Women, Health and Healing: Toward a New Perspective* (London: Tavistock)

Doyal, L. (1988), *Promoting Women's Health*, unpublished article (Bristol: Department of Nursing Health and Applied Social Studies)

Doyal, L. and Elston, M.A. (1983), *Medicine and Health*, Open University Course U221, 'The changing experience of women' (Milton Keynes: O.U. Enterprises)

Dunham, H.W. (1964), 'Social class and schizophrenia', *American Journal of Orthopsychiatry*, 34, pp. 634–42

Dunnell, K. and Cartwright, A. (1972), *Medicine Takers, Prescribers and Hoarders* (London: RKP)

Durward, L. (1984), *Poverty in Pregnancy: The cost of an adequate diet* (London: Maternity Alliance)

Dworkin, R.J. and Adams, G.L. (1984), 'Pharmacotherapy of the chronic patient: gender and diagnostic factors', *Community Mental Health Journal*, 20, pp. 28–61

Eastwood, M.R. and Trevelyan, M.H. (1972), 'The relationship between physical and psychiatric disorder', *Psychological Medicine*, 2, pp. 363–72

Eekelaar, J. and Maclean, M. (1986), *Maintenance after Divorce* (Oxford: Clarendon Press)

Ehrenreich, B. and English, D. (1979), *For Her Own Good: 150 years of the expert's advice to women* (London: Pluto Press)

Eichenbaum, L. and Orbach, S. (1983), *Understanding Women* (Harmondsworth: Penguin)

Elias, P. (1988), 'Family formation, occupational mobility and part-time work', in A. Hunt (ed.), *Women and Paid Work: Issues of equality* (Basingstoke: Macmillan)

English House Condition Survey (1986), (London, HMSO)

Erikson, E. (1965), *Childhood and Society* (Harmondsworth: Penguin)

Ermish, J. (1989), *Welfare Benefits and Lone Parents Employment* (London: National Institute of Economic and Social Research)

Ernst, S. and Goodison, L. (1981), *In Our Own Hands* (London: Women's Press)

Evandrou, M., Falkingham, J., Legrand, J. and Winter, D. (1990), *Equity in Health and Social Care*, paper presented to Social Policy Association Annual Conference, July 1990, Bath

Evason, E. (1980), *Ends that Won't Meet* (London: Child Poverty Action Group)

Eyer, J. and Sterling. P. (1977), 'Stress related mortality and social organization', *Review of Radical Political Economics*, 9, pp. 1–37

Fagin, L. and Little, M. (1984), *The Foresaken Families* (Harmondsworth: Pelican)

Fanning, D.M. (1967), 'Families in flats', *British Medical Journal*, 4, pp. 382–86

Faris, R.E. and Dunham, H.W. (1939), *Mental Disorders in Urban Areas* (Chicago: University of Chicago Press)

Fenton, S. (1986), *Race, Health and Welfare* (Bristol: University of Bristol, Department of Sociology)

Ferguson, A. (1986), 'Women's health in a marginal area of Kenya', *Social Science and Medicine*, vol. 23, pp. 17–29

Field, F. (1981), *Inequality in Britain: Freedom, welfare and the State* (London: Fontana)

Field, F. (1987), *Freedom and Wealth in a Socialist Future* (London: Fontana)

Fisher, G., Joseph, D. and Ward, P. (1986), *Black Single Mothers in Brent: Some issues, policies and responses: A pilot study* (London: Brent Black Workers Support Group)

Focas, C. (1989), 'A survey of women's travel needs in London', in M. Grieco *et al.* (eds.), *Gender, Transport and Employment* (Aldershot: Avebury)

Fondation pour la récherche sociale (1980), *Poverty and the Anti-poverty policies* (France: Fondation pour la Recherche Social)

Forest, R. and Murie, A. (1988), *Selling the Welfare State: The privatization of public housing* (London: RKP)

Foucault, M. (1967), *Madness and Civilisation: A history of insanity in the Age of Reason* (London: Tavistock)

Fox, A.J. and Goldblatt, P.O. (1982), *Longitudinal Study: Socio-demographic mortality differentials, 1971–75, Series L5 (1)* (London: HMSO)

Fox, J. (ed.) (1989), *Health Inequalities in European Countries* (Aldershot: Gower)

Fraser, D. (1984), *The Evolution of the British Welfare State* (London: Macmillan)

French, M. (1985), 'Women and work', in *Women: A world report* (London: Methuen)

Fry, V. and Pashardes, P. (1985), 'Distributional aspects of inflation: Who has suffered most?' *Fiscal Studies*, November 1985, pp. 21–9

Gabe, J. and Williams, P. (1986), *Women, Housing and Mental Health*, paper presented at the conference 'Unhealthy housing: A diagnosis' (University of Warwick)

Galloway, B. (ed.) (1983), *Prejudice and Pride: Discrimination against gay people in Modern Britain* (London: RKP)

*General Household Survey, 1981* (London: OPCS)

*General Household Survey, 1989* (London: OPCS)

*General Household Survey, 1990* (London: OPCS)

General Municipal Boilermakers and Allied Trades Union (GMB) (1987), *Health and Safety for Women* (London: GMB)

George, V. (1988), *Wealth, Poverty and Starvation: An international perspective* (Brighton: Harvester Wheatsheaf)

George, V. and Lawson, R. (eds.) (1980), *Poverty and Inequality in Common Market Countries* (London: RKP)

George, V. and Wilding, P. (1972), *Motherless Families* (London: RKP)

Gillis, A.R. (1977), 'High-rise housing and psychological strain', *Journal of Health and Social Behaviour*, 18, pp. 418–31

Gilloran, J.L. (1968), 'Social health problems associated with "High living"', *Medical Officer*, 120, pp. 117–18

Glendinning, C. and Craig, G. (1990), 'The trickle away effect', *Community Care*, 22 March 1990, pp. 21–3

Glendinning, C. and Millar, J. (eds.) (1987), *Women and Poverty in Britain* (Hemel Hempstead: Harvester Wheatsheaf)

Goffman, E. (1968), *Asylums* (Harmondsworth: Penguin)

Goldberg, D. and Huxley, P. (1980), *Mental Illness in the Community* (London: Tavistock)

Goldberg, E.M. and Morrison, S.L. (1963), 'Schizophrenia and Social Class', *British Journal of Psychiatry*, 109, pp. 785–802

Goldblatt, P. (ed.) (1990), *Longitudinal Study: Mortality and Social Organisation* (London: HMSO)

Goldman, N. and Ravid, R. (1980), 'Community Surveys: Sex differences in mental illness', in M. Guttentag *et al.* (eds.), *The Mental Health of Women* (New York: Academic Press)

Gove, W.R., Hughes, M. and Galle, O.R. (1979), 'Overcrowding in the home: An empirical investigation of its possible consequences', *American Sociological Review*, 44, pp. 59–80

Gove, W.R. and Tudor, J.F. (1973), 'Adult sex roles and mental illness', *American Journal of Sociology*, 78, pp. 813–35

Graham, H. (1984), *Women, Health and the Family* (London: Tavistock)

Graham, H. (1985), 'Providers, negotiators and mediators: Women as the hidden carers', in E. Lewin and V. Oleson (eds.), *Women, Health and Healing: Toward a new perspective* (London: Tavistock)

Graham, H. (1986), *Caring for the Family* (London: Health Education Council)

Graham, H. (1987a), 'Being poor: Perceptions and coping strategies of lone mothers', in J. Brannen and G. Wilson (eds.), *Give and Take in Families: Studies in resource distribution* (London: Allen and Unwin)

Graham, H. (1987b), 'Women's smoking and family health', *Social Science and Medicine*, vol. 25, pp. 47–56

Graham, H. (1987c), 'Women's poverty and caring', in C. Glendinning and J. Millar (eds.), *Women and Poverty in Britain* (Brighton: Wheatsheaf)

Graham, H. (1990), 'Behaving well: Women's health behaviour in context', in H. Roberts (1990), *Women's Health Counts* (London: Routledge)

Graham, H. and Popay, J. (eds.) (1988), *Women and Poverty: Exploring the research and policy agenda* (London: Thomas Coram Research Centre and University of Warwick)

Graheme, H. (ed.) (1987), *Women, Health and Work: Proceedings of a symposium presented by the Medical Women's Federation* (London: Women's Medical Federation)

Gregory, J., Foster, K., Tyler, H. and Wisemen, M. (1990), *Dietary and*

Nutrition Survey of British Adults (London: HMSO)

Grieco, M., Pickup, L. and Whipp, R. (eds.) (1990), *Gender, Transport and Employment* (Aldershot: Gower)

Grimsley, M. and Bhat, A. (1988), 'Health', in A. Bhat, R. Carr-Hill and S. Ohri (eds.), *Britain's Black Population* (Aldershot: Gower)

Groves, D. (1987), 'Occupational pension provision and women's poverty in old age', in C. Glendinning and J. Millar (eds.), *Women and Poverty in Britain* (Brighton: Wheatsheaf)

Gulati, L. (1982), *Profiles in Female Poverty: A study of five poor working women in Kerala* (Oxford: Pergamon Press)

Guttentag, M., Salasin, S. and Belle, D. (eds.) (1980), *The Mental Health of Women* (New York: Academic Press)

Haavio-Mannila, E. (1986), 'Inequalities in health and gender', *Social Science and Medicine*, vol. 22, pp. 141–9

Haines, F.A., and De Looy, A.E. (1986), *Can I afford the diet? The effect of low income on people's eating habits, with particular reference to groups at risk* (Birmingham: British Dietetic Association)

Hakim, C. (1979), *Occupational Segregation* (London: Department of Employment)

Hakim, C. (1987), *Home-based Work in Britain: A report on the 1981 National Homeworking Survey* (London: Department of Employment)

Hamilton, K. and Gregory, A. (1989), 'Women, transport and health', *Radical Community Medicine*, 38, pp. 15–17

Hamilton, K. and Jenkins, L. (1989), 'Why women and travel?' in M. Grieco *et al.* (eds.), *Gender, Transport and Employment* (Aldershot: Avebury)

Hanna, E. (ed.) (1988), *Poverty in Ireland*, 30th Annual Summer School of Social Study Conference (Cork: Social Study Conference)

Harbury, C.D. and Hitchins, D. (1979), *Inheritance and Wealth Inequalities in Britain* (London: Allen and Unwin)

Hare, E.H. (1956), 'Mental illness and social conditions in Bristol', *Journal of Mental Science*, 102, pp. 349–57

Harkey, J., Miles, D.L., and Rushing, W.A. (1976), 'The relation between social class and functional status: A new look at the drift hypothesis', *Journal of Health and Social Behaviour*, 17, pp. 194–204

Harrington, M. (1962), *The Other America: Poverty in the United States* (New York: Macmillan)

Harrington, M. (1977), *The Vast Majority: A journey to the world's poor* (New York: Simon and Schuster)

Harrington, M. (1988), *The New American Poverty* (New York: Firethorn Press)

Hart, N. (1985), *The Sociology of Health and Medicine* (Lancashire: Causeway Press)

Hart, N. (1987), 'Social class still reigns', *Poverty*, 67, pp. 17–19

Hart, N. (1989), 'Sex, gender and survival: Inequalities of life chances between European men and women', in J. Fox (ed.), *Health Inequalities in European Countries* (Aldershot: Gower)

Hewitt, M. (1958), *Wives and Mothers in Victorian Industry* (London: Rockcliffe)

Hewlett, S.A. (1987), *A Lesser Life: The myth of women's liberation* (Harmondsworth: Penguin)

Hill, M. (1990), *Social Security Policy in Britain* (Aldershot: Edward Elgar)

Hodgkinson, N. (1988), *The Screen Test, Sunday Times*, 17 July

Hodgkinson, N. (1989), *Screening the Right Woman, Sunday Times*, 8 January

Holden, K.C. (1990), 'Women's economic status in old age and widowhood', in M.N. Ozawa (ed.), *Women's Life Cycle and Economic Insecurity: Problems and proposals* (New York: Praeger)

Hollingshead, A.B. and Redlich, F. (1958), *Social Class and Mental Illness* (New York: John Wiley)

House of Commons Social Services Committee (1987–88), *Families on Low Incomes: Fourth Report* (London: HMSO)

Howe, G., Westhoff, C. Vesset, M. and Yeales, D. (1985), 'Effects of age, cigarette smoking and other factors on fertility', *British Medical Journal*, 290, p. 1697

Howell, E.D. (1981), 'Women: From Freud to the present', in E.D. Howell and M. Bayes, (eds.), *Women and Mental Health* (New York: Basic Books)

Howell, E.D. and Bayes, M. (eds.) (1981), *Women and Mental Health* (New York: Basic Books)

Hunt, A. (1988a), 'Women and Paid Work', in A. Hunt (ed.), *Women and Paid Work: Issues of equality* (Basingstoke: Macmillan)

Hunt, A. (ed.), (1988b), *Women and Paid Work: Issues of equality* (Basingstoke: Macmillan)

Hunt, S., Martin, C.J. and Platt, S. (1986), *Housing and Health in a Deprived Area of Edinburgh*, paper presented at Conference on Unhealthy Housing, University of Warwick

Hunt, S.M. and McEwan, J. (1980), 'The development of a subjective health indicator', *Sociology of Health and Illness*, 2, pp. 231–46

Huws, U. (1984), *The New Homeworkers* (London: Low Pay Unit)

Hyndman, S.J. (1990), 'Housing damp and health among British Bengalis in East London', *Social Science and Medicine*, vol. 30, pp. 131–41

Illsley, R. (1986), 'Occupational class, selection and the production of inequalities in health', *Quarterly Journal of Social Affairs*, 2, pp. 151–65

Illsley, R. (1987), 'The health divide: Bad welfare or bad statistics?', *Poverty*, 67, pp. 16–17

Illsey, R. and Svenssen, R. (1990), 'Health inequalities in Europe', *Social*

Science and Medicine, vol. 31, 3, Special Issue

Ineichen, B. (1986), *Mental Health and High-rise Housing*, paper presented at Conference on Unhealthy Housing, University of Warwick

Ineichen, B. and Hooper, D. (1974), 'Wives' mental health and children's behaviour: Problems in contrasting residential areas', *Social Science and Medicine*, vol. 8, 6, pp. 369–74

Ingleby, D. (ed.) (1981), *Critical Psychiatry: The Politics of Mental Health* (Harmondsworth: Penguin)

Institute of Fiscal Studies (1986), *The Retail Price Index and the Cost of Living* Report Series no. 22 (London: IFS)

Jacobson, B. (1981), *The Ladykillers: Why smoking is a feminist issue* (London: Pluto)

Jacobson, B. (1986), *Beating the Ladykillers* (London: Pluto)

Joffe, M. (1989), 'Social inequalities and low birth weight: Timing of effects and selective mobility', *Social Science and Medicine*, vol. 28, pp., 613–19

Johnson, P. and Webb, S. (1990a), *Poverty in Official Statistics*, Institute of Fiscal Studies Commentary no. 24 (London: IFS)

Johnson, P. and Webb, S. (1990b), *The Income Support System and the Distribution of Income in 1987*, a study commissioned by the House of Commons Social Services Committee (London: HMSO)

Jones, L. and Cochrane, R. (1981), 'Stereotypes of mental illness: A test of the labelling hypothesis', *International Journal of Psychiatry*, 27, pp. 99–107

Jones, T., Maclean, B. and Young, J. (1986), *The Islington Crime Survey* (Aldershot: Gower)

Jordanova, L. (1981), 'Mental illness, mental health: Changing norms and expectations', in Cambridge Women's Studies Group (eds.), *Women in Society* (London: Virago)

Joshi, H. (1987), 'The cost of caring', in C. Glendinning and J. Millar (eds.), *Women and Poverty in Britain* (Hemel Hempstead: Harvester Wheatsheaf)

Joyce, L. and McCashin, A. (1982), *Poverty and Social Policy* (Dublin: Institute of Public Administration)

Kaplan, A. and Kotler, P.L. (1985), 'Self-reports: Predictive of mortality', *Journal of Chronic Diseases*, 38, pp. 195–201

Kaplan, G.A. and Salonen, J.T. (1990), 'Socio-economic conditions in childhood and ischaemic heart disease during middle age', *British Medical Journal*, 301, pp. 1121–23

Karlekar, M. (1982), *Poverty and Women's Work: A study of sweeper women in Delhi* (New Delhi: Vikos)

Keithley, J., Byrne, D., Harrison, S. and McCarthy, P. (1984), 'Health and housing conditions in public sector housing estates', *Public Health*, 98, pp. 344–53

Kelly, L. (1988), *Sharing a Particular Pain* (London: Virago)

Khoo, D.E. and Habib, N.A. (1990), 'Fats and cancer', *West of England Medical Journal* 300, p. 440, 17 February

Kidd, T. (1989), 'Women and welfare', in I. Reid and E. Strata (eds.), *Sex Differences in Britain*, second edition (Aldershot: Gower)

Klerman, G.L. and Weissman, M.M. (1980), 'Depression among women: Their nature and causes', in M. Guttentag *et al.* (eds.), *The Mental Health of Women* (New York: Academic Press)

Knight, I. and Eldridge, J. (1984), *The Heights and Weights of Adults in Great Britain* (London: HMSO)

Kohn, M.L. (1972), 'Class, family and schizophrenia: A reformulation', *Social Focus*, 50, pp. 295–304

Koskenuvo, M., Kaprio, J., Lonnquist, J. and Sarna, S. (1986), 'Social factors and the gender difference in mortality', *Social Science and Medicine*, vol. 23, pp. 605–9

Laing, R.D. and Esterson, A. (1970), *The Divided Self* (Harmondsworth: Penguin)

Land, H. (1969), *Large Families in London*, Occasional Papers in Social Administration no. 32 (London: Bell)

Land, H. (1977), *Parity Begins at Home: Women's and men's work in the home and its effects on their paid employment* (Manchester: Equal Opportunties Commission)

Land, H. (1981), *Parity Begins at Home: Women and men's work in the home and its effects on their paid employment* (London: Equal Opportunties Commission and Social Science Research Council)

Land, H. (1983), 'Poverty and gender: The distribution of resources within the family', in M. Brown (ed.), *The Structure of Disadvantage* (London: Heinemann)

Land, H. (1986), *Women and Economic Dependency* (Manchester: Equal Opportunties Commission)

Land, H. (1989), 'The construction of dependency', in M. Bulmer, J. Lewis and D. Paichaud (eds.), *The Goals of Social Policy* (London: Unwin Hyman)

Land, H. and Rose, H. (1985), 'Compulsory altruism for some or an altruistic society for all?', in P. Bean, J. Ferris and N. Whynes (eds.), *In Defence of Welfare* (London: Tavistock)

Land, H. and Ward, S. (1986), *Women Won't Benefit: The impact of the Social Security Bill on women's rights* (London: NCCL)

Lang, T. (1984), *Jam Tomorrow* (Manchester: Manchester Polytechnic)

Laws, S., Hey, V. and Eagen, A. (1986), *Seeing Red: The politics of premenstrual tension* (London: Hutchinson)

Legal and General (1990), *What is a Housewife?*

Lennane, K.J. and Lennane, R.J. (1982), 'Alleged psychogenic disorders in women: A possible manifestation of sexual prejudice', in E. Whitelegg (ed.), *The Changing Experience of Women* (Milton Keynes: Open University)

Lewin, E. and Olesen, V. (1985a), 'Occupational health and women', in E. Lewin and V. Oleson (eds.), *Women, Health and Healing: Toward a new perspective* (London: Tavistock)

Lewin, E. and Olesen, V. (eds.) (1985b), *Women, Health and Healing: Toward a new perspective* (London: Tavistock)

Lewis, O. (1964), *The Children of Sanchez* (Harmondsworth, Penguin)

Lewis, J. and Piachaud, D. (1987), 'Women and poverty in the twentieth century', in C. Glendinning and J. Millar (eds.), *Women and Poverty in Britain* (Hemel Hempstead: Harvester Wheatsheaf)

Lidz, T. (1975), *The Origin and Treatment of Schizophrenic Disorders* (London: Hutchinson)

Lister, R. (1973), *As Man and Wife* (London: Child Poverty Action Group)

Llewellyn Davies, M. (1915), *Maternity: Letters from Working Wives* (London: Bell)

Loney, M. (1983), *The Politics of Greed* (London: Pluto Press)

Loney, M. and Bocock, R. (eds.) (1987), *The State of The Market* (London: Sage and Open University)

Loney, M., Boswell, D. and Clarke, J. (1983), *Social Policy and Social Welfare* (Milton Keynes: Open University)

Lonsdale, S. (1987), 'Patterns of paid work', in C. Glendinning and J. Millar (eds.), *Women and Poverty in Britain* (Hemel Hempstead: Harvester Wheatsheaf)

Lonsdale, S. (1990), *Women and Disability: The experience of physical disability among women* (London: Macmillan)

Lovett, A.A., Gatrell, A.C., Bound, J.P., Harvey, P.W. and Whelan, A.R. (1990), 'Congenital malformations in the Fylde Region of Lancashire, England, 1957–73', *Social Science and Medicine*, vol. 30, pp. 103–9

Low Income Families Statistics (1986; 1988), (London: HMSO)

Lynge, E., Andersen, O. and Horte, L.G. (1989), 'Mortality: A comparison of within-country differentials based on selected occupational groups reported in a variety of countries', in J. Fox (ed.), *Health Inequalities in European Countries* (Aldershot: Gower)

Macfarlane, A. (1990), 'Official statistics and women's health and illness', in H. Roberts (1990), *Women's Health Counts* (London: Routledge)

Macfarlane, A. and Mugford, M. (1984), *Birth Counts: Statistics of Pregnancy and Childbirth*, National Perinatal Epidemiology Unit (London: HMSO)

MacGregor, S. (1981), *The Politics of Poverty* (London: Longman)

Macintyre, S. (1986), 'The patterning of health by social position in contemporary Britain: Directions for sociological research', *Social Science and Medicine*, 23, pp. 393–415

Mack, J. and Lansley, S. (1985), *Poor Britain* (London: Allen and Unwin)

Maclean, M. (1987), 'Households after divorce: The availability of resources and their impact on children', in J. Brannen and G. Wilson (eds.), *Give and Take in Families: Studies in resource distribution* (London: Allen and Unwin)

Maclean, M. and Eekelaar, J. (1983), *Children and Divorce: Economic factors* (London: Social Science Research Council)

Maclean, M. and Jefferys, M. (1974), 'Disability and Deprivation', in D. Wedderburn (ed.), *Poverty, Inequality and Class Structure* (London: Cambridge University Press)

Macormack, C.P. (1988), 'Health and the Social Power of Women', *Social Science and Medicine*, vol. 26, pp. 677–83

Main, B.G. (1988), 'Lifetime attachment to the labour market', in A. Hunt (ed.), *Women and Paid Work: Issues of equality* (Basingstoke: Macmillan)

Makosky, V.P. (1980), 'Sources of stress: Events or conditions?', in D. Belle (ed.), *Lives in Stress: Women and depression* (Beverly Hills: Sage)

Makosky, V.P. (1982), 'Stress and the mental health of women: A discussion of research and issues', in M. Guttentag *et al.* (eds.), *The Mental Health of Women* (New York: Academic Press)

Malos, E. (1980), *The Politics of Housework* (London: Allison and Busby)

Marmot, M., Adelstein, A. and Bulusu, L. (1984), *Immigrant Mortality in England and Wales 1978*, OPCS Studies on Medical and Population Subjects 47 (London: HMSO)

Marmot, M.G. and MacDowall, M.E. (1986), 'Mortality decline and widening social inequalities', *The Lancet*, 11, pp. 274–6

Marmot, M.G., Shipley, M.J. and Rose, G. (1984), 'Inequalities in death: Specific explanations of a general pattern', *The Lancet*, 1, pp. 1003–6

Marsden, D. (1969), *Mothers Alone: Poverty and the fatherless family* (London: Allen Lane)

Martin, C.J., Platt, S. D. and Hunt, S.M. (1987), 'Housing conditions and ill health', *British Medical Journal*, 294, pp. 1125–7

Martin, J. and Roberts, C. (1984), *Women and Employment: A lifetime perspective*, Department of Employment (London: HMSO)

Matrix (ed.) (1984), *Making Space: Women and the man-made environment* (London: Pluto Press)

Maynard, A. (1989), 'A very British way of dying', *Health Service Journal*, 825, 6 July

McCarthy, P. *et al.* (1985), 'Respiratory conditions: Effects of housing and other factors', *Journal of Epidemiology and Community Health*, 39, pp. 15–19

McClaughlin, E., Millar, J. and Cooke, K. (1989), *Work and Welfare Benefits* (Aldershot: Gower)

McConville, B. (1983), *Women Under the Influence* (London: Virago)

McDowell, M.E. (1983), 'Measuring women's occupational mortality', *Population Trends*, 34, pp. 25–9

McKeown, T. (1976), *The Modern Rise of Population: Dream, Mirage or Nemesis?* (London: Edward Arnold)

McNaught, A. (1988), *Race and Health Policy* (London: Croom Helm)

McPherson, A. and Anderson, A. (eds.) (1983), *Women's Problems in General Practice* (Oxford: Oxford University Press)

Menchik, P.L. (1990), 'Inheritance and the treatment of women', in M.N. Ozawa (ed.), *Women's Life Cycle and Economic Insecurity: Problems and proposals* (New York: Praeger)

Metress, E. and Metress, S. (1990), 'Socio-political factors that affect women's health in Northern Ireland', *International Journal of Health Services*, 20, p. 2

Miles, A. (1988), *Women and Mental Illness* (Hemel Hempstead: Harvester Wheatsheaf)

Miliband, R. (1974), 'Politics and Poverty', in D. Wedderburn (ed.), *Poverty, Inequality and Class Structure* (London: Cambridge University Press)

Millar, J. (1987), 'Lone Mothers', in C. Glendinning and J. Millar (eds.), *Women and Poverty in Britain* (Brighton: Wheatsheaf)

Millar, J. (1989a), *Poverty and the Lone Parent: The challenge to social policy* (Aldershot: Avebury)

Millar, J. (1989b), 'Social security, equality and women in the UK', *Policy and Politics*, 17, pp. 311–19

Millar, J. and Glendinning, C. (1987), 'Invisible women, invisible poverty', in C. Glendinning and J. Millar (eds.), *Women and Poverty in Britain* (Brighton: Wheatsheaf)

Millar, J. and Glendinning, C. (1989), 'Gender and poverty', *Journal of Social Policy*, 18, p. 3

Mind (1980), *Mental Health Statistics* (London: Mind)

Ministry of Agriculture, Food and Fisheries (1989), *Household Food Consumption and Expenditure: Annual Report of National Food Survey Committee* (London: HMSO)

Mitchell, J. (1974), *Psychoanalysis and Feminism* (Harmondsworth: Penguin)

Mitchell, J. (1984), *Women: The Longest Revolution. Essays in feminism, literature and psychoanalysis* (London: Virago)

Mitter, S. (1986), *Common Fate, Common Bond: Women in the global economy* (London: Pluto Press)

Mitton, R., Willmott, P. and Wilmott, P. (1983), *Unemployment, Poverty* and Social Policy in Europe: A comparative study in Britain, France and Germany (London: Bedford Square Press)

Morgan, H.G., Pocock, H. and Pottle, S. (1975), 'Urban distribution of non-fatal deliberate self-harm', *British Journal of Psychiatry*, 1, pp. 258–305

Moser, K., Fox, A.J. and Jones, D.R. (1984), 'Unemployment and mortality in the OPCS Longitudinal Study', *The Lancet* ii, pp. 1324–9

Moser, K., Fox, A.J. and Jones, D.R. (1986), 'Unemployment and mortality in the OPCS Longitudinal Study', in R.G. Wilkinson (ed.), *Class and Health: Research and Longitudinal Data* (London: Tavistock)

Moser, K. and Goldblatt, P (1985), *Mortality of Women in the OPCS Longitudinal Study: Differentials by own occupation and household and housing characteristics*, Social Statistics Research Unit, Working Paper 26 (London: City University)

Moser, K., Pugh, H. and Goldblatt, P. (1987), *Inequalities in Women's Health: Developing an alternative approach*, Longitudinal Study Working Paper no. 54 (London: Social Science Research Unit)

Munro, M. (1988), 'Housing wealth and inheritance', *Journal of Social Policy*, 17, pp. 417–36

Myers, J.K. and Bean, L.L. (1968), *A Decade Later: A follow-up of social class and mental illness* (New York: Wiley)

National Advisory Committee on Nutritional Education (1983), *Proposals for Nutritional Guidelines in Britain: A discussion paper* (London: Health Education Council)

National Council of Welfare (1979), *Women and Poverty* (Ottawa: National Council of Welfare)

Navarro, V. (1976), *Medicine Under Capitalism* (London: Croom Helm)

New Earnings Survey (1990), (London, HMSO)

Newton, R. and Hunt, L. (1984), 'Psychosocial stress in pregnancy and its relation to low birthweight', *British Medical Journal*, 288, p. 1191

Novak, T. (1984), *Poverty and Social Security* (London: Pluto)

O'Brien, M. (1983), *The Politics of Reproduction* (London: RKP)

Oakley, A. (1974), *Housewife* (Harmondsworth: Penguin)

Oakley, A. (1976), *Housewife*, second edition (Harmondsworth: Penguin)

Oakley, A. (1981), *From Here to Maternity* (Harmondsworth: Penguin)

Oakley, A. (1986), *Telling The Truth About Jerusalem* (Oxford: Basil Blackwell)

Oakley, A. (1987), *Social Welfare and the Position of Women* (London: Thomas Coram Research Unit, Working Paper 5)

Office of Health Economics (1989), *Mental Health in the 1990s: From custody to care?* (London: OHE)

OPCS (1983), *Congenital Malformations Statistics, 1971–80, England and Wales* (London: HMSO)

OPCS (1986a), *Morbidity Statistics from General Practice, 1981–82*, OPCS

Series MB5 (1) (London: HMSO)

OPCS (1986b), *Occupational Mortality, 1979–80, 82–83, Decennial Supplement* (London: HMSO)

OPCS (1990a), *Morbidity Statistics from General Practice, 1981–82: Socioeconomic analysis*, OPCS Series MB5 (1) (London: HMSO)

OPCS (1990b), *Longitudinal Study: Mortality and social organisation, England and Wales, 1971–81*, Series LF6 (London: HMSO)

Oppenheim, C. (1988), *Poverty: The facts* (London: Child Poverty Action Group)

Oppenheim, C. (1990), *Poverty: The facts* (London: Child Poverty Action Group)

Orbach, S. (1978), *Fat is a Feminist Issue* (London: Paddington Press)

Orbach, S. (1986), 'Hunger strike: The anorectic's struggle as a metaphor for our age' (London: Faber)

Osborn, A. (1983), *Maternal Employment, Depression and Child Behaviour*, EOC Research Bulletin no. 8 (Manchester: Equal Opportunities Commission)

Osborn, A. and Butler, N.R. (1985), *Ethnic Minority Children* (London: Commission for Racial Equality)

Osborn, J. (1990), *Psychosocial Effects of Child Sex Abuse in Child Sex Abuse*, University of Norwich Social Work Monographs (Norwich: University of Norwich)

Pagel, M.D., Smilksten, G., Regen, H. and Montano, D. (1990), 'Psychosocial influences on new born outcomes: A controlled prospective study', *Social Science and Medicine*, vol. 30, pp. 597–660

Pahl, J. (1980), 'Patterns of money management within marriage', *Journal of Social Policy*, 9, pp. 313–35

Pahl, J. (1983), 'The allocation of money and the structuring of inequality within marriage', *Sociological Review*, 13, pp. 237–62

Pahl, J. (1985), *Private Violence and Public Policy* (London: RKP)

Pahl, J. (1989), *Money and Marriage* (London: Macmillan)

Pahl, J. and Vaile, M. (1988), 'Health and health care among travellers', *Journal of Social Policy*, 17, pp. 195–214

Parsons, T. (1951), *The Social System* (London: RKP)

Pascall, G. (1986), *Social Policy: A feminist analysis* (London: Tavistock)

Passanante, M.R. and Nathanson, C.A. (1985), 'Female labor force participation and female mortality in Wisconsin, 1974–78', *Social Science and Medicine*, vol. 21, pp. 655–65

Paterson, C.M. and Roderick, P. (1990), 'Obstetric outcome in homeless women', *British Medical Journal*, 301, pp. 263–6

Payne, S. (1987), *Did she fall or was she pushed: A study of material and social deprivation amongst female psychiatric out-patients* (Bristol: University of Bristol, PhD thesis)

Pearce, D. (1978), 'Feminisation of Poverty: Women, work and welfare', *Urban and Social Change Review*, 2, 1 & 2

Pearlin, L. and Johnson, T. (1977), 'Marital status, life strains and depression', *American Sociological Review*, 42, pp. 704–15

Pember-Reeves, M.S. (1913), *Round about a Pound a Week* (London: Bell, reprinted by Virago)

Phillimore, P. (1989), *Shortened Lives: Premature death in North Tyneside*, Bristol Papers in Applied Social Studies no. 12 (Bristol: University of Bristol)

Phillips, D.L. (1968), 'Social class and psychological disturbance: The influence of positive and negative experiences', *Social Psychiatry*, 3, pp. 41–6

Phoenix, A. (1991), *Young Mothers* (Cambridge: Polity Press)

Piachaud, D (1979), *The Cost of a Child* (London: Child Poverty Action Group)

Piachaud, D. (1981a), *Children and Poverty* (London: Child Poverty Action Group)

Piachaud, D. (1981b), 'Peter Townsend and the Holy Grail', *New Society*, 10 September, pp. 419–21

Pill, R. and Stott, N.C. (1982), 'Preventive Procedures and Practices among Working Class Women: New data and fresh insights', *Social Science and Medicine*, 21, 9. pp. 975–83

Platt, S. (1984), 'Unemployment and suicidal behaviour: A review of the literature', *Social Science and Medicine*, 19, pp. 93–115

Platt, S. and Kreitman, N. (1984), 'Unemployment and parasuicide in Edinburgh 1968–82', *British Medical Journal*, 289, pp. 1029–32

Pollert, A. (1981), *Girls, Wives, Factory Lives* (London: Macmillan)

Popay, J. and Jones, G. (1987), 'Women's health in households with dependent children', in H. Graheme (ed.), *Women, Health and Work* (London: Women's Medical Federation)

Popay, J. and Jones, G. (1988), *Gender Inequalities in Health: Explaining the sting in the tail*, paper presented to Social Policy Association Annual Conference, Edinburgh, July 1988.

Popay, J. and Jones, G. (1990), 'Patterns of health and illness amongst lone parents', *Journal of Social Policy*, 19, pp. 499–534

Porter, R. (1987), *A Social History of Madness: Stories of the insane* (London: Weidenfeld and Nicolson)

Posner, T. and Vessey, M. (1988), *Prevention of Cervical Cancer: The patient's view* (London: The King's Fund)

Pringle, R. (1988), *Secretaries Talk: Sexuality, power and work* (London: Verso)

Prior, L. (1989), *The Social Organisation of Death* (London: Tavistock)

Pugh, H. and Moser, K. (1990), 'Measuring women's mortality differences', in H. Roberts (ed.), *Women's Health Counts* (London: Routledge)

Radloff, L. (1975), 'Sex differences in depression: The effects of occupation and marital status', *Sex Roles*, 1, pp. 249–65

Radloff, L. (1980), 'Risk factors for depression: What do we learn from them?', in M. Guttentag *et al.* (eds.), *The Mental Health of Women* (New York: Academic Press)

Raikes, A. (1989), 'Women's health in East Africa', *Social Science and Medicine*, vol. 28, pp. 447–59

Ramirez, A.J. *et al.* (1989), 'Stress and relapse of breast cancer', *British Medical Journal*, 298, pp. 291–3

Reese, M.F. (1982), 'Growing up: The impact of loss and change', in D. Belle (ed.), *Lives in Stress: Women and depression* (Beverly Hills: Sage)

Reid, I. (1989), 'Vital statistics', in I. Reid and E. Strata (eds.), *Sex Differences in Britain*, second edition (Aldershot: Gower)

Reid, I. and Strata, E. (eds.) (1989), *Sex Differences in Britain*, second edition (Aldershot: Gower)

Ricker, P.P. and Carmen, E.H. (1984), *The Gender Gap in Psychotherapy* (New York: Plenum Books)

Rimmer, L. (1988), 'Intra-family distribution of paid work', in A. Hunt (ed.), *Women and Paid Work: Issues of equality* (Basingstoke: Macmillan)

Roberts, H. (1985), *The Patient Patients* (London: Pandora Press)

Roberts, H. (1990), *Women's Health Counts* (London: Routledge)

Roberts, H. and Barker, R. (1987), *What are People Doing when they Grade Women's Work?*, LS Working Paper no. 52 (London: Social Statistics Research Unit)

Robertson, H. (1988), 'AIDS: A trade union issue', in P. Aggleton and H. Homans (eds.), *Social Aspects of Aids* (Lewes: Falmer Press)

Robinson, J. (1982), 'Cancer of the Cervix: Occupational risk of husbands and wives and possible preventive strategies', in J.A. Jarden, F. Sharp and A. Singer (eds.), *Proceedings of the Ninth Study Group of the Royal College of Obstetricians and Gynaecologists* (London: RCOG)

Rogers, B. (1980), *The Domestication of Women: Discrimination in developing countries* (London: Tavistock)

Roll, J. (1986), *Dear Mother? Maternity payments reform* (London: Family Policy Studies Centre)

Room, G., Lawson, R. and Laczko, F. (1989), 'New poverty in the European Community', *Policy and Politics*, 17, pp. 165–76

Rose, G. and Marmot, M. (1981), 'Social class and coronary heart disease', *British Heart Journal*, 45, pp. 13–19

Rosenfeld, S. (1980), 'Sex differences in depression: Do women always have higher rates?', *Journal of Health and Social Behaviour*, 21, pp. 33–42

Rowntree, S. (1922), *Poverty: A study of town life* (London: Thomas Nelson and Sons)

Rowntree, S. (1941), *Poverty and Progress: A second social survey of York* (London: Longman)

Rubinstein, W.D. (1986), *Wealth and Inequality in Britain* (London: Faber)

Rutter, D.R. and Quine, L. (1990), 'Inequalities in pregnancy outcome: A review of psychosocial and behavioural mediators', *Social Science and Medicine*, vol. 30, pp. 553–68

Savage, W. and George, J. (1989), *A Survey of Women's Knowledge, Attitudes and Experience of Cervical Screening in the Tower Hamlets Health District* (London: Department of General Practice and Primary Care, Medical College, St Bartholomew's Hospital)

Savel-Cubizolles, M.J. and Kanuskin, M. (1982), 'Work in pregnancy: Its evolving relationship with perinatal outcome', *Social Science and Medicine*, vol. 22, pp. 431–42

Scheff, T. (1966), *Being Mentally Ill: A sociological theory* (New York: Aldine)

Scott, H. (1984), *Working Your Way to the Bottom: The feminisation of poverty* (London: Pandora)

Scull, A. (1979), *Museums of Madness: The social organisation of insanity in nineteenth-century England* (London: Allen Lane)

Scully, D. and Bart, P. (1983), 'A funny thing happened on the way to the orifice: Women in gynaecology textbooks', in J. Huber (ed.), *Changing Women in a Changing Society* (Chicago: University of Chicago Press)

Seligman, H.E.P. (1975), *Helplessness: On depression, development and death* (San Francisco: Freeman)

Selye, H. (1956), *The Stress of Life* (New York: McGraw Hill)

Sen, A. (1983), *Poor Relatively Speaking* (London: Economic and Social Research Institute)

Sharpe, S. (1984), *Double Identity: The lives of working mothers* (Harmondsworth: Penguin)

Sharples, P.M., Storey, A., Aynsley-Green, A. and Eyre, J.A. (1990), 'Causes of fatal childhood accidents involving head injury in Northern Region', 1979–86, *British Medical Journal*, 301, pp. 1193–7

Showalter, E. (1987), *The Female Malady: Women, madness and English culture* (London: Virago)

Sinfield, A. (1986), 'Poverty, privilege and welfare', in P. Bean and N. Whynes (eds.), *Barbara Wootton: Social Science and Public Policy: Essays in her honour* (London: Tavistock)

Skegg, D.C.G., Doll, R. and Perry, J. (1977), 'Use of medicines in general practice', *British Medical Journal*, pp. 1561–3

Sluka, J.A. (1989), 'Living on their nerves: Nervous debility in Northern

Ireland', in D.L. Davis and S.M. Low, *Gender, Health and Illness: The case of nerves* (New York: Hemisphere)

Smart, C. (1976), *Women, Crime and Criminology: A feminist critique* (London: RKP)

Smith, A. (1989), 'Letter', *The Lancet*, pp. 392–3

Smith, A. and Jacobson, B. (1989), *The Nation's Health* (London: King's Fund)

Smith, G.D., Bartley, M. and Blane, D. (1990), 'The Black Report on socio-economic inequalities in health ten years on', *British Medical Journal*, pp. 301, 373–7

Smith, R. (1987), *Unemployment and Health* (Oxford: Oxford University Press)

Smith, T. (1990), 'Poverty and health in the 1990s', *British Medical Journal*, pp. 301, 349–50

Smith-Rosenberg, C. (1974), 'Puberty to menopause: The cycle of feminity in nineteenth-century America', in M. Hartman and L. Banner (eds.), *Clio's Consciousness Raised* (New York: Harper and Row)

Social Trends (1989), (1990), (London: HMSO)

Sorenen, A. and McLauchan, S. (1987), 'Married women's economic dependency', *American Journal of Sociology*, 93, pp. 659–87

Spring-Rice, M. (1939), *Working Class Wives: Their health and conditions* (London: Virago)

Srole, L., Langner, T.S., Michael, S.T., Opler, M.K. and Rennie, T.A.C. (1961), *Mental Health in the Metropolis: The Midtown Manhatten Survey* (New York: McGraw Hill)

Stark, T. (1990), *Income and Wealth in the 1980s: An update* (London: The Fabian Society)

Stellman, J. (1977), *Women's Work, Women's Health: Myths and realities* (New York: Pantheon)

Sterling, P. and Eyer, J. (1981), 'Biological basis of stress-related mortality', *Social Science and Medicine*, 15E, pp. 3–42

Stewart, M.B. and Greenhalgh, C.A. (1984), 'Work history patterns and the occupational attainment of women', *Economic Journal*, 93, pp. 493–519

Stitt, S. (1990), *Testing the Adequacy of the Income Support Scale Rates by Disaggregated Weekly Budget Standards*, paper presented at the Annual Conference of the Social Policy Association, Bath

Stott, N.C.H. and Pill, R. (1983), *A Study of Health Beliefs and Health Behaviour among Working-Class Mothers* (Cardiff: Department of General Practice, Welsh National School of Medicine)

Strachan, D. (1986), *The Home Environment and Respiratory Morbidity in Children*, paper presented at the Conference of Unhealthy Housing, University of Warwick

Sullivan, O. (1986), 'Housing movements of the divorced and separated',

*Housing Studies*, 1, pp. 35–48

Szasz, T. (1973), *The Manufacture of Mental Illness: A comparative study of the inquisition and the mental health movement* (London: Paladin)

Taylor, D. (1985), 'Women: An analysis', in *Women: A World Report* (London: Methuen)

Taylor, J. and Taylor, D. (1989), *Mental Health in the 1990s: From custody to care?* (London: Office of Health Economics)

Taylor, N. (ed.) (1986), *All in A Day's Work: A report on anti-lesbian discrimination in employment and unemployment in London* (London: Lesbian Employment Rights)

Terry, P.B. *et al.* (1980), 'Analysis of ethnic differences in perinatal statistics', *British Medical Journal*, pp. 281, 1307–8

Thane, P. (1978), 'Women and the Poor Law in Victorian and Edwardian England', *History Workshop Journal*, pp. 6, 29–51

Thane, P. (1982), *The Foundation of the Welfare State* (London: Longman)

The Black Report (1980), *Inequalities in Health: Report of a Research Working Party* (London: DHSS)

*The Guardian*, 'Make or break?', 20 March 1990

*The Observer*, 'Food worker report reveals additive risk', 29 October 1989

Thorogood, N. (1987), 'Race, class and gender: The politics of housework', in J. Brannen and G. Wilson (eds.), *Give and Take in Families: Studies in resource distribution* (London: Allen and Unwin)

Titmuss, R. (1963), 'The social division of welfare: Some reflections on the search for equity', in *Essays on the Welfare State, Second Edition* (London: University Books)

Torkington, P.N. (1983), *The Racial Politics of Health: A Liverpool Profile* (Liverpool: Liverpool University)

Townsend, P. (1957), *The Family Life of Old People* (London: Routledge and Kegan Paul)

Townsend, P. (1974), 'Poverty and relative deprivation: Resources and style of living' in D. Wedderburn (ed.), *Poverty, Inequality and Class Structure* (London: Cambridge University Press)

Townsend, P. (1979), *Poverty in the United Kingdom* (Harmondsworth: Penguin)

Townsend, P. (1981), 'Peter Townsend Replies', *New Society*, 17 September, pp. 477–8

Townsend, P. (1987), 'Deprivation', *Journal of Social Policy*, 16, pp. 125–46

Townsend, P. (1989), 'Slipping Through the Net', *The Guardian*, 30 December

Townsend, P. (1990a), 'Individual or social responsibility for premature death: Current controversies in the British debate about health', *International Journal of Health Studies*, 20, pp. 373–92

Townsend, P. (1990b), 'Living standards and health in the inner cities', in

S. MacGregor and B. Pimlott (eds.), *Tackling the Inner Cities* (Oxford: Oxford University Press)

Townsend, P. (1990c), *Poverty and Deprivation in Britain 1979–90: A problem in policy analysis*, paper presented to Social Policy Association Annual Conference, July 1990, Bath

Townsend, P. (1990d), 'Widening inequalities of health: A rejoinder to Rudolph Klein', *International Journal of Health Studies*, 20, pp. 363–74

Townsend, P. (1990e), *Deprivation and Ill-Health: New scientific evidence and the implications for policy*, Institute for Health Policy Studies (London: IHPS)

Townsend, P. (ed.) (1970), *The Concept of Poverty* (London: Heinemann)

Townsend, P., Corrigan, P. and Kowarzik, U. (1987), *Poverty and the London Labour Market* (London: Low Pay Unit)

Townsend, P. and Davidson, N. (eds.) (1982), *Inequalities in Health: The Black Report* (Harmondsworth: Penguin)

Townsend, P., Davidson, N. and Whitehead, M. (1988), *Inequalities in Health: The Black Report and The Health Divide* (Harmondsworth: Penguin)

Townsend, P. and Gordon, D. (1989), *What is Enough? New evidence on poverty in Greater London allowing the definition of a minimum benefit*, memorandum of evidence to the House of Commons Social Services Committee, August 1989

Townsend, P., Phillimore, P. and Beattie, A. (1988), *Health and Deprivation: Inequality and the North* (London: Croom Helm)

Townsend, P., Simpson, D. and Tibbs, N. (1984), *Inequalities of Health in the City of Bristol: A preliminary review of the statistical evidence* (Bristol: Department of Social Administration: University of Bristol)

Turner, R.J. and Wagenefeld, M.O. (1967), 'Occupational mobility and schizophrenia: An assessment of the social causation and social selection hypotheses', *American Sociological Review*, 32, pp. 104–13

United Nations Development Programme (UNDP) (1990), *Human Development Report* (New York: UNDP)

Verbrugge, L.M. (1986), 'From Sneezes to Adieux: Stages of health for American men and women', *Social Science and Medicine*, vol. 22, pp. 1195–1212

Verreault, R., Brisson, J. *et al.* (1990), 'Body weight may affect prognosis in breast cancer', *International Clinical Review*, 10, p. 288

Victor, C. (1990), *Whose Responsibility? Health Care Provision and the Homeless*, paper presented to Social Policy Association Annual Conference, July 1990, Bath

Victor, C.R. (1989), 'Health inequality in later life: Age, gender or class?' in C.J. Martin and D.V. McQueen (eds.), *Readings for a New Public Health* (Edinburgh: Edinburgh University Press)

Vogel, J.,Anderssen, L.G., Davidsson, U. and Hall, L. (1988), *Inequality in Sweden: Trends and current situation* (Stockhom: SCB)

Wadsworth, M. (1986), 'Serious illness in childhood and its association with later life achievement', in R. Wilkinson (ed.), *Class and Health: Research and longitudinal data* (London: Tavistock)

Walby, S. (1986), *Patriarchy at Work: Patriarchal and capitalist relations to employment* (Cambridge: Polity Press)

Waldron, I. (1980), 'Employment and women's health: An analysis of causal relationships', *International Journal of Health Services*, 10, 3

Walker, A. (1987), 'The Poor Relation: Poverty among old women', in C. Glendinning and J. Millar (eds.), *Women and Poverty in Britain* (Hemel Hempstead: Harvester Wheatsheaf)

Walker, A. and Townsend, P. (eds.) (1981), *Disability in Britain: A Manifesto of Rights* (Oxford: Martin Robertson)

Walker, L. E. (ed.) (1984), *Women and Mental Health Policy* (London: Sage)

Walker, R., Lawson, R. and Townsend, P. (eds.) (1984), *Responses to Poverty: Lessons from Europe* (London: Heinemann)

Walker, R. and Parker, G. (1988), *Money Matters: Income, wealth and financial welfare* (London: Sage)

Watkins, S.J. (1986), 'The effect of workplace health services on sex-specific morbidity rates', *Social Science and Medicine*, vol. 22, pp. 517–20

Watson, S. (1985), *Matrimonial Property Research Paper Housing After Divorce* (Australia: The Law Reform Commission)

Watson, S. (1986), 'Women and housing or feminist housing analysis', *Housing Studies*, 1, pp. 1–10

Watson, S. (1988), *Accommodating Inequality: Gender and housing* (London: Allen and Unwin)

Watson, S. and Austerberry, H. (1986), *Housing and Homelessness: A feminist perspective* (London: RKP)

Weeks, J. (1985), *Sexuality and its Discontents: Meanings, myths and modern sexualities* (London: RKP)

Weissman, M.M. and Klerman, G.L. (1977), 'Sex differences and the epidemiology of depression', *Archives of General Psychiatry*, 34, pp. 98–111

Weisstein, N. (1970), 'Kinde, kuche, kirche as scientific law: Psychology constructs the female', in R. Morgan (ed.), *Sisterhood is Powerful* (New York: Vantage Books)

Wells, N. (1987), 'The health of Britain's women', in H. Graheme (ed.), *Women, Health and Work* (London: Women's Medical Federation)

West, P., Macintyre, S., Annendale, E. and Hunt, K. (1990), 'Social class and health in youth: Findings from the West of Scotland Twenty 07 Study', *Social Science and Medicine*, vol. 30, pp. 665–73

Westwood, S. and Bhachu, P. (eds.) (1988), *Enterprising Women: Ethnicity, economy and gender relations* (London: Routledge)

Whitehead, M. (1987), *The Health Divide* (London: Health Education Council)

Whiteside, N. (1988), 'Unemployment and health: An historical perspective', *Journal of Social Policy*, 17, pp. 177–94

Wilkinson, R. (ed.) (1986), *Class and Health: Research and longitudinal data* (London: Tavistock)

Wilkinson, R.G. (1989), 'Class mortality differentials, income distribution and trends in poverty 1921–81', *Journal of Social Policy*, 18, pp. 307–35

Wilson, E. (1977), *Women and the Welfare State* (London: Tavistock)

Wilson, G. (1987a), *Money in the Family* (London: Avebury)

Wilson, G. (1987b), 'Money: patterns of responsibility and irresponsibility in marriage', in J. Brannen and G. Wilson (eds.), *Give and Take in Families: Studies in resource distribution* (London: Allen and Unwin)

Wilson, G. (1989), 'Family food systems, preventive health and change: A policy to increase the health divide', *Journal of Social Policy*, 18, pp. 167–86

WISH (1988), *Single Women and Homelessness in Bristol* (Bristol: Bristol City Housing Department)

Wolf, E. (1987), *International Comparisons of the Distribution of Household Wealth* (Oxford: Clarendon)

Women in Medicine Group (1982), *Women in Medicine: Planning and pitfalls* (London: Women in Medicine Group)

Women of Europe (1990), *Women of Europe Supplement no. 31: Childcare in the European Communities* (Brussels: Commission of the European Communities)

Women: A World Report (1985), 'Women: A world report: Women to women', in *Women: A World Report* (London: Methuen)

Wright, P. (1990), 'Pollution in Czechoslovakia', *New Society*, 1 June, pp. 16–20

Wynn, M. and Wynn, A. (1979), *Prevention of Handicap and the Health of Women* (London: RKP)

Wynne, L.C. and Singer, M.T. (1963), 'Thought disorder and family relations of schizophrenics', *Archives of General Psychiatry*, 9, pp. 191–98

Young, B. (1980), 'Health and housing infestation', *Roof*, July/August, pp. 111–12

Young, G. (1981), 'A woman in medicine: Reflections from the inside', in H. Roberts (ed.), *Women, Health and Reproduction* (London: RKP)

Zopf, P. (1989), *American Women in Poverty* (New York: Greenwood Press)

Zweig, F. (1961), *The Worker in an Affluent Scoiety* (London: Heinemann)

# INDEX